AF798120

The Politics of the Dreamscape

Seth Rogoff

The Politics of the Dreamscape

palgrave
macmillan

Seth Rogoff
Departments of History and English
University of Southern Maine
Portland, ME, USA

ISBN 978-3-030-74795-4 ISBN 978-3-030-74796-1 (eBook)
https://doi.org/10.1007/978-3-030-74796-1

© The Editor(s) (if applicable) and The Author(s), under exclusive licence to Springer Nature Switzerland AG 2021
This work is subject to copyright. All rights are solely and exclusively licensed by the Publisher, whether the whole or part of the material is concerned, specifically the rights of translation, reprinting, reuse of illustrations, recitation, broadcasting, reproduction on microfilms or in any other physical way, and transmission or information storage and retrieval, electronic adaptation, computer software, or by similar or dissimilar methodology now known or hereafter developed.
The use of general descriptive names, registered names, trademarks, service marks, etc. in this publication does not imply, even in the absence of a specific statement, that such names are exempt from the relevant protective laws and regulations and therefore free for general use.
The publisher, the authors and the editors are safe to assume that the advice and information in this book are believed to be true and accurate at the date of publication. Neither the publisher nor the authors or the editors give a warranty, expressed or implied, with respect to the material contained herein or for any errors or omissions that may have been made. The publisher remains neutral with regard to jurisdictional claims in published maps and institutional affiliations.

Cover illustration: kenkuza_shutterstock.com

This Palgrave Macmillan imprint is published by the registered company Springer Nature Switzerland AG.
The registered company address is: Gewerbestrasse 11, 6330 Cham, Switzerland

Acknowledgments

I am happy to take this opportunity to thank some of the many people who supported me in the conceptualizing and writing of this book.

Huge thanks to the editorial team at Palgrave, who diligently and professionally moved this project from draft to final form. Special thanks to Brendan George, Rebecca Hinsley, and Asma Azeezullah for their support throughout the process, and to the anonymous reviewers for their fascinating and helpful suggestions and feedback.

I am very pleased to take this opportunity to thank Esther Peeren for her tremendous guidance. Her profound insights and precise comments on the structure of the project and the individual chapters were critical for the shaping of my work. I am grateful that she dedicated so much time to reading drafts and correcting problems, large and small. I would like to thank Thomas Vaessens. His feedback was immensely valuable at all stages of the process, propelling me to think more deeply about theoretical and structural issues of this work. Incredibly valuable for the revision of my manuscript was the advice of Mieke Bal, Stefan Besser, Carrol Clarkson, Yra van Dijk, and Marie-Aude Lous Baronian—thank you.

Thanks to Eloe Kingma and the community at the Amsterdam School for Cultural Analysis (ASCA) and the University of Amsterdam. ASCA is a model of an amazing academic community. There should be more places like it.

Many people where I have taught over the years supported this project. I would like to give special thanks to Dave Susman at York County Community College for supporting my successful application for the National Endowment for the Humanities grant that began my work on dreams, and to Adam Tuchinsky at the University of Southern Maine for giving me the opportunity to teach seminars on dream studies at USM. I would also like to thank Adam and for his intellectual support and friendship.

I would like to thank Dan Byers at Harvard's Carpenter Center and the Harvard libraries for permitting me to view archival materials related to the *Dreamstage* exhibition.

Many friends and colleagues helped me with this project. They include Lou Porta, Nick Nesbitt, Eva Cermanova, Matthew Specter, Joel Revill, Jon Calame, Luisa Greenfield, Ming Tsao, Martin Kley, Liz Stern, Michel Gribenski, Camilla Bork, Ewa Kara, Shiva Darbandi, Alex Waterman, and Stephan Delbos.

I would like to thank my parents, Martin and Linda Rogoff, and my children, Adina and Saul.

Jana, thank you for your guidance, patience, and love.

Contents

List of Figures

1

Introduction

In May of 1958, the activist and singer Paul Robeson took to the stage of New York's Carnegie Hall. For the previous decade, Robeson had been the target of US government, McCarthyite, and other right-wing attacks, including the confiscation of his passport and a singular ban on traveling outside of the United States to prevent him from engaging in political speech abroad. A combination of racially and politically motivated oppression hindered Robeson from performing freely within the country. Right-wing violence, most famously in the Peekskill riots (1949), targeted Robeson as a symbol of racial and political progressivism (O'Dell 2010: 153–163). During the Carnegie Hall concert, Robeson performed the African American spiritual "We Are Climbing Jacob's Ladder," which he refers to in his autobiographical manifesto *Here I Stand* as containing a "driving power" (Robeson 1958: 100). Though Robeson does not elaborate on what he means by this, I suspect that the "driving power" of the spiritual in Robeson's performance emanates from the repeated evocation of its central image, Jacob's ladder, a reference to the biblical Jacob's dream of a ladder or staircase in Genesis 28:12.

The spiritual begins with the repetition of the line, "We are climbing Jacob's ladder." In Robeson's rendition, each repetition increases in

© The Author(s), under exclusive license to Springer Nature Switzerland AG 2021

S. Rogoff, *The Politics of the Dreamscape*,
https://doi.org/10.1007/978-3-030-74796-1_1

volume and intensity—the texture and fullness of Robeson's voice resounding through the hall. While seemingly straightforward, the spiritual is, in fact, proposing a set of complex ideas. First, the repetition of the line serves to locate the singer, and the collective "we," inside of the space of Jacob's dream—his *dreamscape*. Jacob's ladder, after all, is an artifact of Jacob's dream and fades when the dream gives way to waking life. On the other hand, the dreamscape, as the spiritual implies, does not just disappear. It maintains its integrity as a parallel space, available to new subjects thousands of years after its original manifestation. Second, the *reopening* of Jacob's dreamscape in the spiritual allows for the ladder to be redefined—or, perhaps, (re)activated. In Jacob's dream in Genesis, the future patriarch does not climb the ladder, remaining instead a passive spectator of angels going up and down it. The collective subject, the "we" of the spiritual, on the other hand, transforms the ladder through action—the climbing of the ladder—thereby effecting an unstated type of transformation of the collective, an emancipation, a freeing, a gaining of access to the divine space, and an escape from hierarchy, oppression, and violence. The lack of specificity with regard to what is at the bottom and at the top of the ladder pushes the spiritual toward a universality without needing to claim one. The final line in the opening stanza of the spiritual emphasizes the idea of struggle: "We're soldiers in this fight." The climbing of the ladder, then, is not only an act of self-emancipation; it is a struggle, a process, a battle against opposing forces. The transition to the second stanza of the spiritual zooms in on the theme of process, struggle. The climb is now rung by rung as the collective "we" moves upwards with steady determination: "Every round goes higher and higher." Again, Robeson performs the stanza with increasing volume, building toward the repetition of the same final line that ended the first stanza.

The action remains in the space of Jacob's dream when the third stanza opens, though the imagery of the stanza's key line straddles the spaces of dream and wakefulness. The spiritual continues, "Rise and shine and give God the glory." The phrase "rise and shine" is typical of the coming of morning—but here the meaning is ambiguous. The "rise" refers to the "climb," to the "higher and higher." The "rise" could also refer to Jacob's rise, the moment of wakefulness, reflection, experience, and epiphany that comes in Genesis and which I will discuss later in Chap. 3. The "shine" could mean the inner glow of the spirit in its newly won state of freedom, a state that is not a metaphorical heaven or divine realm but the actualization of emancipation and freedom among the subjects in the dreamscape. God's glory contributes to the impulse to shatter oppression, to surmount hierarchy—to rise beyond the ladder.

In the case of Robeson's 1950s America, this oppression meant Cold War political persecution (anti-communism), corporate domination, and the continuation and intensification of extremist racial-political terror in the face of rising grassroots, legal, and political demands for racial equality (Perucci 2012; Lowndes 2008). When Robeson invites the Carnegie Hall audience to sing along with him after the third stanza, the collective "we" becomes a true multiplicity, a social force, a current of energy that further radicalizes the space of Jacob's dream, which has suddenly become open and democratic in the truest sense, a space of harmony and collective purpose. Robeson's singing of the slave spiritual—created at some point in the late colonial or antebellum period of American history—renewed what I will show centuries of religious exegesis had all but discarded: the anarchic energy and political potency of Jacob's dream. Robeson's voice casts the dreamscape as a radical *political space*, and his performance constitutes a poetic response to the many overlapping authoritarian impulses of the late 1950s. It is a mistake to see the spiritual as using the image of Jacob's ladder as mere metaphor. In Robeson's rendition, the song draws on not only the legacy of the slave's fight against the tyrannical system of slavery, but it calls on the reservoir of the anarchic politics of Jacob's dreamscape itself, reigniting its force, asserting its space against the counterforce, the counter-space, of the oppressive, hierarchical "real." The following chapters take up Robeson's insight that the space of the dream, what I call in this book the dreamscape, is a site of politics, a space in and around which ideas and forces vie for power.

This book focuses on the politics of the dreamscape as a space contested by two archetypal modes of thinking about dreaming, one authoritarian and the other anarchistic. These modes, importantly, rarely, if ever, exist in a pure form as either completely anarchistic or totally authoritarian—nor does one single political mode ever fully control or define the dreamscape. Each instance of the politics of the dreamscape is a complex and contextually situated blend of political logics. The chapters that follow attempt to break down specific paradigmatic moments of dreaming in literature and culture in order to identify and describe the precise interplay of political forces converging in and around them. Because of the complexity of each instance of dreaming, this book eschews an attempt at a synthetic history of the politics of dreaming or dream interpretation. Instead, it focuses, in detail, on a limited number of illustrative examples of the politics of the dreamscape that establish or reflect important and influential ways of thinking about dreaming. Within this structure, the analysis proceeds more or less chronologically. It begins by proposing an "origin myth" of dreaming in Genesis's Garden of Eden story and ends with the dreamscape's neurobiological "erasure." Between these two poles, I discuss the multifaceted nature of biblical dreaming, the rise of Freudian psychoanalytic dream interpretation, and a set of modernist alternatives to the Freudian paradigm in the work of Philip Roth, Carl Jung, Jean Rhys, and Franz Kafka. This methodology reveals the different dimensions of the dream as a site of politics. Far from marginal or peripheral, discourses on dreaming have been central to the operation and challenging of power.

Throughout this book, I argue that the authoritarian tendencies of presenting dreaming work to reinforce hierarchical structures, to reify conceptions of identity that limit freedom and promote social and cultural conformity, and to support coercive institutional and personal power. As I demonstrate in Chap. 2, even radical artists like William Blake fall into an authoritarian mode when they deploy dream interpretation in ways that overlap with repressive discourses. In the case of Blake's *Illustrations of the Book of Job*, the dream-texts (illustrations 11 and 12 of the cycle), though containing powerful disruptive and radical elements, connect to the discursive history of European anti-Semitism through its drive for narrative cohesion. The example of Blake points to what seems to be a structural issue in the politics of the dreamscape: the authoritarian conquest of the dreamscape tends to be more prominent—and the moments or expressions of an anarchic politics of the dreamscape fragile and fleeting. Anarchic moments can, moments later, give way to or co-exist with authoritarian structures, especially as the norms of narrative and the allure or demands of interpretation seep in. I demonstrate this process with Blake's *Job* as well as in a discussion of Robert Frost's poem "After Apple-Picking." At the same time, the process of overwriting and marginalizing these anarchic moments is never complete. As I suggest with Robeson's performance above, and in my analysis of Jacob's dream of the ladder later in the book, the anarchic potential and energy of the dreamscape remain alongside or buried beneath these authoritarian interpretive and narrative constructs and apply pressure on them. Jacob's dreamscape maintains its radicalism, and it is there to be reanimated by Robeson's millennia after its seeming capture or erasure by authoritarian forces. The nature of the dreamscape itself, which I will discuss below, helps explain this anarchic potency.

Much of what Susan Sontag writes about the interpretation of art can be said about the interpretation of dreams. In "Against Interpretation," Sontag writes:

> Today is such a time, when the project of interpretation is largely reactionary, stifling. Like the fumes of the automobile and of heavy industry which befoul the urban atmosphere, the effusion of interpretations of art today poisons our sensibilities. In a culture whose already classical dilemma is the hypertrophy of the intellect at the expense of energy and sensual capability, interpretation is the revenge of the intellect upon art. (1969: 17)

Sontag's notion that interpretation works against "energy" and "sensual capacity" aligns with the manner in which dream interpretation drains the dreamscape of its partiality, instability, chaos, and intensity—the very attributes that form the basis of its anarchic potential, which I discuss in the sections of this book on Jacob's dream of the ladder (Chap. 3), Jean Rhys (Chap. 5), and Franz Kafka (Chap. 6). At the same time, this book does not do away with interpretation. This would hardly be possible. Rather, it insists on reinterpretations that illuminate the workings of the dreamscape as an anarchic space. Sontag, too, does not reject all interpretations, only types of interpretations that "destroy" the interpreted object by coopting it into a dominating interpretive logic. Sontag contrasts this destructive mode of interpretation with a type of interpretation that functions as a "liberating act," interpretation as "a means of *revising*, of *transvaluing*, of *escaping* the dead past" (1969: 17, emphasis mine).

The anarchism of the dreamscape, as I define it, is related to but not the same as anarchism as a political theory, which Robert Graham defines, using a "historical-contextual approach," as a "political doctrine based on anti-authoritarianism, anti-statism, anti-parliamentarianism, voluntary association, libertarian methods and direct action" (2018: 32). Though anarchistic conceptions of the dreamscape challenge authority, they do not propose a usable political model, system, or vision. Rather, the anarchism of the dreamscape can be understood on a more fundamental level as a force for rupture or disruption that calls into question the building blocks of authoritarian, coercive power. In this book, the anarchism of the dreamscape is mainly conceived of as a mode of radical critique. This mode has common features that present themselves in sources ranging from Biblical times to modernist literature, though the precise operations of these features vary from case to case. This diversity of strategies of rupture or disruption is an important element of the dreamscape's anarchism. Absent the formation of a radically reinvented society, anarchism can remain vital primarily as a mode of radical critique—and this vitality depends precisely on its diversity and flexibility. These modes of critique work to destabilize the normative logic of the dominant, quotidian operations of power, thus opening up spaces—whether real or imagined—for alternative understandings and enactments of subjectivity and social arrangements.

Chuang Tzu's "Butterfly Dream"

An important example of the dreamscape's anarchistic attributes appears in the second chapter of the *Book of Chuang Tzu* (late fourth century/early third century BCE). A brief discussion of Chuang Tzu's "Butterfly Dream" in relation to his notion of chaos (*hundun*) will help frame the dimensions of this book. In the key passage, Chuang Tzu writes:

> Once upon a time, I, Chuang Tzu, dreamt that I was a butterfly, flitting around and enjoying myself. I had no idea I was Chuang Tzu. Then suddenly I woke up and was Chuang Tzu again. But I could not tell, had I been Chuang Tzu dreaming I was a butterfly, or a butterfly dreaming I was

> now Chuang Tzu? However, there must be some sort of difference between Chuang Tzu and a butterfly! We call this the transformation of things. (2006: 20)

Chuang Tzu's "Butterfly Dream" calls into question the nature and stability of the self and, from an epistemological point of view, the dream can be understood as challenging Descartes's response to the regression into total skepticism through the postulation of the *Cogito, ergo sum* formulation (Han 2009). The dream has been read by Harold Roth as reflecting Chuang Tzu's mystical orientation in which self-based knowledge or identity/perspective is an imposition to the mystical union with the universe and the gaining of a greater type of knowledge of the totality of being (1999). More radically, Kai-Yuan Cheng asserts that the butterfly dream is Chuang Tzu's formulation of the non-existence of the self—what Cheng calls the "no-self" position. Cheng asserts that, for Chuang Tzu, even though a space or "arena" of selfhood can be described, it must be seen as being "empty" or without a "true ruler" in the sense of a core, stable, and discernible notion of selfhood. Cheng's notion of the "no-self" goes beyond others who see in the butterfly dream an indication of a self-in-flux. Cheng writes: "Zhuangzi [Chuang Tzu] is strongly opposed to self-attachment and egocentrism... Knowing that self is an illusion gives us an intellectual understanding that there is nothing about me that needs to be protected with all my power and resources" (2014: 588).

Other scholars develop further the idea that the butterfly in the butterfly dream represents a kind of ethical example, one in line with the non-hierarchical, anti-egoistic notions expressed by Cheng. Sandra A. Wawrytko, for example, compares Chuang Tzu to Nietzsche to emphasize the creative, non-hierarchical, and playful nature of his philosophy:

> Zhuang Zi [Chuang Tzu] is a fluttering yin butterfly, who invites us to play. Ever receptive and flexible, imbued with *wu-wei* effortless action, the butterfly has no purpose beyond its own play... The newly awakened Zhuang Zi is at first uncertain whether he is a human who dreamed of being a butterfly or a butterfly dreaming of being a human. Zhuang Zi ultimately rejects this false dilemma, embracing the underlying harmony

> of the "Transformation of Things" (*wu-hua*). He is both butterfly and human, the dreamer and the dream. (2008: 528)

Like Roth, Wawrytko's idea of the "false dilemma" and an "underlying harmony" points to the more general Daoist conception of the limitation of the individual perspective on apparent reality. For Chuang Tzu, the finding of the Dao requires a discovery of the unity of the universe in its undifferentiated state. The freedom of the non-self is part of the discovery of the inherent falsity of all individuated things. This idea is expressed most famously by Chuang Tzu's in the *Hundun* or Chaos parable at the end of his Chap. 7. Chuang Tzu writes:

> The Emperor of the South Sea is known as Change. The Emperor of the North Sea is called Dramatic. The Emperor of the Centre is called Chaos [Hundun]. Change and Dramatic met every so often in the region of Chaos. Chaos always treated them kindly and virtuously. Change and Dramatic said: "Everyone has seven orifices so they can see, hear, eat, and breathe. Chaos does not have these. Let us bore some holes into him." Each day they bored a hole into Chaos…but on the seventh day Chaos died. (2006: 64)

In the parable, the center is the zone of chaos and defined by its unrefinement, lack of form, and failure to adhere to the norms of subjectivity and, thus, action in the world. Change (also translated as "speed") and Dramatic (or "sudden"), on the other hand, are words of action. These forces are welcomed in the center with kindness and virtue. Instead of understanding the world of *Hundun* or Chaos, the emperors Change and Dramatic seek to improve their host by giving Hundun an individuality, a singularity, and a recognizable subjectivity. The creation of form from the void of chaos, then, is tantamount to death. The process of the creation of form and individuation of things means the destruction of a harmonious world and a greater good—a state of being that knows no division between one thing and another, oneself and another. With the death of *Hundun*, it would seem like this center, this vital space for discovering the harmony of chaos and the ethics and virtues of pre-creation and non-differentiation—a space that houses the breakdown of boundaries and definitions—has been destroyed. This collapse of the zone of the center leads back to the "Butterfly Dream," because it is here that the space of chaos, the center, reopens—inspiring again the recognition of the ethics of the dreamspace as the "transformation of things," the instability of creation, and the ultimate artificiality and tenability of definitions and distinctions. In an article on the eighteenth-century Chinese novel *Dream of the Red Chamber*, Zuyan Zhou points to the political implications of the death of *Hundun* by juxtaposing its chaos and "primeval harmony" with the acts of the legendary Chinese leaders "whose imposition of rules, order, government and conventions gave rise to hierarchy and ambition, thereby disrupting the primordial chaos/harmony" (2001: 255).

As Eugene Eoyang points out, the word *hundun* references the movement of water: "the rhymed compound conveys the sense of the turbulence, the whirling action of water currents, the turbid flowing, yet unfathomable rhythms of swirling action" (1989: 275). This reference to water connects the Chinese *hundun* to the biblical notion of chaos as characteristic of the pre-creation "deep," which I discuss in Chap. 2 as a vital anarchistic component of the dreamscape. This is a fascinating convergence of the Daoist and biblical texts. In the Hebrew Bible, the "deep" (*tehom*) carries with it reference to Tiamat, the goddess of the primeval ocean and the principal antagonist to the creator God in the pre-biblical traditions. In the Hebrew Bible, the deep is an ungodly state and the setting of God's miraculous process of creation. The taming of chaos, in Genesis, engenders the coming of the "good," while in Chuang Tzu, the death of chaos signifies the destruction of virtue and the rise of differentiation and, thus, falsity, inequality, and hierarchy. Eoyang approaches the essential connection between chaos or *hundun* and anarchism when he writes, "Understanding hun-dun as something physically and metaphysically impenetrable probably harks back to the parable in Zhuangzi, which reminds us that hun-dun, once penetrated, dies; the suggestion is that chaos once understood is no longer chaos" (1989: 275). If we draw these two parables together, the "Butterfly Dream" and "Hundun," we can posit that the dreamscape recreates or even preserves the "center kingdom" as a space ruled by benevolent or virtuous chaos, which hosts without judging, categorizing, or dominating. In other words, the dreamspace as a kingdom of chaos is an anarchistic space in an absolute sense, but to remain so, it, too, must remain, like *hundun*, impenetrable, "whirling," "flowing"—unfixed by any specific paradigm or agenda of interpretation. Here the dreamscape connects to the central Daoist concept of "the way," which, Ellen Marie Chen argues, in its "emptiness" and "pure motion" forms the basis for creation: "…*Tao* is…indefinable, nameless, shape of no-shape, sign of no-thing, illusive and evasive…exactly because *Tao* is motion, a motion that produces all things" (1969: 396). It might seem paradoxical to refuse interpretive systems and at the same time to call for an understanding of the dreamscape as anarchistic. I would like to suggest, however, that the dreamscape's anarchism is an attribute of its emergence as a rupture in the landscape of the "real" and the fleeting creation by this rupture of a "center kingdom" in the sense of the Hundun parable—not a quality conferred on it through interpretation. Following Sontag, an emancipatory type of interpretation seeks to preserve this anarchic attribute rather than to reorganize the dreamscape in the service of authoritarian and hierarchical political modes.

Defining the Dreamscape

I use the term dreamscape purposefully but with a certain amount of hesitation. The word dreamscape implies the existence of a space separate from the "territory" or "territories" of waking life and discrete from the consciousness of the dreamer. In the theoretical literature in the field of geography, the difference between "space" and "territory" is generated by the assertion of power (authority) and the continuous (re)organization of politics and society. Stuart Elden, for example, asserts that "creating a bounded space is already a violent act of exclusion and inclusion; maintaining it as such requires constant vigilance and the mobilization of threat; and challenging it necessarily entails a transgression" (2010: 806–807). The dreamscape as a space or field, in this sense, is a non-territory—a space resistant to boundaries (both of space and time) and strategies of control.

A dreamscape has been defined as a "scene that is reminiscent of a dream," as a "representation of a dream in a painting or other work of art," and as a "landscape or image seen in a dream" (OED 2017). These three definitions, though seemingly complimentary, are in tension with each other. The first purports to extrapolate the qualities of oneiric space in order to define a non-dream space as dream-like. This points to the blurred boundaries between dreaming and waking life, ultimately calling into question the existence of two states of consciousness opposed in binary fashion, as displayed in the example of Chuang Tzu's "Butterfly Dream" and in the third stanza of Robeson's "Jacob's Ladder" ("rise and shine"). The second definition maintains that the dreamscape is synonymous with its graphic and/or literary representation. The third stands opposed to the second: here the dreamscape is not a secondary representation but rather the space of the dream itself, the dream's environment, its world. According to this definition, representations of dreamscapes are not dreamscapes; they are descriptions or *translations* of dreamscapes into (audio) visual or written language. This distinction is critical, because the politics of the dreamscape as discussed in this book concern precisely the translation or transformation of the oneiric field into dream-image, dream-text, dream-data, and so on. As I will show, the tools for fashioning such a representation of the dreamscape—the "mapping" of the dreamscape and its transformation into "territory"—are not only the pen and paintbrush but also interpretive paradigms and ideological positions.

The dreamscape is a space, but not a clearly delineated space or zone. A critical feature of a dreamscape is precisely, because its shape is not fixed or fixable, it cannot be represented or translated fully or perfectly into image, text, or audio-visual experience. Amorphousness and borderlessness are core attributes of the dreamscape. The dreamscape, in other words, is a *disordered* space, and the imposition of order onto it is a political act. Where, for example, are the boundaries of a dream? They are always beyond view, shifting, dissolving, reforming. This notion of the dreamscape as disordered—lacking clear form or borders—might seem obvious, but it is often reduced or ignored in the push toward explicating the meaning of a dream.

At the same time, the concept of the dreamscape runs in parallel to the concept of landscape, which seems to imply a hardening of boundaries, order, and a domination of space by the gaze of the viewer. My hesitation with the concept of dreamscape comes in the context of its relationship to landscape. On the other hand, landscape is not the same as landscape painting or photography. The latter representations equate with my notion of dream-text. Rather, landscape in its pre-representational form is just as borderless and amorphous as the dreamscape. As such, the space of the dream reminds us precisely of the irreducibility, complexity, ungraspability, fluidity, and interconnectedness of nature. The fluid state of the dream is, at the same time, the underlying and anarchic fluidity (the chaos, the *hundun*, the *tehom*) of the real, both zones inhabited by Chuang Tzu's butterfly-subjects, subjects without "true rulers" or defined, unitary, stable, and identifiable "selves."

Jorge Luis Borges refers to dreams as works of fiction and rightly points out that when one speaks of dreams, one is speaking only of a partial memory of a dream or a distorted version of the dream transformed into narrative or image (1984: 26–27). Access to an original, chaotic dreamscape is impossible—as is access to an equivalent boundless "landscape." Accordingly, this book on the politics of the dreamscape aims to explore representations of dreamscapes (dream-texts) by positing the presence of tensions between structures of authoritarianism in dream representations and a countervailing impulse toward anarchy contained in the pre-organized (non-territorial) dreamscape. While the vast majority of dream-texts are concerned with transforming the dreamscape into discernible territory through the application of structures of coercive power, other dream-texts attempt to preserve or articulate elements of the pre-territorial dreamscape. My work, following Borges, takes all dream-fictions—from those purportedly objective reports of "real" dreams (Freud's dream of Irma's injection or Dora's dream of the jewelcase) to seemingly invented dreams (like K.'s dream of wrestling an official in Kafka's *The Castle* or Sasha Jensen's "Exhibition Dream" in Jean Rhys's *Good Morning, Midnight*)—as manifestations of the same phenomenon: attempts to represent a dreamscape by refashioning it as a dream-text.

Chapter 2 presents a theoretical discussion of the politics of the dreamscape in its authoritarian and anarchistic tendencies. In this chapter, I define what I consider the main features of the anarchism of the dreamscape. The dreamscape, I argue (as I have presented above in the case of Chuang Tzu), contains remnants of the state of chaos or pre-creation, a state that preceded the imposition of authority, structure, and hierarchy.

My reading of what I call "dreamscape origins" through the Garden of Eden narrative maintains that the dreamscape opens up only after the expulsion of Adam and Eve from the Garden of Eden. Dreaming—a state different from being awake and from the emptiness of prelapsarian sleep—contains the force of the entropic dissolution of order toward a primordial state of chaos, symbolized by the notion of the "deep" (*tehom*) and the Edenic character of the serpent. The force of chaos and the presence of the pre-creation deep in the dreamscape connect to the fundamental disordering act in Genesis, Eve's rebellion against God's authority by eating the fruit of the tree of knowledge. Eve's rebellion, I argue, is one of multifaceted desire against the hierarchies and circumscriptions of the Edenic order. In the postlapsarian world, this disordering impulse, or urge toward chaos, finds its home in the dreamscape.

If the dreamscape preserves the disordered space and entropic force of chaos (*hundun*, *tehom*), it is also home to radically destabilized subjects, resistant, though ultimately vulnerable, to fixed identity constructions. Subjects in the dreamscape are fluid—they fracture, double or triple, mirror, combine, and dissolve into airy nothingness. All subjects emerge as vaporous or spectral and solidify and rigidify only through the imposition of the representative dream-text and its corresponding interpretation. The lack of solidification, separateness, and clarity of subjectivity stages an equality of dream-subjects, undercutting hierarchical assertions.

This understanding of the anarchism of the dreamscape as a mode of critique—critique of structures of order, hierarchical relationships, fixed identities, independent subjectivities, assertions of interpretive or narrative control—allows for a shift of focus away from the interpretation of a narrative or graphic dream-text and toward elements such as the movement, instability, and intensity. My discussions of texts by Robert Frost, Jean Rhys, and Franz Kafka engage with these elements. Dreaming, when seen in this light, acts as an anarchic force that is woven into the textures of daily life and can be seen as a model for rethinking space and subjectivity in the realm of waking "reality." In fact, it is imperative that this rethinking be done—both for the sake of the dreamscape's waking parallel, nature, which is being systematically destroyed by the compounded effects of hierarchical arrangements that seek to territorialize the world in Elden's sense, and for the sake of waking subjects, who could start to imagine the world of Hundun's Center Kingdom, one of hospitality, caring, virtue, the equality of subjects, the interconnectivity (not in a false techtopian sense but in a real Levinasian ethical sense) of subjectivities—subjectivities constantly shifting, changing, or *becoming* in relation to the world. The anarchic force of the dreamscape, as I demonstrate in the subsequent chapters, provokes authoritarian interpretive models of dream analysis designed to quash or contain these "chaotic" pressures.

After presenting a theoretical framework for thinking about the politics of the dreamscape in Chap. 2, Chaps. 3 and 4 discuss two important paradigms in the history of dream analysis: biblical dream interpretation and Freudian psychoanalysis. Chapter 3 develops the biblical dream interpretation introduced in Chap. 2 by offering a speculative critique of the dominant interpretation of the stories of Jacob and Joseph in the book of Genesis. While the standard narrative views Joseph as the chosen son of Jacob and as the continuation of the divinely ordained patriarchal line leading from Abraham to Moses, I propose that the biblical text contains two incompatible portraits of Joseph and that the best way to understand the narrative logic of these conflicting portraits is through close analysis of the ways the dream-texts work in the story. In the case of Joseph, the dream-texts support a philosophy of history that foregrounds the subsequent Exodus story, the founding myth of ancient Israelite religion, statehood, and identity. I speculate in this chapter that an alternative tradition can be traced in the Joseph story that sees Joseph not as a continuation of the patriarchal line, and as a heroic figure in Jewish history, but as a tyrannical figure and enemy of the faith of Jacob. By seeing Joseph in this light, I propose a new reading of Jacob and specifically his vision of the ladder as suggesting a more immediate, non-hierarchical, and more personal and open conception of faith. It is precisely this anarchistic conception of faith, I contend, that the Joseph tradition seeks to bury in the text through the interpolation of the dream-texts and, with it, the idea of divinely controlled history. In Genesis, an authoritarian conception of dreaming overwrites the more radical and immediate politics of Jacob's dreamscape. As I say above with the example of Paul Robeson, however, the radical politics of Jacob's dreamscape continue to present emancipatory possibilities despite the authoritarian exegetical tradition.

Chapter 4 looks at Sigmund Freud as the first part of a discussion of modernist and contemporary conceptions of dreaming. The subsequent sections on Carl Jung, Philip Roth, Jean Rhys, Franz Kafka, and sleep/dream science all implicitly or explicitly draw on and critique Freud's work. Chapter 4 focuses on Freud's reading of two dreams, the so-called specimen dream or dream of Irma's injection in *The Interpretation of Dreams* (1900) and Dora's first dream in *Fragment of an Analysis of a Case of Hysteria* (1905). I argue that Freud's creation and analysis of the dream-text express the developing politics of the dreamscape in the emerging theory and practice of psychoanalysis. Evoking the analogy of late nineteenth-century European imperialism—a movement concurrent with the development of psychoanalysis—I discuss Freud's "colonization" of the space of the dreamscape, the transformation of this space into "territory," and the importance of this territorial construction and occupation in terms of psychoanalysis's relative position in the medical field and the position of the analyst in relation to the patient. The occupation of the dreamscape sets the stage for a "civilizing process" by which the analyst attempts to assert order and control over the "sick" psyche. With the specimen dream, Freud maps the general terrain of the dreamscape, understanding it as the site of a complex multiparty contestation between psychoanalyst, patient, medical institutions and discourses, and the social norms governing the public and private spheres. In the case of Dora's first dream, Freud's weaving of scientific methods and hermeneutical analysis aspires to total occupation and control of the territory of the dreamscape and represents a complexly articulated expression of the authoritarian structure of psychoanalytic dream interpretation. In attempts to reanalyze *Dora*, critics of the case study have contested nearly all of Freud's conclusions without, however, calling into question the political nature of the structure of his dream analysis. As a consequence of this neglect, the search for dream meaning in contemporary culture remains anchored to professionalized psychological discourse and dependent on the relationship between scientific and hermeneutical logics—a blending that is often enacted through the hierarchical nature of therapy and iterated in the story or text of the case study, whether it be in the form of a written report or as an oral construct produced by the therapeutic communication.

Chapter 5 builds on the analysis of Freud's dream interpretation by analyzing two cases, Philip Roth and Carl Jung, in which dream-texts act as a force for narrative and thematic integration. My analysis of the integrative function of dream-texts in terms of narrative and thematic structure is based on Neil Klugman's "Island Dream" from Philip Roth's novella *Goodbye, Columbus* (1959) and the sequence of dream reports from Carl Jung's "Individual Dream Symbolism in Relation to Alchemy" (2010). These two texts represent bookends to the thinking about dreaming at the height of psychoanalytic power within the scientific community and society at large. With Roth, my aim is to show how the integrative functions of the dream-text are deployed in popular literary narratives (Roth's collection won the National Book Award in 1959). Jung's piece on dreams and alchemy, on the other hand, represents one of the most sophisticated uses of the dream-text in the quest for wholeness or totality in the modernist era. The chapter contrasts these integrative approaches with Jean Rhys's novel *Good Morning, Midnight* (1939). In the latter, the dream-text becomes a potential site of disintegration, gesturing toward anarchistic possibilities. The chapter proposes that *Good Morning, Midnight* challenges dominant and authoritarian models of modernist integrative dream interpretation, and asserts, as a counter-position, the emancipatory possibilities of disintegration.

Chapter 6 continues the discussion of the dreamscape as a site of radical politics and argues that one of Franz Kafka's most anarchic political expressions, the expression of freedom in *The Castle*'s dream scene, relies on an understanding of dream experience that is grounded in notions of disintegration, intensity, and escape. The analysis pivots around the politics of dreaming in the single dream-text in *The Castle* (written in 1922, published in 1926). I contextualize my discussion of the novel by offering a detailed analysis of the dynamics of power in Kafka's short stories "The Judgment" (written in 1912, published in 1913) and "In the Penal Colony" (written in 1914, published in 1919), as well as in his unfinished novel *The Trial* (written in 1914–1915, published in 1925). This analysis identifies key characteristics of Kafka's conceptions of power, including the hermetic quality of systems of power in his work, the expression of power as performance or everyday practice, the inherent fragility (despite their apparent invulnerability) of power structures, and the tendency of one system of power to overtake, displace, or marginalize competitors. I then present an analysis of Kafka's writings on dreaming, reading passages from his diaries as containing anarchic impulses. The chapter concludes with a close reading of K.'s dream in *The Castle* against Kafka's conception of power in the novel.

The final chapter, Chap. 7, turns from modernist conceptions of dreaming to what I term the neurobiological "erasure" of the dreamscape. The chapter focuses on dream science and its relationship to scientific and popular discourses of neurobiology, including those related to the marketing of psychotropic drugs and sleep medication. The focal point in this chapter is an analysis of an exhibition held at Harvard's Carpenter Center for the Arts in 1977 called *Dreamstage*. *Dreamstage* was the brainchild of the Harvard psychiatrist J. Allan Hobson and combined popular science with art in order to publicly present recent neurobiological discoveries in relatable terms. The chapter argues that *Dreamstage* and related discourses helped to transform dreaming from primarily an illusory or imaginative construct into a physical and biochemical process, thus stripping it of "meaning" and rendering it part of the sleep cycle (coterminous with REM sleep). This stripping away of the illusory realm works to obliterate the dreamscape as a space apart and different from any physical manifestation, in effect denying or erasing its existence. The chapter places this erasure of the dreamscape in the context of the rise of 24/7 consumer capitalism and the increasing technophile society of the late 1970s and 1980s—developments continuing (and further accelerating) today.

References

Borges, Jorge L. *Seven Nights*. Trans. Eliot Weinberger. New York: New Directions, 1984.

Chen, Ellen M. "Nothingness and the Mother Principle in Early Chinese Taoism." *International Philosophical Quarterly* 9.3 (1969): 391–405.

Cheng, Kai-Yuan. "Self and the Dream of the Butterfly in the Zhuangzi." *Philosophy East and West* 64.3 (2014): 563–597.

Elden, Stuart. "Land, Terrain, Territory." Progress in Human Geography 34.6 (2010): 799–817.

Eoyang, Eugene. "Chaos Misread: Or, There's Wonton in My Soup." *Comparative Literature Studies* 26.3 (1989): 271–284.

Graham, Robert. "(Mis)conceptions of Anarchism," *Anarchist Studies* 26.2 (2018): 32–55.

Han, Xiaoqiang. "Interpreting the Butterfly Dream." *Asian Philosophy* 19.1 (2009): 1–9.

Jung, Carl. "Individudal Dream Symbolism in Relation to Alchemy." *Dreams*. Trans. R.F.C. Hull. Princeton: Princeton UP, 2010.

Lowndes, Joseph E. *From the New Deal to the New Right: Race and the Southern Origins of Modern Conservatism*. New Haven: Yale University Press, 2008.

OED Online. Oxford: Oxford UP. 3 November 2017.

Perucci, Tony. *Paul Robeson and the Cold War Performance Complex: Race, Madness, Activism*. Ann Arbor: U of Michigan P, 2012.

O'Dell, Jack. *Climbin' Jacob's Ladder: The Black Freedom Movement Writings of Jack O'Dell*. Ed. Nikhil Pal Singh. Berkeley: University of California Press, 2010.

Robeson, Paul. *Here I Stand*. Boston: Beacon, 1958.

Roth, Harold D. *Original Tao: Inward Training (Nei-Yeh) and the Foundations of Taoist Mysticism*. New York: Columbia UP, 1999.

Sontag, Susan. *Against Interpretation and Other Essays*. New York: 1969.

Tzu, Chuang. *The Book of Chuang Tzu*. Trans. Martin Palmer. New York: Penguin, 2006.

Wawrytko, Sandra A. "Deconstructing Deconstructions: Zhuang Zi as Butterfly, Nietzsche as Gadfly." *Philosophy East and West* 58.4 (2008): 524–551.

Zhou, Zuyan. "Chaos and the Gourd in *The Dream of the Red Chamber*." *Y'oung Pau* 87.4 (2001): 251-288.

2

Dreams and Power: Authoritarian Territory, Anarchistic Space in the Garden of Eden, William Blake's *Illustrations of the Book of Job*, and Robert Frost's "After Apple-Picking"

Introduction

The dreamscape has long been a site of political contestation. Regimes of power, from ancient Near and Middle Eastern kings to medieval religious authorities and more contemporary psychological and scientific discourses, have attempted to occupy this space by relying on modes of interpretation and structures of interpretive legitimacy (Oppenheim 1956). Within these regimes, the dream interpreter becomes an agent of authority—establishing or reinforcing dynamics of power and concomitant ideologies.

The desire to control the dreamscape for the purposes of developing hierarchy and aggrandizing authoritarian power runs through a wide array of ancient sources—from the first recorded dream on the Stele of the Vultures[1] to the Sumerian cuneiform text of the Gudea cylinders describing the building of a temple for the god Ningirsu[2] to Solomon's dream at Gibeon after rising to occupy King David's throne in the Bible.[3] In the "Legend of Sargon," a third millennium BCE Akkadian account, the interpretation of dreams plays a pivotal role in the rise of Sargon against the kings Urzababa and Lugal-zage-si. Though the story sets the

© The Author(s), under exclusive license to Springer Nature Switzerland AG 2021

S. Rogoff, *The Politics of the Dreamscape*,
https://doi.org/10.1007/978-3-030-74796-1_2

stage for Sargon's seizure of the throne of Kish and his subsequent campaigns to dominate Akkad, and is therefore one of rebellion against entrenched power, the authoritarian structure remains unchanged: the dream-texts in the legend serve to legitimize the power of the newly chosen leader and his religious cult (Noegel 2001: 47; Heinz and Feldman 2006: 67–86).

A countercurrent exists to the authoritarian politics of representing the dreamscape—what I call a radical current or an anarchism of the dreamscape. While this anarchistic current is as shifting and heterodox as the authoritarian side, it differs in that it calls into question or undermines authoritarian paradigms. The anarchic possibilities of the dreamscape have not yet been the focus of scholarly attention. By uncovering and theorizing the anarchism of the dreamscape, this and subsequent chapters contribute new concepts to the history of dream interpretation, anarchist theory, and theories and practices of resistance to authoritarian and hierarchical power structures.

Definitions of anarchism have ranged from those rooted in historically contingent contexts (nineteenth-century Europe and Russia, for example) to those grounded in a set of transhistorical principles. In English, the concept of anarchy/anarchism first emerged in the sixteenth century and for the following centuries was used to describe a state of lawlessness and chaos (OED Online). In Book Two of *Paradise Lost*, for example, Milton evokes the concept of anarchy in the description of the "deep" that Satan and Sin encounter when the gates of hell are unlocked and thrown open:

> So wide they stood, and like a Furnace mouth
> Cast forth redounding smoak and ruddy flame.
> Before thir eyes in sudden view appear
> The secrets of the hoarie deep, a dark
> Illimitable Ocean without bound,
> Without dimension, where length, breadth, and highth,
> And time and place are lost; where eldest Night
> And Chaos, Ancestors of Nature, hold
> Eternal Anarchie, amidst the noise
> Of endless Warrs and by confusion stand. (Milton 1975: 50–51)

Milton's mention of anarchy as the basic condition of nature without the steady and creative hand of God endows the concept with transhistorical meaning. Anarchy is a condition that precedes power, authority, and social organization. It is the negative of creation, which means in this sense the imposition of order and the elimination of chaos. The notion of a condition preceding the ordering and structuring of the world provides the starting point for other articulations of anarchism. In *Demanding the Impossible*, Peter Marshall attempts to compile some general principles common to many strains of anarchism:

> If you dive into an anarchist philosophy, you generally find a particular view of human nature, a critique of the existing order, a vision of a free society, and a way to achieve it. All anarchists reject the legitimacy of external government and of the State, and condemn imposed political authority, hierarchy and domination. (2009: 3)

For Marshall, anarchism can be found among ancient writings in most civilizations and is especially pronounced in Daoism and Zen Buddhism. Leonard Williams echoes the central thrust of Marshall's definition, claiming, "Through it all, anarchism seems to retain its central character as a viewpoint opposed to the presence of coercion, hierarchy, and authority in human affairs" (2007: 300).

Lucien van der Walt gives a more specific "origin" point for the emergence of anarchism, which he locates in middle to late nineteenth-century Europe. "The historical record shows very clearly," he argues, "that a specific, self-defined, consciously anarchist movement, only and first, emerged in the First International around Mikhail Bakunin and the International Alliance of Social Democracy. That puts it in the period from 1864, around 150 years ago—not in the Garden of Eden and not in the ancient world" (2016: 92). This dating is key, van der Walt argues, because it shows anarchism's inherent connections to the broader workers' movement. "A historical approach points us to the First International. That locates anarchism, as a consequence," he writes, "as rooted in the working class and socialist movement" (2016: 92). Such historical definitions of anarchism link anarchist theory to movements of resistance to the emerging modern nation-state. Thus, Leonard Williams writes, "At the most basic level, anarchism is fundamentally opposed to the existence of the State and the authority relations that the State codifies, legitimates, or represents" (2007: 300).

While from a historical perspective, anarchism as a modern political philosophy emerged in the revolutionary and post-revolutionary period in Europe, the deeper roots of anarchist concepts point to the existence of anarchistic strategies of resistance dating back to ancient times. These strategies have animated resistance movements across the globe and stem from combinations of political theory and localized practices. The anarchism of the dreamscape calls on these traditions of resistance, thus eluding strict historical periodization (which could itself be seen as a means of narrative control) and pointing toward the transhistorical and global nature of anti-authoritarianism. I contend that the dreamscape offers an a-systematic conception of power and resistance that presents combinations of the following two key general anarchistic assertions.

First, the dreamscape hosts unstable subjects—Chuang Tzu's butterflies. Because of this, identity cannot be fixed in the space of the dreamscape; any momentarily coalesced identity is immediately questioned, unraveled, or dismantled. In many cases, the emerging dreamscape serves as a moment of rupture, breaking apart a notion of a unified, atomistic subjectivity. On the contrary, attempts to transform the dreamscape into dream-text serve to solidify subjectivity and fix identity, thereby re-inscribing the anarchistic potential of the dreamscape into the logic of authoritarian power. This process of re-inscription can be seen below in the example of Blake's *Illustrations of the Book of Job*. While Job's terror in the dreamscape is an anarchic moment—it is a fracturing, destabilizing dislocation of selfhood and its concomitant ideology—the application of the Jewish/Christian binary (even in its Blakean form) puts the terror in the context of religious power dynamics, subsuming the narrative into anti-Jewish polemic.

The dreamscape, as a space for inter-subjective encounters between fluid and unstable subjects, breaks down barriers between self and other. The subject's lack of fixedness, its constructed nature, fluidity, and even its tendency to merge with others during an antagonistic (or erotic) encounter call into question attempts to establish hierarchy between dream-subjects; in the dreamscape, all subjects are *equal.* Blake's visual mirroring of Job and God works anarchically in this way, Job at once individual and universal. Ideology might permeate the dream-text—but the broken nature of dream-logic, the fluidity of the dreamspace, and the instability of dream-subjects render that ideology unstable and open to diverse strategies of resistance. In the field of the dreamscape, constructs of authority seem brittle and crumbling at best. It is precisely the intrusion of interpretive schema as dream-text, inevitable as it may be, that disrupts the underlying equality of subjects in the dreamscape.

Second, the emergence and formation of the dreamscape create a rupture in the authoritarian and hierarchical structures of everyday life and fashion, an anarchic zone—a kingdom of *hundun*, a space of fragmentation (but, importantly, not individuation), disruption, and disorder. The organized territory of wakefulness immediately and inevitably encroaches on the dreamscape through the fashioning of representation in its dominant terms, producing the dream-text. The political moment, then, orients around two possibilities. The first is the crystallization of the dream-texts in support of authoritarian (broadly speaking) narratives or constructs. The second possibility is the attempt to work back out of the dream-text toward the irrecoverable field of the dreamscape, which, though vanished, has left traces of its anarchistic potential—the residue of Job's terror in Blake's work, for example.

This chapter is divided into three parts. The first part of the chapter presents an origin myth of the dreamscape as a zone of refuge from the post-Edenic order established after the expulsion of the human pair from the Garden of Eden. This *imagined* moment of dreamscape origins contains the potentiality for anarchistic relationships in everyday life based on the fashioning of a zone of freedom, one analogous to the pre-creation state of chaos and symbolized by the notion of the "deep" (*tehom*) and comparable (or at least compatible) with Chuang Tzu's notion of *hundun* outlined in the introduction. The relationship between the nature of dreamscape origins and the secondary dream-text, I argue, puts pressure on representations of dreamscapes and seeks paths back into the raw, unrecoverable, chaotic zone of the dreamscape. The residue of the dreamscape in the dream-text contains an impulse toward "chaos" or "uncreation," a kind of self-effacing or disintegrative quality that challenges or destabilizes hierarchical relationships and assumptions. The second and third parts of this chapter look at two case studies of dream-texts that contain fascinating blends of authoritarian and anarchist currents. Section "An Origin Myth of the Dreamscape in Genesis 2-3" focuses on William Blake's *Illustrations of the Book of Job*, in which the dream-text (illustrations 11 and 12) creates a narrative rupture that precipitates transformation and enlightenment. On the one hand, this rupture destabilizes Job's subjectivity and fixed identity and opens space for radical spiritual formulations. On the other hand, it connects narratively and discursively to long-standing European anti-Jewish traditions, thus operating in an authoritarian manner. The third and final part of the chapter draws on the origin myth of the dreamscape to frame a reading of Robert Frost's poem "After Apple-Picking" as a dream-text that, like Blake's *Job*, moves in both authoritarian and anarchistic directions.

An Origin Myth of the Dreamscape in Genesis 2-3

Origin myths, even when perceived as fictions or allegories, serve to construct and perpetuate structures of authority (Walker-Jones 2008). The Garden of Eden story (Genesis 2-3) has been fundamental in forming the foundation for numerous hierarchies, dualisms, and ideological concepts, including patriarchy, sin/evil, anthropocentrism, and the subordination of the human to the divine. In recent decades, readings of the Garden of Eden narrative have presented a more nuanced picture of the story in order to destabilize traditional assumptions (Trible 1978; Jobling 2005; Armour and St. Ville 2006; Walker-Jones 2008). Mieke Bal, for example, reads Genesis 2-3 in ways that challenge two fundamental positions articulated in Paul's *I Timothy*, namely the primacy of Adam over Eve (hence Eve's/woman's subordinate status) and the notion that Eve alone, not Adam, was deceived by the serpent and (alone) transgressed God's prohibition. Together, these two Pauline ideas reinforce patriarchy not only within the traditions of Christianity but also in the broader culture of the West. Bal counters the Pauline tradition by equalizing the creation moment—both male and female are created together and in relation to the other—and rejecting the notion of Eve's deception (Bal 1985).

The project of fracturing monolithic ideological implications of origin myths opens up pathways for asserting counternarratives. In the discussion that follows, I propose an origin myth of the dreamscape. This proposition of dreamscape origins imagines that the dreamscape opens up as a consequence of Adam and Eve's expulsion from Eden, the beginnings of agricultural toil/work and thus recuperative sleep, and the imposition of a new paradigm of power that ties humanity to hierarchical arrangements based on a combination of force, morality, and the formation of rigid dualisms/identities (male/female, divine/mundane, human/animal, etc.). From its origins, this disorderly dreamscape contains traces of the primal chaos of the serpent and the multifaceted desire that enables Eve to overcome God's authority by eating the forbidden fruit. At the very moment of the formation of a new ideology and structure of power, in other words, comes the space for radical opposition: the dreamscape ruptures and destabilizes postlapsarian reality. On the edge of postlapsarian order and authoritarian power (of Adam, of God), the dreamscape presents a distinct type of anarchy (of Eve, of the serpent).

Genesis 2 sets in motion the historical story of humanity within the structures of paradisiacal authoritarianism.[4] The generic human being—the being of dust—turns into the flesh and blood Adam. The God of Genesis is unlike other ancient Near Eastern God-kings; it is not an uncaring, ruthless, or amoral deity concerned mainly with its own comfort and luxury (Sarna 1966: 16–18). God is described as a "good" being, a just and loving presence. As such, Adam is not first given the spade or the hoe; rather, he is set down in an environment, Eden, in which there is no difference between work and play or work and leisure. Umberto Cassuto's translation of the "creation of man" verses (2:5–7) is attuned to man's original labor-less existence. "Now no thorns of the field were yet in the earth," Cassuto begins, emphasizing the juxtaposition between this prelapsarian state of creation and the condition after the expulsion from Eden ("thorns and thistles it [the ground] shall sprout for you"). The juxtaposition continues with "no grain of the field had yet sprung up...." In Eden, sustenance is there for the taking as fruits from the trees. After the expulsion from Eden, sustenance must be earned through work (grains from the ground). The paradisiacal qualities of Eden are stressed further, according to Cassuto, in the text's mentioning of the watering of the ground: "but the waters of the deep went up from the earth and watered the whole face of the ground" (1961: 100). As Cassuto argues, the original state of the human being in the Garden of Eden is free of work, suffering, hardship, and worry. It is a life of splendid ease, in which all is provided by the natural cycles of irrigation and fructification, liberated from the fickleness of rain and the necessity to labor.

Only one thing is required of Adam for a life of perpetual (and perhaps immortal) luxury and ease—absolute obedience to God's authority and renunciation of any claim to challenge the authority or singularity of God's divine status. This authority and singularity are represented by the tree of the knowledge of good and bad, and the prohibition to eat from it. "The Lord God took the man and placed him in the Garden of Eden, to till and tend it. And the Lord God commanded the man, saying, 'Of every tree of the garden you are free to eat; but as for the tree of the knowledge of good and bad, you must not eat of it; for as soon as you eat of it, you shall die'" (Berlin and Brettler 2004: 16). Cassuto replaces "to till and tend it" with "to serve and to guard" (1961: 121), which seems more fitting, as the requirement that humans work for food (tillage) is only imposed on them as punishment for disobedience. Moreover, Cassuto's translation emphasizes the hierarchical relationship implicit in the prelapsarian Edenic moment ("to serve").

Until this point in the story, Adam exists only in the state of wakefulness. This is not surprising, considering that in the time after the creation there is no mental or physical exhaustion to make sleep necessary. Adam's existence does not weary him and thus there is no need for replenishment. Sleep is introduced into the story as part of the process of God fashioning a second being, Eve, out of the original human. God comes to Adam and induces a trance-like sleep, the first sleep, which Adam experiences as a dreamless and empty state of being: "So the Lord God cast a deep sleep upon the man" (Berlin and Brettler 2004: 16). During Adam's empty sleep, God dissects part of him (commonly considered a rib) and constructs a second human being out of this flesh—a woman, Eve. The fact that Eve is constructed during Adam's empty sleep and therefore completely beyond his consciousness is notable. It is as if the trance-like sleep reopens the period of creation that seemed to end with the creation of human beings in Genesis 1 and the day of cessation on the seventh day. This act of creation during sleep represents a type of *slippage* that I will highlight again when discussing the serpent. Woman, Eve, is the artifact of this slippage and symbolically connects the state of sleep with the act of creation and a time of (at least partial) chaos. In other words, the creation of Eve in the zone of empty sleep points to an entropic force, a tendency of creation to dissipate and then for things to be recreated.

In the voluminous commentary on Genesis 2, the empty sleep has been seen as having little significance. Cassuto sees Adam's sleep as necessitated by the aesthetics of the narrative; to cut into human flesh while Adam is awake would have been to destroy the poetics of the piece and to traumatize Adam (1961: 133–134). The Jewish legends compiled by Louis Ginzberg emphasize that the deep sleep was necessary in order to shield Adam from witnessing Eve's creation. Such a witnessing would have provided Adam a type of familiarly incompatible with amorous desire, "…God had created a wife for Adam [Lilith] before Eve, but he would not have her, because she had been made in his presence. Knowing well all the details of her formation, he was repelled by her" (Ginzberg 1909: 67–68). In terms of the power structure of prelapsarian Eden, another passage from the legends on Adam's sleep is more on point, because it makes manifest one of the central themes in the Garden of Eden story: the total yet tenuous nature of God's authority over creation, first and foremost over the human being. According to this passage, God's grasp on total authority was undermined by the creation of the first human being:

> And not alone the creatures of the earth, even the angels thought Adam the lord of all, and they were about to salute him with "Holy, holy, holy, is the Lord of Hosts," when God caused sleep to fall upon him, and then the angels knew that he was but a human being. (Ginzberg 1909: 64)

The prohibition of eating from the tree of knowledge of good and bad, the inducement of the first sleep, and the fashioning of Eve create the context for the great morality play of Genesis 3, the serpent's "seduction"—I would say, rather, the serpent's *provocation*—of Eve and the move of

Adam and Eve from the original paradisiacal state and into the realm of struggle, pain, and immutable mortality (God, of course, did not initially forbid Adam from eating from the tree of life). The rebellion of Eve and then Adam against God, and the need to find a new structure of divine authority in postlapsarian time, begins with the serpent's provocation of Eve to eat the fruit of the forbidden tree.

The serpent possesses some form of understanding greater than either of the two humans. While the humans bask in their innocence—knowing no shame, blissfully oblivious—the serpent is the "shrewdest of all the wild beasts that the Lord God had made" (Berlin and Brettler 2004: 16). When the serpent questions Eve about the forbidden fruit, Eve tells it of God's injunction. The serpent reveals to Eve that God has deceived them, saying, "You are not going to die, but God knows that as soon as you eat of it your eyes will be opened and you will be like the divine beings who know good and bad" (Berlin and Brettler 2004: 16). The serpent's words recognize the lie inherent in all relationships of power—in this case, the lie is that there is an inherent and impenetrable boundary between God (ruler) and human (ruled). In this case, the boundary consists of knowledge. Adam and Eve eat from the tree of the knowledge of good and bad, and thereby gain the knowledge formerly reserved for God.

The nature of what the serpent knows is unclear—he is described as "shrewd," "cunning." Analysis of serpents in Ancient Near East and the biblical literature points to a multitude of possible meanings—both positive and negative. As for relatively positive associations, Nahum Sarna writes, "In the Near East the serpent was a symbol of deity and fertility, and the images of the serpent-goddesses have been found in the ruins of many Canaanite towns and temples" (1966: 26). Jewish traditions also portray the serpent in a relatively positive light:

> Among the animals the serpent was notable. Of all of them he had the most excellent qualities, in some of which he resembled man…Had it not been for the fall of man, which brought misfortune to them, too, one pair of serpents would have sufficed to perform all the work man has to do…As a matter of fact, it was the very ability of the serpent that led to the ruin of man and his own ruin. (Ginzberg 1909: 71–72)

On the other hand, contextual parallels frequently contain notions of serpents as something like Manichean antagonists to God. Cassuto and others argue that Genesis transforms the notion of the serpent as divine antagonist in line with its broader monotheistic revolution. Usually the strictest of readers with regard to the literal statements of Genesis, Cassuto explains the serpent through metaphor:

> But since in the popular thought and language the concept of *evil* was strongly associated with that of the *serpent*, it was possible for the Torah, without changing its attitude to the ancient poetic tradition, to use the accepted folk ideas and phraseology that were a *product* of that tradition, and hence to choose specifically the serpent out of the animal world as the symbol of evil. And in order to make it quite clear that we have here only a symbol, and that we must not regard the serpent as an independent entity in opposition, as it were, to the Creator of the world, as the ancient tradition of the poets narrated, the Torah stressed at the very outset that the serpent belonged to the category of the *beasts of the field that the Lord God had made*. (1961: 142, italics in text)

By reading the "serpent" as a symbol of evil and not as a fully embodied character, Cassuto is able to make a psychological move. The serpent, he argues, is in fact a dimension of Eve. The dialogue between the serpent and Eve is actually a dialogue *within* Eve, "between her wiliness and her innocence, clothed in the garb of a parable. Only in this way is it possible to understand the conversation clearly; otherwise it remains obscure" (Cassuto 1961: 142).

Rather than following Cassuto and viewing the serpent as symbolic of the potential for evil within Eve, it seems more plausible to me to see the serpent as a discrete character that represents the environment from which serpents in the ancient Near East originally came—the *deep*. In these ancient traditions, the deep represents the primal antagonist to the creator god, a watery being that the creator god is forced to conquer in order to fashion the universe. In the case of Genesis 2, reference to the deep through the serpent (a creature—like Leviathan—associated with the watery domain) indicates, like the slippage during Adam's sleep/trance, the presence of the inherent potential for chaos in the post-creation world, the likes of which are found in the state of pre-creation, when "the earth being unformed and void, with darkness over the surface of the deep..." (Berlin and Brettler 2004: 12). Sarna, while holding on to the notion of evil, makes precisely this link between the "deep," the Leviathan/serpent, and primal chaos:

> The role of the creature [serpent] is that of seducer, laying before the woman the enticing nature of evil and fanning her desire for it. The use of the serpent symbolism in this situation has most likely been conditioned by the place of the serpent in the old cosmic combat myth...There, be it noted, the serpent is one of the epithets of Leviathan, one of the chief opponents of God and the representative of cosmic chaos. (1966: 26)

The serpent, then, is far from being simply a symbol of Eve's inherent potential for evil—or even necessarily a symbol of evil itself (despite what Sarna claims); it is an allusion to the primal chaos of the deep, a state of resistance to the acts of creation and to the order and hierarchy fashioned by God to overcome the primal chaos as narrated in Genesis 1. Thus, the serpent's statements to Eve are meant specifically to introduce an element of primal chaos into the world by asserting that the hierarchies of creation are not inherent or primary but were fashioned by the will of God for the purpose of establishing and maintaining authority. It is this notion that sets in motion the development of Eve's act of eating the fruit.

Eve's embrace of the serpent's kernel of chaos provokes her to begin to reflect on God's prohibition. For the briefest moment, the Garden of Eden has the potential to become an anarchistic paradise instead of an authoritarian one; once the hierarchy of God and human breaks down, so too does that between human and animal, god and angels, and so on. God, however, has no intention of submitting to the rising power of the human being. He displays his profound distrust of human power—and the structure of the rest of the Pentateuch shows an attempt to replace the original paradisiacal authoritarianism of creation with the development of a type of ideological authoritarianism, one that now has to deal with the radicalism unleashed by the rebellion of the human pair.

God recognizes in the eating of the fruit of the tree of knowledge a profound threat to the hierarchical, authoritarian order of creation and rushes through the garden to confront Adam and Eve. Some commentators' notion that God preordained the breaking of his one command and then feigned disappointment or anger (Bechtel 1995; Bal 1985) drains the dramatic power of the story. I disagree with this reading, which renders God's jealousy and his expulsion of the human pair from Eden too sedate. Rather, when God finds the human pair with the knowledge once reserved for him, he knows he needs to punish them before they use this wisdom to eat from the tree of life. If they eat from the tree of life and combine knowledge with immortality, man and woman would be God's equal, and his reign over them would come to a swift end: "And the Lord God said, 'Now that the man has become like one of us, knowing good and bad, what if he should stretch out his hand and take also from the tree of life and eat and live forever!'" (Berlin and Brettler 2004: 17) This is a terrified God—an authoritarian trembling before a potentially imminent revolution from below. This moment is the dramatic core of the narrative: the threat of the human rebellion against the order of creation, which is tantamount to a rebellion against creation itself.

God punishes Adam and Eve by casting them out of Eden, the place where there is no work, where sleep has to be induced, and where dreams do not exist. At the garden's entrance, God places insurmountable barriers to prevent the human beings from returning to Eden and gaining access to the tree of life. Paradisiacal authoritarianism is replaced by a type of authoritarian sovereignty backed up by violence: "So the Lord God banished him from the garden of Eden to till the soil from which he was taken. He drove the man out and stationed east of the garden of Eden the cherubim and the fiery ever-turning sword, to guard the way to the tree of life" (Berlin and Brettler 2004: 18). Not only is the new hierarchy based on *territorial* division (inside Eden versus beyond) and backed up by enforcing police (the cherubim) and military technology (the fiery ever-turning sword), it also leads to a radically new mode of existence for human beings. Humans shift from being sybaritic if subservient creatures to subservient and abject toilers. God's punishment of Adam rings out, "Cursed be the ground because of you; by toil shall you eat of it all the days of your life: Thorns and thistles shall it sprout for you. But your food shall be the grasses of the field; by the sweat of your brow shall you get bread to eat..." (Berlin and Brettler 2004: 18).

Eve's punishment seems even more severe. Not only does she have to endure the agricultural revolution that turns human beings from fruit-pickers and creatures of abundance to tillers and creatures of scarcity, she is also punished in two other ways. First, God decrees that Eve will experience pain in childbearing. Second and more important for my purposes here, Eve's relative social position becomes fixed in the new post-Edenic hierarchy as subordinate to Adam—the "original" articulation of patriarchy, a patriarchy that is based on the circumscription and unidirectional channeling of her desire. God tells Eve, "Yet your urge shall be for your husband, and he shall rule over you" (Berlin and Brettler 2004: 17). This is of major significance, because it is an attempt to instrumentalize the selfsame desire encountered as the force behind the eating of the fruit—Eve's startling act of rebellion and emancipation. God's decree re-inscribes desire back into the authoritarian paradigm. Once a multivalent substance that could combine diverse impulses and migrate across sensory and cognitive boundaries, desire becomes fixed in the realm of sexuality (or at the very least domesticity) and is utilized as a tool of oppression and the creation of hierarchical social formations. This circumscription of desire plays a key role in the patriarchal structure that develops beyond Eden. This structure, in turn, sets the stage for the development of full-fledged ideology, the likes of which is presented in the remainder of Genesis and the subsequent books of the Pentateuch. The core dualisms that form around the ultimate authority of God's presence in the post-Edenic world include God/human, life/death, good/bad, male/female, human/animal, human/nature, pleasure/pain, and obedience/punishment. In addition, it could be postulated that a key element of the development of the patriarchal system was predicated on the politics of desire set forth in the postlapsarian moment of punishment. The descendants of Adam subordinate themselves to God, collaborate with God, and thus lord over the descendants of Eve.

Beyond the gates of Eden, Adam and Eve's toil and suffering give rise to regenerative sleep. The link between sleep, toil, and the need for replenishment appears in the Jewish traditions collected by Ginzberg. The implication of the following quotation is that regenerative sleep is a product of the fall:

> The purpose of the sleep that enfolded Adam was to give him a wife, so that the human race might develop, and all creatures recognize the difference between God and man. When the earth heard what God had resolved to do, it began to tremble and quake. "I have not the strength," it said, "to provide food for the herd of Adam's descendants." But God pacified it with the words, "I and thou together, we will find food for the herd." Accordingly, time was divided between God and the earth; God took the night, and the earth took the day. Refreshing sleep nourishes and strengthens man, it affords him life and rest, while the earth brings forth produce with the help of God, who waters it. Yet man must work the earth to earn his food. (Ginzberg 1909: 64–65)

Though temporally confusing, this passage clearly sets the origins of regenerative sleep in post-Edenic time. With the beginning of a type of sleep that comes from toil/exhaustion as opposed to inducement, the dream emerges as a third state of being different from both prelapsarian empty sleep and wakefulness, for it is only after the expulsion in Genesis that the human first dreams. This "origin myth" of dreaming is not meant to reflect biblical literalism—there is no specific claim in the text about the rationale for the creation of the dreamscape as a space separate from sleep and wakefulness. Rather, it is proposed in order to open up dominant cultural formulations of authority and hierarchy to new radical potentialities for critique. If, as in Adam's first slumber, sleep is nothingness, a fall into oblivion, and wakefulness in the postlapsarian world is the (divinely) constructed territory beyond the gates of Eden, then the dreamscape could be seen as a zone beyond or antecedent to God's power that preserves the primary knowledge gained from the eating of the fruit from the tree of knowledge: that there exists thc potential for a return to conditions that include an element of the chaotic deep. The dreamscape, in other words, is a space of anarchy, in the Miltonian sense, in the post-creation world.

In the realm beyond Eden, ruled by sovereign and ideological instead of paradisiacal authoritarianism, the field of the dreamscape becomes a redoubt of human resistance to the domination of a new paradigm of subjugation, created by a God concerned above all with controlling his "knowing" subordinates—the authoritarian ideal. But if the dream can be seen as an anarchic space, it is hardly a secure one. It comes under siege as soon as it emerges as a space distinct from postlapsarian territory—as I will show below in Blake's *Job* and Frost's "After Apple-Picking." The notion of the dreamscape as a besieged space of freedom that is potentially beyond the grasp of authoritarian power and yet also subject to the encroachments, intrusions, and conquests of authoritarianism provides a new conception of anarchistic resistance. The movement from the territory of wakefulness to the space of the dreamscape contains a profound and yet diurnal rupture, one which evokes anarchy while often decisively weaving it back (at least partially) into the fabric of submission as the dreamscape gives way to its representation, the dream-text. In the daily rhythms of wakefulness, sleep, and dreaming, in other words, freedom and equality (anarchy) are radically proposed just as submission is reconstructed and reinforced.

The radicalism of the dreamscape, understood as the post-Edenic space of chaos-in-creation opened up by Eve's rebellion, provides an alternative political conception to the liberal or traditional anarchistic view of power. While the liberal/anarchist origin myth of the individual rests on the "natural" right of freedom, the biblical origin myth of the dreamscape proposes that, rather, the human being is first created into a structure of authoritarian power—albeit a seemingly benign and materially comfortable one, a paradisiacal authoritarianism. The first act of resistance comes in the form of a multifaceted desire, one that combines material, aesthetic, and intellectual impulses. Genesis describes Eve's radical action in the following way: "When the woman saw that the tree was good for eating and a delight to the eyes, and that the tree was desirable as a source of wisdom, she took of its fruit and ate" (Berlin and Brettler 2004: 17). This rebellion of corporeal (good for eating), aesthetic or sensorial (delight to the eyes), and intellectual (source of wisdom) desire results in a fundamental shift—what Genesis calls the gaining of "knowledge." Freedom, then, is not outside of power. It is, rather, the product of action/resistance won through the rebellion of multifaceted desire.

The reading of Eve's act as radical—and of her own volition (provoked not seduced)—cuts against attempts to read Genesis 2-3 in more harmonious ways. Specifically, the radical interpretation of Eve's act challenges the understanding of Genesis 2-3 as a tale of human maturation (Bechtel

1995; Bal 1985). In the maturation story, Eve plays a key role in the transition from a preliminary state of being into a fully articulated human form—an inevitable transition into a state that includes differentiation, procreation, work, and death. In this reading, Eve's act does not seem radical (anti-authoritarian) but desirable, a necessary plot device in line with God's ultimate plan.

This argument seems to me to tame Eve's desire. It avoids the strong traces of antagonism between serpent and God, and thus between forces of chaos and creation, accepting the monotheistic "revolution" as a total process of remaking the older poetic and New Eastern traditions. This more harmonious interpretation explains God's swift and angry reaction not as authentic but as histrionic. In short, to argue that the scenario from the creation of Eve to the eating and sharing of the fruit was God's design would mute key tensions in the text and empty the story's dramatic core. Alternatively, the tensions can be accounted for if Eve's desire is connected with the serpent as an agent of primal chaos. Together, desire and chaos threaten the order of creation and the hierarchy of authority in the world. The opening of the dreamscape does not promise such a radical act as Eve's eating of the fruit, but by creating a rupture with, or a shattering of, the constructed, authoritarian world of wakefulness/reality it works to open up an anarchic space. The difficulty, however, comes with preserving the potential of this space when moving from the dreamscape back into the "real." The challenges of this can be seen by looking at the radical articulations and authoritarian re-inscriptions of the dream in William Blake's *Illustrations of the Book of Job* and Robert Frost's "After Apple-Picking."

Anarchist Radicalism and Authoritarian Discourse in Blake's *Illustrations of the Book of Job*

William Blake's *Illustrations of the Book of Job* (1825) provides a particularly interesting example of how the interpretation of the dreamscape can undermine authoritative structures in quite radical ways, while at the same time intersecting with authoritarian discourses of power through the dream-text's absorption or reflection of hierarchical narrative structures or elements. Blake (1757–1827) was an English artist and poet who straddled the ages of Enlightenment and Romanticism, a transitional era marked by political radicalism and revolution, intellectual exploration, and renewed religious fervor (Hobsbawm 1996: 1). One of the most hotly contested spheres of intellectual and creative inquiry in this period was the relationship between an individual's rational side and the spiritual or non-rational side embodied by emotion, intuition, longing, and religious exaltation (Izenberg 2001: 1–17; Michael 2016: 2). Dreams were an important site of this relationship, because, as one can see, for example, in Goya's etching *The Sleep of Reason* (1799), they represented a state of being in which the rational mind was thought to have lost control and to be subordinated to fears, impulses, and desires. Goya's visual dream-text stages the crux of the debate between rationalists and their critics about how far reason could take a person in the search for higher, greater, or even total understanding of the "self" and the universe. On the one hand, that an owl in the etching attempts to hand the sleeping man a stylus might indicate that creative inspiration comes from the nightmarish zone of irrationality.[5] On the other hand, the sleeper cannot take the stylus from the owl; only a mind awake and rational can translate the impulses of this nightmare vision into art—can create.

The *Book of Job*, a text from the Hebrew Bible, presented Blake with a testing ground to explore the intersection of (and tensions between) reason, traditional religious faith, and a type of individual inspiration or spiritual enlightenment that pushed toward an anarchist critique of authority and hierarchy.[6] In a series of twenty-one illustrations, Blake visualizes and re-invents the story of Job, an "innocent" man whose faith, upon the request of an accuser, is tested by God through intense suffering. Two dream scenes come around the mid-point of the book, illustrations 11 and 12, and play a pivotal role in Job's ultimate acceptance of his "guilt" and his subsequent spiritual conversion (Figs. 2.1 and 2.2).

Blake's cycle of illustrations begins by depicting Job as a prosperous and godly man, though with hints that all might not be right with his conception of righteousness. In the text below the image in illustration 1, Blake adds, following Paul's Second Epistle to the Corinthians: "The

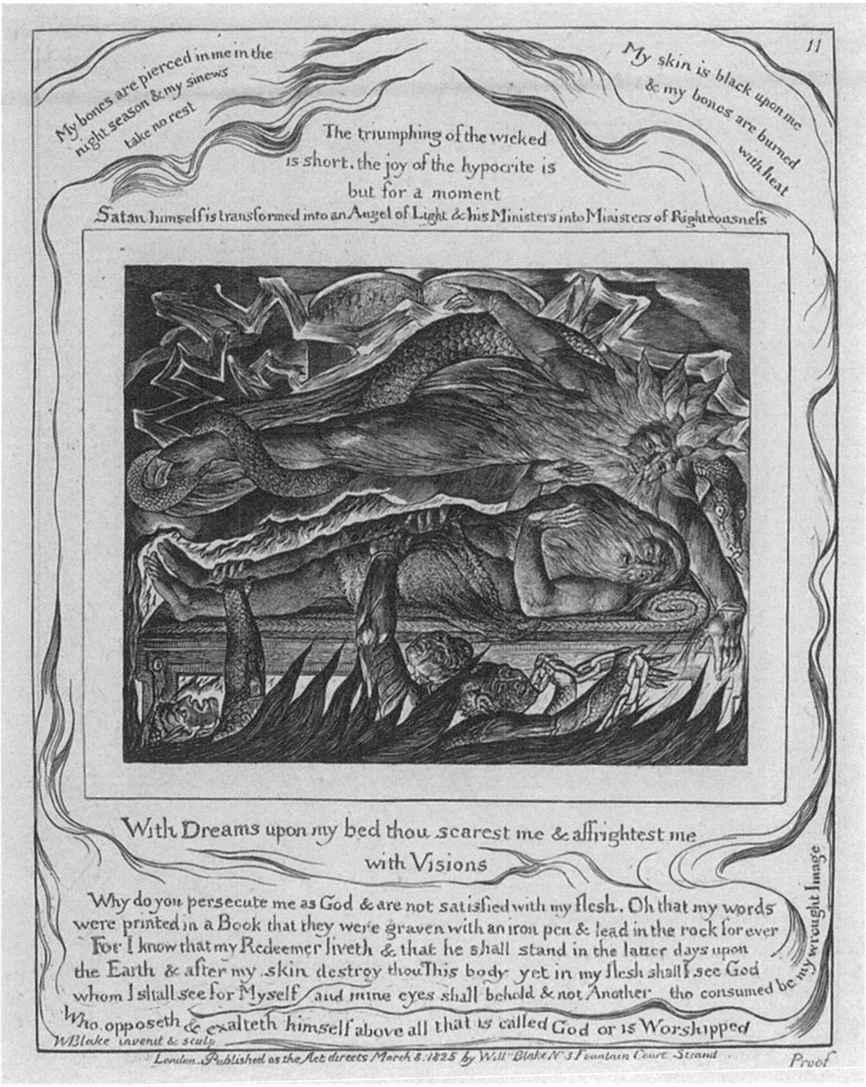

Fig. 2.1 William Blake, Illustration 11 "Job's Evil Dreams" of *Illustrations of the Book of Job* (Wikimedia Commons)

Fig. 2.2 William Blake, Illustration 12 "The Wrath of Elihu" of *Illustrations of the Book of Job* (Wikimedia Commons)

letter killeth/The spirit giveth life/it is spiritually discerned," foreshadowing the central conflict in the cycle of illustrations between the moral law and spiritual faith.[7] In illustration 2, the drama begins. The scene is split into two halves. On top, Satan (the accuser) appeals to God to allow him to afflict Job with suffering to test his faith. God agrees. In the bottom half, Job is portrayed discussing religious matters with angels and his family. Illustration 3 depicts the beginning of Job's miseries as Satan falls upon his sons and has them killed. In illustration 4, Job hears about these misfortunes from messengers. Illustration 5 is again split. In the bottom half, Job, though afflicted with misery, is upholding his religious duty by giving to the poor and downtrodden. Nonetheless, in the upper part of the illustration, God allows Satan to turn on Job directly. Illustration 6 finds Satan torturing Job by blighting him with boils as the sun sets on the horizon. In the next illustration, as darkness envelopes the scene, friends come to comfort Job. Job, however, does not find comfort, and in the next illustration, shrouded by night, he lashes out in despair, cursing the day he was born. The next two illustrations show Job discussing his case with his three best friends, all of whom side with God against him. Job rejects their reasoning (that he is to blame for his misfortune) and takes his case directly to God. The rejection of the friends' accusations sets the stage for illustrations 11 and 12, in which Job has the two dreams that allow him the insight necessary to begin his journey to enlightenment and redemption.

The scene in illustration 11 of Blake's *Job* is divided into three zones. In the middle of the scene, Job lies sleeping. He is being afflicted by nightmares happening below and above him. The implication is that, as he is in waking life, Job is being tortured in his sleep. Below Job is the pit of hell. Demons (perhaps the demonic doubles of his three friends) reach up and grasp his sleeping body, threatening to pull him down into the fiery abyss of eternal damnation and suffering. The demonic beings are hideous creatures with scaly flesh, long fingers, and brutish faces. They carry chains—symbolic of confinement and torture. Above Job, a figure swoops down wrapped in a serpent. The figure is recognizable both as the God who sat on the throne in illustration 1 and as a demonic character, a false God. Around Job, ribbons of light or jagged lightning bolts cut through the sky. Looming above the serpent-wrapped figure is a stone tablet, a clear reference to the commandments or covenant given to Moses by God on Mount Sinai, the covenant that forms the basis of Hebrew law and the Jewish religion.

In the dream, as Blake imagines it, Job experiences a type of utter terror he is not able to experience in his waking life, even under the most severe emotional and physical distress. Only in the dreamscape, according to Blake, can Job achieve such a state of terror, a state that opens up the possibility for eventual enlightenment and redemption. As in the rest of the series, symbols pervade the scene. The serpent wrapped around the false god indicates his demonic nature, evoking the serpent from the Garden of Eden. The flying man also has a cloven hoof instead of a normal human foot, indicating that this "god" is the devil in disguise. The text above the divine/demonic figure states, "Satan himself is transformed into an Angel of Light." Though in a literal sense this would imply that this "god" is, in fact, Satan, the likeness between the divine figure and the God of the previous illustrations compels the reading that this being represents a fusion of God and Satan into a unified being—a direct contrast to the unification of the divine being that will occur after the dream sequence. The dark sky and stormy weather show that this "god" is not friendly and not coming in peace. Finally, the tablets above the flying devil-god refer to the Hebrew Bible, and in the watercolor versions of the illustration it is clear that these are God's commandments. "God" has one finger pointed to the Hebrew law and the other pointed to the hellish inferno.

Why would the Satan-God be drawing Job's attention to the Mosaic Law, the foundation of Judeo-Christian monotheism? In illustration 2 of the engraved, printed version, in which the accuser is appealing to God to test Job's faith, Blake adds the Hebrew words "King Jehovah" (Wicksteed 1910: 51). Blake is indicating that this God is specifically the Hebrew or Old Testament God. This is emphasized by the image of God sitting on a throne with a book (the "legalistic" Torah) on his lap. In the dream, Job sees that this king/God is not the almighty source of good in the world. Rather, he is a vengeful, capricious, demonic force, who is interested only in strictly upholding his oppressive laws. Obey the law, he seems to tell Job in the dream, or suffer in hell—indeed, both are part of the same system, the reflections of each other that represent the fusion of

God and Satan. The stage is now set for Job to differentiate between the demonic Old Testament God (a unity of God and Satan) and a type of God, who does not oppress through the "Law" but who opens one up to the spirit. Indeed, as Henry Summerfield argues, this tension between legalistic religion and inner experience of the Gospel is a recurring motif in Blake's *Job* (1987: 97). Following his dream vision in illustration 11, Job realizes that while he previously had adhered to the law, he had not embraced the spirit of faith, an unmediated inner experience of creative illumination and total unity of being. Job, in Blake's re-invention, can now be successfully converted from an Old Testament dogmatist into a believer in (a Blakean) Christ.

In Blake's version of the story, Job's nightmare in illustration 11 transforms into the calm dream of illustration 12, in which Job, his wife, and Job's three friends are visited by a young man named Elihu, who starts to reveal to them the truth of the divine message: that faith does not come from one's actions or adherence to a set of laws but rather flows out from the inner being of the individual. Once Job starts down this path, the process of enlightenment begins, culminating in a visit to Job by the unified figure of God-Christ, who discloses to him the unity of all things, especially that of the material and the divine (the individual being and universal being), bringing about the final conversion. Job, now aware of this unity, sees his good fortune restored. This stands in contrast with the biblical story of Job in numerous respects, most centrally, the biblical *Book of Job* presents Job's submission to God as a product of the recognition of the supreme *difference* between the power of the creator God and the limited perspective of a single human being. The only bridge between the two entities could be one of faith—faith in God's moral perfection and the righteousness of a life lived through faith (Kaufmann 1972: 334–338).

In Blake's re-interpretation of the *Book of Job*, the connection to radical theology is clear: Job's task is to probe his innermost self to discover the essence of the divine being and thus the unity of all things. It is a quest that can only occur in the deepest spirit of the person; it cannot be legislated from outside or grasped rationally. As Summerfield summarizes, "In Blake's system a fall into moral legalism is accompanied by a lapse from imaginative vision into the Lockean philosopher's and the Newtonian scientist's acceptance of the external objects the senses perceive as constituting reality" (1987: 94). The choice of dreams as the catalyst for this transformation is important. Whereas the earlier scenes show Job making a rational defense of his piety, the dreams allow his non-rational, emotive, intuitive senses to take over. As opposed to the religious disputation in illustration 2, which finds representatives of the Gospel attempting to sway Job away from legalistic faith, it is in the dreams, freed from the strictures of reason, that Job can experience the basic truth that leads to redemption.

The arc of spiritual transformation leads Blake to reposition the dream sequence at the center of the narrative. In the biblical story, the dream is a fairly insignificant detail, a part of Job's lament in the first part of the story, which sets up his charge against God. In chapter 7:14–15, Job says, "You frighten me with dreams, and terrify me with visions till I prefer strangulation, death, to my wasted frame" (Berlin and Brettler 2004: 1514). In Blake's reimagining, this line comes to mark the transition point from one set of beliefs to another, from a life of unrighteousness to a life of redemption, from legalistic guilt to spiritual illumination, and with it, a liberation of the imagination.

Blake's translation of Job's dreamscape into dream-text allows him to radically challenge structures of religious authority as well as to postulate the limits of reason in relation to faith. Before the dream, Job cannot break free of the religious law's hold on him and cannot see what Blake considers the falsity and inherent slavery of this system. It is only in the terrifying dream that Blake's religious understanding can be shattered, making way for the revelation that comes in the subsequent illustrations. The core of this revelation moves the story into the heat of Blakean religiosity: that real faith is not legal or ethical in the Old Testament sense but an embrace of one's relationship to the universality of humanity through imagination and love. For Blake, the individual identity gains meaning as an aspect of the universal, while the universal gains meaning through the individual identities that together form it (Wicksteed 1910: 109–117). In this sense, Blake's dream-texts are consistent with anarchistic ideas. They create a rupture in the narrative by shattering the hold of authoritarian structures over Job's notions of faith. The dream-texts then present what seems like a deeply egalitarian vision of faith—the true reciprocity of the individual and the universal, the celebration of the bonding nature of imagination and love, the recognition of oneself in everyone, everyone in each other (absolute and unqualified equality). Blake's (now Job's) anarchist morality replaces the legalistic ethics of Old Testament life.

Nonetheless, despite his radicalism Blake's vision in *Illustrations of the Book of Job* remains vulnerable to two authoritarian constructs. Both of these constructs stem from Blake maintaining New Testament concepts as the framing for his radical theology. The first authoritarian element in Blake's Job is the theme of submission, represented compositionally in illustration 17, in which God-Jesus comes to Job (Fig. 2.3). Here, Job and his wife kneel before God-Jesus to receive or gain enlightenment, which is symbolized by the brilliant sun in the background. The pair gazes up at the figure of divine unity, fully immersed in his message. Job's three friends provide contrast, as they turn their backs to the figure and shield their eyes from the sunlight; they choose to remain in darkness. That God-Jesus's head is contained within the circle of the sun while his feet remain on the ground indicates that he provides the bridge between the material and the spiritual, the very bridge that was absent in Job's previous conception of faith. The composition in illustration 17 acts as the visual counterpart to Elihu's text in illustration 12, "Lo all these things worketh God oftentimes with Man to bring back his Soul from the pit to be enlightened with the light of the living." In illustration 12, Elihu comes to Job as the emissary charged with announcing the coming of Christ. However radically Blake defines "Jesus" or the notion of the divine unity, the compositional power of the scenes in 12 and 17 derives from the hierarchical relationship between Job and the divine. There can be no faith, it seems, without submission.

More important than Job's submission, Blake's reimagining of the biblical story—and especially of the dream in illustration 11—betrays influences of long-standing anti-Jewish polemic in its narrative logic. In the broader Protestant context, the contrast between Jewish legalism and Christian faith, as well as the links between the Jewish God and demonic forces, stretches back to Martin Luther and other early Reformation figures (Rowan 1985: 88–90; Oberman 1989: 292–297).[8] In turn, these Reformation polemics rely on older medieval anti-Jewish traditions

Fig. 2.3 William Blake, Illustration 17 "The Vision of Christ" of *Illustrations of the Book of Job* (Wikimedia Commons)

(Trachtenberg 1983; Menache 1985). One of the key medieval polemics against Jews was precisely the claim that the God of the Jews was not God but the devil—and that the Jews worked in the service of the devil and his false messiah, the Antichrist. The link between Jew, devil, and Antichrist formed one of the central pillars of anti-Jewish sentiment, which in turn was linked to eruptions of violence and constant discrimination. In the case of Luther and others, the anti-Jewish polemic seeks to establish a clear hierarchy of faiths, to introduce a progressive interpretation of religious history (Christianity overcoming Judaism), and to legitimize the social, political, and legal exclusion and/or subordination of Jews in Christian realms. In the context of the early nineteenth century, Blake's conjoining of Jewish religiosity with Enlightenment rationalism (especially deism) could thus be seen as an attack on the politics of Jewish legal emancipation of the Napoleonic era and as a legitimization of the post-Napoleonic reaction against Jewish integration, a reaction often dressed in Christian garb (Shabetai 1996).

I have so far discussed two distinct types of authoritarian representations of the dreamscape. The first type acts to directly buttress existing hierarchical power relationships. The example of King Solomon in the book First Kings is an apt one here. Solomon is already king when he goes to Gibeon to incubate a dream. The dream-text acts as a powerful legitimation of his rule by elevating his status and linking him intimately with the patron God. The second type of authoritarian representation acts to both challenge authoritarian constructs and either to rebuild them in an opposing, but still hierarchical, manner or to locate the new construct within a hierarchical or authoritarian narrative logic. Blake's representation of Job's dreamscape provides an interesting example of the latter. Blake's Job is emancipated from legalistic rationalism and discovers a radical form of faith, only to find himself within the visual logic of hierarchical Christianity and, much more significantly, subsumed into the discursive logic of long-standing anti-Jewish polemic. The main authoritarian thrust of Blake's Job comes when he utilizes anti-Jewish traditions to present the Jew as the prototypical "other" to the Blakean Christian. Blake's use of John 10:30 in illustration 17 (Job's submission to God-Jesus) is telling in this regard. While the quoted text, "I and the Father are one," seems rather uncontroversial and points to anarchistic possibilities. Those familiar with the Christian writings, however, would understand that the statement comes amid a scene of incredible tension between Jesus and the Jews. In the Gospel of John, Jesus's statement about divine unity is followed by conflict in the subsequent verse 10:31: "The Jews took up stones again to stone him" (Gospel of John n.d.). Here the Jew has become, in the Christian imagination, the tormenter and murderer of Christ—and one might add *in the service of the devil*. Even a radical spiritual thinker like Blake falls into identity constructs with deep social and political implications that configure hierarchical structures of power.

The Self, Lost and Regained, in Robert Frost's "After Apple-Picking"

Robert Frost's poem "After Apple-Picking" (1914) demonstrates the complexity of the political contest over the dreamscape outlined above—between the potential for a radical opening of an anarchistic space and submission to subjugating authoritarian constructs. The poem opens with a scene of abandoned labor—a toiling scene reminiscent of the type of work God decrees to be Adam's fate after the eating of the fruit of the tree of knowledge. Two images in the opening of the poem connect to Genesis. First, the "two-pointed ladder" that is "sticking through a tree" indicates the human attempt to aspire to a higher realm—one that gels with the irreversibility of the banishment from Eden and the subsequent inaccessibility of the divine space (Frost 1969: 68). The aspiration, in other words, is as constant or fixed as it is hopeless. More importantly, second, the apples gesture to the fruit of the tree of knowledge, which in the Western imagination is typically characterized as an apple (Júnior 2006). The relevant aspect here is that the narrator of the poem has no thought of eating the fruit—"there may be two or three/Apples I didn't pick upon some bough" (1969: 68). The fruit is to be harvested and processed and/or sold. The eating of the fruit, an act of pleasure or desire, seems directly opposed to the harvesting of fruit as an act of work. The juxtaposition between pleasure/desire and work shows that this narrator has fully assimilated to the post-Edenic world. Meaning and a sense of self are gained through one's labor.

The essence of agricultural labor is incompleteness—work begets work in an endless cycle—"And there's a barrel that I didn't fill..."—leading to dissatisfaction. The line "but I am done with apple picking now" is nicely ambiguous—meaning either a daily cessation or a stopping forever, a termination (1969: 68). It could be that the poem is suggesting that all cessations are potential terminations. This chafing against the world of toil acts as a prelude to the oncoming of a dream: "Essence of winter sleep is on the night,/ The scent of apples: I am drowsing off" (1969: 68). The accentuation of "winter" sleep works in a similar way as "done with apple picking now." It could resonate with literal meaning, a sleep during wintertime—and the autumnal New England is certainly wintery. Alternatively, it can imply a last sleep, a death. A third option is that "winter sleep" can mean hibernation, the long regenerative sleep built into the cycle of nature. The literal meaning suggests an ordinary recuperative night's sleep after a long day of labor—a bucolic image. Reference to hibernation adds a darker tint to the scene—for we know that hibernation is extremely unlikely and that the life rhythms of this toiler do not align with surrounding forces of nature. Even when nature retreats into a long slumber, in other words, this narrator must wake up each day and continue his work. The theme of death is even darker still and could be related to Adam and Eve's ultimate punishment, the placing of an eternal obstacle blocking the tree of life and its promised immortality. The dominant concepts of work, nature, and sleep/death define the realm of wakefulness in the poem before the slip into the dream.

Frost's poem captures the moment of transition between wakefulness and dream—that very moment when the pillars of reality crumble and new potentialities emerge. As the narrator drifts off to sleep, he pauses at the border between memory and the dreamscape. "I cannot rub that strangeness from my sight," the narrator says, "I got from looking through a pane of glass/I skimmed this morning from the drinking trough/And held against the world of hoary grass" (1969: 68). This ice-screen distorts the gaze, and the narrator, the looker, is cast into uncertainty. All of a sudden, from the ordinary work-a-day world nothing can be known, nothing is sure. The momentary failure of vision brings forth the dreamscape, despite the almost instinctual attempt to defend against it by rubbing "the strangeness" away. The ice sheet begins to melt in the narrator's hands. He lets it "fall and break" (1969: 68). This shattering of the ice simultaneously creates and announces the presence of the dreamscape. This is the anarchistic moment, as the shattering of the ice sheet indicates the fracturing of constructed "reality" and the spiraling toward a state of unbound chaos, which resonates with the moment in Genesis 1, discussed above, directly preceding creation when the earth was "unformed" (Berlin and Brettler 2004: 12). The shattering, in this sense, announces the presence of the metaphoric "serpent" of creation, the entropic force of un-ordering within the constructed order.

Not only does the melting and subsequent shattering (a combination of a metamorphosis and a destruction or annihilation) of the ice sheet usher the narrator forward into the dream, it casts turbulence back onto the other side of the border—calling into question the ability to clearly and cleanly distinguish one state of being (dreaming) from the other (wakefulness). "It melted, and I let it fall and break," the speaker says, adding the qualification, "But I was well/Upon my way to sleep before it fell,/And I could tell/What form my dreaming was about to take" (1969: 68). This qualification of the melting and shattering of the ice sheet circles the poem back to its beginning and to the image of "My long two pointed ladder's sticking through a tree/Toward heaven still" (1969: 68). The images of the ladder, of the apples still clinging to the boughs of the tree, and the partially filled barrel now sway between waking memory and dream, making it impossible to draw a temporally absolute line between them. The claim that the narrator could "tell what form [his] dreaming was about to take" is rendered highly questionable. Most likely, he can tell what will take place in the dream because he is there experiencing it. The ice sheet has already been shattered. The temporal confusion and the blurred distinction between memory and dream add to the narrator's dislocation. The content of the reported dream continues to blur the dreamscape with memory. This blurring is not confined to thoughts, but includes traces of the senses—touch, smell, hearing, and even one's very equilibrium.

Magnified apples appear and disappear,
Stem end and blossom end,
And every fleck of russet showing clear,
My instep arch not only keeps the ache,
It keeps the pressure of the ladder-round.
I feel the ladder sway as the boughs bend.
And I keep hearing from the cellar bin
The rumbling sound
Of load on load of apples coming in. (Frost 1969: 68–69)

Individual images in this dream-text could be analyzed in a multitude of ways, but instead I want to point to the way the narrator of the poem offers the first inklings of an interpretation even while, seemingly, still at least half-immersed in the dreamscape. In so doing, the narrator presents the anarchic potential of the dreamscape and then proceeds to weave it into the fabric of subjugating power through the dream-text.

The critical moment comes directly after the flood of sensory images presented above. With the rumbling sound of apples still resonating in the narrator's ear, he states, "For I have had too much/Of apple-picking: I am overtired/Of the great harvest I myself desired" (1969: 69). The dream, then, inspires in the narrator an expression of weariness. It is a nightmarish replaying of the daily sensorium of harvesting. In this nightmare, work loses its bearing on a higher purpose, and the collapse of the notion of purposeful work in turn calls into question the purpose of sleep as an act of strengthening and rejuvenation. If work and therefore sleep have no greater purpose, then the picking of apples appears nothing but an endless repetition of the same act, as the narrator says, "There were ten thousand thousand fruit to touch,/Cherish in hand, lift down, and not let fall" (1969: 69). The doubling of the word "thousand" transforms the description from one of ordinary labor into one of a behavior bordering on the mechanistic. If the act of harvesting has lost meaning, the division between good apples and cider apples is also meaningless—as is the extreme care taken in inspecting and preserving each individual specimen. These are economic decisions, decisions about value and fungibility—and there is no doubt that the work of harvesting has transformed this man into a being guided and organized by economic concerns. Even if the apple picking can (or should) be read metaphorically, the logic is still that of the market.

Aspects of the dream-text, however, undermine this logic by presenting to the narrator the apple as an aesthetic object rather than an economic unit: "Magnified apples appear and disappear,/Stem end and blossom end,/And every fleck of russet showing clear…" (1969: 68). Henry David Thoreau, too, makes the distinction between apples as market objects and their nature as wild fruit when he describes the farmer carting his harvest to market for sale: "Though [the farmer] gets out from time to time, and feels of [the apples], and thinks they are all there, I see the stream of their evanescent and celestial qualities going to heaven from his cart, while the pulp and skin and core only are going to market. They are not apples, but pomace" (Thoreau 1999: 75). Thoreau continues:

> Almost all wild apples are handsome. They cannot be too gnarly and crabbed and rusty to look at. The gnarliest will have some redeeming traits even to the eye. You will discover some evening redness dashed or sprinkled on some protuberance or in some cavity. It is rare that the summer lets an apple go without streaking or spotting it on some part of its sphere. It will have some red stains, commemorating the mornings and evenings it has witnessed; some dark and rusty blotches, in memory of the clouds and foggy, mildewy days that have passed over it; and a spacious field of green reflecting the general face of Nature,—green even as the fields; or a yellow ground, which implies a milder flavor,—yellow as the harvest, or russet as the hills. (1999: 87)

Glimmers—but just glimmers, and maybe mere suggestions—of Thoreau's thoroughly anti-economic view of the human's relationship to the apple—and by extension to nature—are contained in Frost's narrator's interpretation.

Of the radical implications of the dreamscape in the poem, however, the anti-market economic one is the safest. The anarchic elements—the distorting/failure of vision, the melting and shattering of the ice sheet, the blurring of the boundaries between memory and dream, the collapse of the linearity of time—are pushed aside in order for the narrator to turn back to the opening question of the poem—whether the essence of his sleep touches on ordinary daily routines, the relationship between the individual and nature, or whether it evokes the notion of death:

> One can see what will trouble
> This sleep of mine, whatever sleep it is.
> Were he not gone,
> The woodchuck could say whether it's like his
> Long sleep, as I describe its coming on,
> Or just some human sleep. (1969: 69)

The clear allusion to death with the phrases "long sleep" and "human sleep" re-solidifies the subjectivity of the narrator and pulls him out of the dreamscape, even though this thought could very well have occurred within it. Vision is reaffirmed ("one can see") as the dreamscape becomes an interruption of recuperative sleep and therefore bothersome and useless ("what will trouble/This sleep of mine"). Seemingly within the dream, or at the very least on the border of the dreamscape, the narrator begins to interpret the dream (to create a dream-text of it) in ways that lessen or ignore its radical implications, its anarchic moments, and instead focus on inscribing meaning back into the broader system of power that the dream seems to be chafing against—the world of diurnal toil guided by market-economic logic.

If "long sleep" and "human sleep" with their allusions to regeneration and/or death point to the re-solidifying and fixing of subjectivity, the moment with the ice sheet indicates the opposite: the potential fragility and fragmentation of the self, the unreliability of vision, and the heightening and at the same time confusion of the senses, which inverts or at least equalizes the relationship between reason and affect. The radical moment, in other words, calls unified or crystalized subjectivity into question by forcing it to exist simultaneous to the shattered self. It calls vision into question—and with it the whole system of cognition based on knowledge and judgment. The radical moment, the shattering, topples the hierarchical dominance of reason over affect, without, however, inverting the hierarchy to claim the primary of the senses over thought. Here, Frost is closer to Thoreau's description of transcendence and self-becoming as the dissolution of identity. How similar is Thoreau's notion of dissolution of the self to Chuang Tzu's butterfly!

> Drifting in a sultry day on the sluggish waters of the pond, I almost cease to live and begin to be. A boatman stretched on the deck of his craft and dallying with the noon would be as apt an emblem of eternity for me as the serpent with his tail in his mouth. I am never so prone to lose my identity. I am dissolved in the haze. (Thoreau 2009: 7)

Authority is, at least in part (if not in great measure), built on the hardening of identity as part of a broader structure of power that supports hierarchy and material inequality. The anarchism opened up by the emergence of the dreamscape ruptures this structure of power by calling into question—or radically challenging—its basic assumptions about selfhood, relationships, time, space, and perception. Frost's narrator experiences such a moment of radical possibility. As my analysis of the poem indicates, however, this anarchism is fleeting and fragile. It is immediately challenged by the intrusion of authoritarian impulses. On the other hand, the authoritarian concepts cannot fully displace the primary anarchism, and thus Frost's poem, like Blake's *Job*, exists in a state of tension between its radical impulses and its authoritarian implications. The following chapters will explore this tension across an array of dream-texts, mapping the twin trajectories of anarchism and authoritarianism in the traditions of thinking about dreaming.

Conclusion

The dreamscape's potential as a site of anarchy in the sense described above positions it as a contested field or political space. Regimes of power recognize this anarchistic potential and seek to impose ideological/territorial structures on the dreamscape, foremost by establishing interpretive schemata and utilizing them for the production of dream-texts. Such interpretive schemata become embedded in culture and consciousness, making it difficult to think about dreaming without immediately applying narrative logic and interpretive concepts. This logic and these concepts shift over time—though not necessarily in a progressive sense. Elements of ancient dream interpretation still infuse popular consideration of dreaming today, as evidenced by Jungian dream theory's reliance on a set of traditional symbols or concepts that reflect the "collective unconscious."

However, despite attempts of regimes of power to invade, dominate, or conquer the dreamscape, thus banishing or limiting its potential as an anarchistic site of resistance, the dreamscape continues to evade total occupation and to assert a counterforce against interpretive circumscriptions. This counterpressure can be productively understood as a product of the origin of the dreamscape, in other words as the remnant of the chaos-in-creation contained in Eve's desirous rebellion against the authoritarianism that structured the prelapsarian Garden of Eden. This chaos can be understood in two ways. The first is as an entropic force against all fixed orders, definitions, and identities. This is the chaos of the primal "deep," represented by the serpent (or Chuang Tzu's *hundun*). This "serpent" *enacts* the principles of radical equality, freedom from authority, and the disintegration of selfhood. There can be no "self" before the creation of a cosmic order that houses it. At the same time, the second force, the force of desire, is an integrating one—a momentary bringing together of affective, intellectual, and aesthetic impulses in order to act. Eve *becomes* a free self through this emancipatory act, in a similar way as the subject of Chuang Tzu's butterfly dream becomes free through the embrace of the "transformation of things." The origins of the dreamscape in the aftermath of the humans' expulsion from Eden mirror the development of the authoritarian structures of postlapsarian life: the development of a controlling and internalized ideology, a regime of work together with the hierarchical structures of agrarian life, and a social structure built on clear lines of power, with the patriarchal formation as one of the first articulations.

As the following chapters demonstrate, these anarchistic impulses of the primal dreamscape put pressure on their representative dream-texts. Dream-texts, therefore, despite their ideological implications, are fundamentally unstable—containing within themselves the metaphorical serpent, that entropic or disintegrative force of disorder and deconstruction of hierarchy. This anarchistic potential can be almost entirely circumscribed, as I argue is the case with Freud and Jung. It can also be minimized in the (witting or unwitting) service of supporting authoritarian structures, as I demonstrate with Blake's *Job*, Frost's "After Apple-Picking," and, in the following chapter, Jacob's dream of the ladder in Genesis. Close analysis of the dream elements in these works situates them as hovering between radical and authoritarian impulses and presents a new framework for understanding their politics. Other works, like those of Jean Rhys and Franz Kafka, undermine to a greater extent the stable status of the dream-text to gesture toward the anarchic attribute of the dreamscape. Both Rhys and Kafka have been described as anarchists without much specificity. By focusing on dreams in their works, I aim to articulate a more developed understanding of what type of anarchism their work represents. Finally, while the neurobiological discourse on dreaming presents a possible opportunity to escape the narrative logic of the dream-text partially or even fully, it often does so by immersing itself into the discursive streams of pharmacological capitalism and technophile fantasy.

Notes

1. Around 2450 BCE, the Sumerian ruler Eannatum I of Lagash commissioned the production of a stele to glorify his military victory over the kingdom of Umma. Known as the "Stele of Vultures" (because of the depiction of vultures carrying off the severed heads of the defeated) and currently housed in the Louvre Museum in Paris, the pillar contains fragments of the first recorded dream. In the dream, Ningirsu, god of war and patron deity of Lagash, stands by Eannatum's head and blesses the fight against Umma. The messages of the dream are clear—Eannatum's aggression is being done in the righteous name of Ningirsu and the expansion of the power of Lagash is in line with the will of the gods. This fusion of the secular ruler with the religious cult represents an important aggrandizement of the power of the king, as has been addressed by Scott Noegel (Noegel 2001: 46) and by Irene Winter, who writes: "Thus, the primary, official state message presented through the innovative use of historical narrative on the Stele of the Vultures is that of the legitimate claim of Lagash over the Gu'eden.... The secondary message presented through the historical narrative is that of the centrality of the ruler in maintaining the state. It is our assessment that the stele would have been set up in the major temple to Ningirsu as a votive to the patron deity, who was given

titular credit for the victory at the very time his authority was being eroded and his territorial prerogatives encroached upon by the secular city ruler. The god is given pride of place on the obverse; the king is on the reverse. But the challenge to the older, nominally theocratic base of the city-state is there. The hierarchy of the religious system is no longer identical with the administrative hierarchy of the state" (1985: 27).

2. The idea and strategies for building Ningirsu's temple presented in the Gudea Cylinders are largely revealed to Gudea in dreams. The authority of the dream revelations is crucial for Gudea to justify the incredible social costs of the temple's construction, which, as in the Stele of the Vultures, serves to solidify the king's relationship to, and perhaps domination of, the religious cult.
3. In I Kings, Solomon goes to Gibeon to incubate a dream (a communication with God) in order to gain legitimacy from Yahweh for the consolidation of his political rule after the death of David and the battle over succession. Clearly, Solomon's military and political victory over his enemies is not enough to safeguard his new position as king. The dream provides the bridge between monarchy and theocracy, spurring the development (like in Gudea's account) of the building of the Jerusalem temple. As Noegel states: "Like the Mesopotamian kings, this dream aims to remove doubt concerning Solomon's fitness to rule" (2001: 55). For an interesting alternative reading of Solomon's dream at Gibeon, which maintains that the dream is laced with anti-monarchical irony, see Wozniuk (1997: 1997).
4. James Kennedy sees in Genesis 2 a political allegory for the submission of the peasantry to the elite: "Similarly, the Eden story of Genesis 2-3 is not a dispassionate rendering of how the world came to be, but a narrative describing creation in terms conducive to the Israelite elite's preservation of political power and privilege" (1990: 4).
5. The benefits and dangers of accessing a "dark side" of the human mind are highlighted by Thomas de Quincey in the sequel to his *Confessions of an English Opium-Eater*. He writes, "Among the powers in man which suffer by this too intense life of the social instincts, none suffers more than the power of dreaming. Let no man think this a trifle. The machinery for dreaming planted in the human brain was not planted for nothing. That faculty, in alliance with the mystery of darkness, is the one great tube through which man communicates with the shadowy. And the dreaming organ, in connection with the heart, the eye and the ear, compose the

magnificent apparatus which forces the infinite into the chambers of a human brain, and throws dark reflections from eternities below all life upon the mirrors of the sleeping mind" (1868: 149).

6. A.D. Nuttall writes: "Blake oscillates between the words 'imagination' and 'vision', as terms commanding his fundamental allegiance. This of itself suggests that he, like other Romantics, wished to reinterpret imagination as an organ of knowledge rather than a trivially fictive faculty. If imagination, reinterpreted in this way, is deemed to have been raised in status, the presupposition is clear: knowledge must be a good thing. But Blake's obstinate hostility to reason remains" (1998: 239).
7. This quote is an adaptation from 2 Corinthians 3:5–6. The full verse is: "Not that we are competent of ourselves to claim anything as coming from us; our competence is from God, who has made us competent to be ministers of a new covenant, not in a written code but in the Spirit; for the written code kills, but the Spirit gives life" (Revised Standard Version).
8. Trachtenberg, in his discussion of Luther's *On the Jews and their Lies*, quotes Luther, "Those compassionate saints whose misguided benevolence enabled the Jews to murder and to blaspheme sinned against God, for as Christ is His son and the New Testament His book, so has He through the course of world history rejected the Jews together with their father, the hellish devil. Therefore Christians must undertake energetically, in all earnestness, and not in a spirit of levity, to burn their synagogues, to seize their books, to prohibit their religious exercises and their blasphemies; yes, to settle the matter once for all, the Jews must be driven out of Christian society altogether" (219).

References

Armour, Ellen, and Susan St. Ville. *Bodily Citations: Religion and Judith Butler*. New York: Columbia UP, 2006.

Bal, Mieke. "Sexuality, Sin and Sorrow: The Emergence of the Female Character (A Reading of Genesis 1-3)." *Poetics Today* 6.1 (1985): 21–42.

Bechtel, Lyn M. "Genesis 2.4B-3.24: A Myth About Human Maturation." *Journal for the Study of the Old Testament* 20.67 (1995): 3–26.

Berlin, Adele, and Marc Z. Brettler, eds. *The Jewish Study Bible*. New York: Oxford UP, 2004.

Cassuto, Umberto. *A Commentary on the Book of Genesis: Part One from Adam to Noah*. Trans. Israel Abrahams. Jerusalem: Magnes, 1961.

De Quincey, Thomas. *Literary Reminiscences: From the Autobiography of an English Opium-Eater*. Boston: Ticknor and Fields, 1868.

Frost, Robert. *The Poetry of Robert Frost*. Ed. Edward Connery Lathem. New York: Owl, 1969.

Ginzberg, Louis. *The Legends of the Jews I: Bible Times and Characters from the Creation to Jacob*. Trans. Henrietta Szold. Philadelphia: Jewish Publication Society of America, 1909.

Gospel of John. *Bible, Revised Standard Version*, n.d. Accessed 6 March 2019. https://quod.lib.umich.edu/cgi/r/rsv/rsv-idx?type=DIV1&byte=4926419

Heinz, Marlies, and Marian H. Feldman. *Representations of Political Power: Case Histories from Times of Change and Dissolving Order in the Ancient near East*. Winona Lake: Eisenbrauns, 2006.

Hobsbawm, Eric. *The Age of Revolution: 1789–1848*. New York: Vintage, 1996.

Izenberg, Gerald N. *Impossible Individuality: Romanticism, Revolution, and the Origins of Modern Selfhood, 1787–1802*. Princeton: Princeton UP, 2001.

Jobling, J'annine. "Falling in Love Again: Interpreting Transgression and Transgressive Interpretations of Genesis 2-3." *Critical Quarterly* 47.3 (2005): 79–89.

Júnior, Hilário Franco. "Between the Fig and the Apple: Forbidden Fruit in Romanesque Iconography." *Revue de L'Histoire des Religions* 223.1 (2006): 1–37.

Kaufmann, Yeḥezkel. *The Religion of Israel: From Its Beginnings to the Babylonian Exile*. New York: Schocken, 1972.

Kennedy, James M. "Peasants in Revolt: Political Allegory in Genesis 2-3." *Journal for the Study of the Old Testament* 15.47 (1990): 3–14.

Marshall, Peter. *Demanding the Impossible: A History of Anarchism*. Oakland: PM Press, 2009.

Menache, Sophia. "Faith, Myth, and Politics: The Stereotype of the Jews and Their Expulsion from England and France." *The Jewish Quarterly Review* 75.4 (1985): 351–374.

Michael, Timothy. *British Romanticism and the Critique of Political Reason*. Baltimore: Johns Hopkins UP, 2016.

Milton, John. *Paradise Lost: An Authoritative Text, Backgrounds and Sources, Criticism*. Ed. Scott Elledge. New York: Norton, 1975.

Noegel, Scott. "Dreams and Dream Interpreters in Mesopotamia and in the Hebrew Bible (Old Testament)." *Dreams: A Reader on the Religious, Cultural and Psychological Dimensions of Dreaming*. Ed. Kelly Bulkeley. New Hampshire: Palgrave, 2001. 45–71.

Nuttall, A. D. *The Alternative Trinity: Gnostic Heresy in Marlowe, Milton, and Blake*. New York: Clarendon Press, 1998.

Oberman, Heiko A.. *Luther: Man Between God and the Devil.* Trans. Eileen Walliser-Schwarzbart. New Haven: Yale UP, 1989.

OED Online. Oxford: Oxford UP. 3 November 2017.

Oppenheim, A. Leo. "The Interpretation of Dreams in the Ancient Near East. With a Translation of an Assyrian Dream-Book." *Transactions of the American Philosophical Society* 46.3 (1956): 179–373.

Rowan, Steven. "Luther, Bucer and Eck on the Jews." *The Sixteenth Century Journal* 16.1 (1985): 79–90.

Sarna, Nahum M. *Understanding Genesis, vol. 1*. New York: Jewish Theological Seminary of America, 1966.

Second Corinthians Revised Standard Version

Shabetai, Karen. "The Question of Blake's Hostility Toward the Jews." *Elh* 63.1 (1996): 146–152.

Summerfield, Henry. "Beards, Disputations and Revelry: Observations on Blake's 'Job' Engravings with Special Reference to Plates 2 and 3." *Colby Library Quarterly* 23.2 (1987): 89–98.

Thoreau, Henry David. *The Journal 1837–1861*. New York: New York Review Books, 2009.

Thoreau, Henry David. *Wild Fruits*. New York: Norton, 1999.

Trachtenberg, Joshua. *The Devil and the Jews: The Medieval Conception of the Jew and Its Relation to Modern Antisemitism*. Philadelphia: Jewish Publication Society of America, 1983.

Trible, Phyllis. *God and the Rhetoric of Sexuality*. Philadelphia: Fortress, 1978.

van der Walt, Lucien. "Global Anarchism and Syndicalism: Theory, History, Resistance." *Anarchist Studies* 24.1 (2016): 85–106.

Walker-Jones, Arthur. "Eden for Cyborgs: Ecocriticism and Genesis 2–3." *Biblical Interpretation* 16.3 (2008): 263–293.

Wicksteed, Joseph H. *Blake's Vision of the Book of Job*. New York: Dutton, 1910.

Williams, Leonard. "Anarchism Revived." *New Political Science* 29.3 (2007): 297–312.

Winter, Irene J. "After the Battle Is Over: The 'Stele of the Vultures' and the Beginning of Historical Narrative in the Art of the Ancient Near East." *Studies in the History of Art* 16 (1985): 11–32.

Wozniuk, Vladimir. "The Wisdom of Solomon as Political Theology." *Journal of Church and State* 39.4 (1997): 657–80.

3

Dreams and Power Between Jacob and Joseph, a Speculative Interpretation

Introduction

In the previous chapter, I discussed the idea of the "origins of the dreamscape" in terms of a space that opens up with the expulsion of Adam and Eve from the Garden of Eden and the creation of the postlapsarian conditions of labor. In these circumstances, the dreamscape offers an alternative to the new ideological and economic order, retaining elements of the primordial chaos or "deep"—the force of disorder or non-creation—as well as the multifaceted desire that provokes Eve's rebellion against the Edenic order, or what I term paradisiacal authoritarianism. In the rest of Genesis and the subsequent Hebrew scriptures, the dangers of the opening of the dreamscape toward these radical forces are mitigated by the intrusion of God either directly into the realm of dreaming or indirectly by means of fashioning and interpreting dream-texts, with the latter often done by surrogates like Joseph and Daniel. In this chapter, I focus on how the tension between the dreamscape as radical space and the dreamscape as the terrain of God's conquest opens up a critical faultline in the Joseph story—a faultline that splits the narrative into two interpretive layers. The first layer forms the basis of the conventional understanding of the

© The Author(s), under exclusive license to Springer Nature Switzerland AG 2021

S. Rogoff, *The Politics of the Dreamscape*,
https://doi.org/10.1007/978-3-030-74796-1_3

Joseph story, which I will outline below. The second layer, concealed beneath the first as what I call a "spectral ur-text,"[1] contains the remnants of a more radical tradition, one that stands opposed to the narrative logic of the final redaction of the Pentateuch and to nearly the entirety of later monotheistic traditions, with the exception of some gnostic or mystical variants. In the conventional story, Joseph emerges as a fourth patriarch and national hero. In the radical version, Joseph is a tyrant and the chief opponent to Jacob. While there has been extensive discussion of Joseph as a tyrant in the political sense, I argue that the tensions go much deeper and relate to two alternate concepts of faith. Joseph is the powerful transitional force that pushes the biblical story away from the type of religiosity presented in Jacob's dream-vision of the ladder and toward the binding of the Hebrew people to God through a conception of the Lord's control of history and the divine law, a binding that also gives rise to the power structure of the priesthood and ultimately to the political might of the kings.[2]

By identifying a deeper conflict between Jacob and Joseph in Genesis, I am able to propose a new way of contrasting the dreams related to each character. Joseph's dreams and his role as a dream interpreter create the structure for the divinely controlled philosophy of history that sets the stage for the Exodus story. This leaves Jacob's dream of the ladder as the only moment of dreaming in Genesis that cannot be assimilated into this structure. I do not think this is accidental. The continued existence of Jacob's dream of the ladder in the text points to its inherent power in the context of pre-Joseph faith. Its marginalization by the overlaying of Joseph's dream structure indicates that its power is dangerous to the new theological structure. While there is no way to definitively define the nature of the power or meaning of Jacob's dream of the ladder, this chapter argues that the dream offers a glimpse of an anarchic religiosity based on notions of equality, immediacy, and intensity of experience. The slave spiritual "We Are Climbing Jacob's Ladder" discussed in the introduction, which understands Jacob's dream of the ladder as a vision about power and the challenging of the structures of domination, comes closer to its essence than did either the post-biblical exegetes or the liberal academicians of the nineteenth and twentieth centuries.

Joseph the Provider

In his introduction to the book of Genesis in the *Jewish Study Bible*, Jon Levenson says of the story of Joseph that it "represents a narrative so coherent and so continuous that it has justly been termed a novella" (2004: 10). Levenson contrasts the coherence and continuity of the Joseph tale to the fractured and contradictory nature of much of the first book of the Bible. While the fractured and contradictory parts of Genesis have received a steady stream of commentary for thousands of years, the seemingly straightforward Joseph story has garnered relatively little theological or philosophical interest.

Exposition of the Joseph "novella," the sequel to the story of Jacob, has followed the plot and logic of the biblical narrative. This conventional view runs along the following basic lines, picking up the story with Jacob in his uncle Laban's camp. While in camp, Jacob has a total of thirteen children, seven with his first wife Leah, two with Leah's handmaiden, two with the handmaiden of Rachel, his second wife and Leah's younger sister, and finally two with his preferred Rachel. It is clear from the biblical account that since Rachel is Jacob's preferred wife (he was tricked by Laban into marrying Leah), Joseph and his younger brother Benjamin, Rachel's offspring, are his favored children. As the oldest son of Jacob's favored wife, Joseph becomes the most favored son and heir apparent to the patriarchal lineage stretching back to Abraham. Rachel dies from complications from the birth of Benjamin as the family journeys from Bethel to the land of Canaan.

The story picks up again with Joseph tending the family flocks together with the children of Bilhah and Zilpah, the handmaidens of Rachel and Leah. We learn that Joseph tells on his brothers for some sort of bad behavior. We also learn that Jacob has demonstrated his preference for Joseph by making him an "ornamented tunic"—the famous coat of many colors.[3] The point of this opening to the Joseph story is on the surface quite obvious: there is seething conflict brewing between Joseph and his older brothers. Importantly, Joseph's narration of his first dreams acts as the catalyst for transforming the brothers' jealousy and hostility into active violence:

> Once Joseph had a dream which he told to his brothers; and they hated him even more. He said to them, "Hear this dream which I have dreamed: There we were binding sheaves in the field, when suddenly my sheaf stood up and remained upright; then your sheaves gathered around and bowed low to my sheaf." His brothers answered, "Do you mean to reign over us? Do you mean to rule over us?" And they hated him even more for the talk about his dreams.
>
> He dreamed another dream and told it to his brothers, saying, "Look, I have had another dream: And this time, the sun, the moon, and eleven stars were bowing down to me." And when he told it to his father and brothers, his father berated him, "What," he said to him, "is this dream you have dreamed? Are we to come, I and your mother and your brothers and bow low to you on the ground?" (Berlin and Brettler 2004: 75)

The brothers, fueled by Joseph's seeming declaration of superiority—and a perhaps veiled threat to vault from his place in the birth order to claim the mantle of Jacob's primary heir—conspire to harm him: "They said to one another, 'Here comes that dreamer! Come now, let us kill him and throw him into one of the pits; and we can say, 'A savage beast devoured him.' We will see what comes of his dreams!'" (Berlin and Brettler 2004: 75). Persuaded by one of the brothers, Reuben, not to kill Joseph, the brothers instead sell him into slavery to a passing caravan of Ishmaelites. The Ishmaelites take Joseph to Egypt, where he is sold again to Potiphar, a member of the Pharaoh's court.

Joseph's dreams combine two basic ancient dream types (Oppenheim 1956; Noegel 2001: 45–46). First, they are symbolic dreams, containing a hidden or coded message. The sheaves of wheat stand for something, as do the celestial bodies. At the same time, these dreams are prophetic; they indicate something about the future. In the dreams, it is revealed that Joseph will lord over his family, which indeed happens later on. The message presents accurate information that seems to have a divine source. The existence of both symbols and prophecy in a dream points to a divine origin. Though Jacob and the brothers do not explicitly recognize it (and perhaps do not understand it) readers know that the dreams predict what follows—Joseph's rise to power in Egypt and the family's (and the region's) salvation by his intervention on their behalf. These first dreams establish

Joseph as a person with a relationship to God and access to the divine realm. This immediately substantiates his favored status by Jacob. Jacob and God see Joseph as the next in line, a line that runs from Abraham and Isaac, through Jacob, to Joseph and eventually to Moses. The first dreams place Joseph squarely in this history, thrusting him forward as the continuation of the patriarchal tradition. This status is sealed in the Genesis account, Michael Avioz argues, through Joseph's public kiss of his dead father after the reconciliation in Egypt. After the death of the head of the family, Joseph receives an exalted status, and as a result,

> his brothers fear him greatly (Gen. 50,15). Joseph's status as the preferred son was constructed gradually: in chapter 37 he receives the striped shirt; in chapter 48 Jacob actually adopts Joseph's sons; in chapter 49,22–26 Jacob gives him a special blessing. Chapter 50 continues this line and *Joseph actually becomes the patriarch*, immediately after the kiss. Nonetheless, Joseph does not abuse his power against his brothers. (Avioz 2015: 245, emphasis mine)

At the same time, the story seems to present Joseph in a fairly unsympathetic way. When the story first presents him in Canaan, he is bringing "bad reports of [his brothers] to their father" (Avioz 2015: 74). In both the ancient and modern imagination, there is little good that can be said of being a tattletale. Instead of being humble and gracious as the favored son, Joseph seems to act in an arrogant fashion. His inability to take a more thoughtful or considered approach when dealing with his brothers strikes the reader (and Jacob) as dangerous and stupid.

The portrait that emerges from these early accounts of Joseph in Canaan seems to present a nuanced view. He is a young man who is chosen by both God and Jacob, the patriarch of God's chosen people. The implication is that Joseph is a man of God, a man of righteousness. Despite this, he seems little aware of his position. He does not or cannot interpret his own dreams. The reader does not get a sense that Joseph understands the dreams or that he is aware of their divine significance. He betrays his brothers, shows off his tunic, and seemingly innocently narrates his dreams. The conventional understanding of Joseph accepts this composite portrait as being one of unusual emotional and psychological depth, which causes it to stand out in Genesis (Carr 1996: 273). The good, godly, though young, naïve, and perhaps arrogant Joseph has been treated ruthlessly by his ungodly and much less sophisticated brothers. The elderly Jacob is cast as the secondary victim, receiving the torn and bloody tunic from the brothers with deep lamentations.

The link between God and Joseph becomes explicit when Joseph arrives in Egypt and is sold to the house of Potiphar, a courtier of the Egyptian Pharaoh. Joseph is placed as head of Potiphar's household, and because the "Lord was with him," everything of Potiphar's starts to thrive (Berlin and Brettler 2004: 78). Unfortunately for Joseph, his good looks and healthy physique get him into trouble by attracting the attention of Potiphar's wife. She will not leave Joseph alone and, upset by his constant rejections, falsely accuses him of trying to rape her. Potiphar, incensed, responds to the accusation by siding with his wife and putting Joseph in prison.

But God is with Joseph—meaning that God is watching over Joseph and orchestrating events, even seemingly untoward events, with an eye on their grander purpose. Under God's benevolent eye, Joseph manages to excel even in prison, becoming the caretaker of other prisoners. This status is important because after some time, the Pharaoh's cupbearer and personal baker are placed under his charge. Each servant of the Pharaoh, after being in prison for some time, has a dream that he cannot understand. Joseph, seeing the dour expressions of their faces, offers to help. When they tell him the two dreams, Joseph correctly predicts that the cupbearer will be spared and returned to Pharaoh's service while the baker will be tortured and killed. Unlike before, Joseph is now able to interpret dreams, to understand their symbolism, to determine the nature of the prophecy, and, more broadly speaking, knows that the dreams are messages constructed by God. God has planted these dreams in order for Joseph to reveal their meaning. In prison, Joseph comes to understand that his fate is determined by the unfolding of God's will.

Two years after the cupbearer's return to Pharaoh (at which time he forgets about Joseph completely) Pharaoh experiences troubling dreams. He sends for his court magicians and wise men, but none can make any sense of them. At this point, the cupbearer remembers Joseph and his ability to discern the meaning of dreams and the nature of the prophecy they contain. Pharaoh immediately sends for Joseph and tells him his famous two dreams:

> Then Pharaoh said to Joseph, "In my dream, I was standing on the bank of the Nile, when out of the Nile came up seven sturdy and well-formed cows and grazed in the reed grass. Presently there followed them seven other cows, scrawny, ill-formed, and emaciated—never had I seen their likes for ugliness in all the land of Egypt! And the seven lean and ugly cows ate up the first seven cows, the sturdy ones; but when they had consumed them, one could not tell that they had consumed them, for they looked just as bad as before. And I awoke. In my other dream, I saw seven ears of grain, full and healthy, growing on a single stalk; but right behind them sprouted seven ears, shriveled, thin, and scorched by the east wind. And the thin ears swallowed the seven healthy ones. I have told the magicians, but none has an explanation for me." (Berlin and Brettler 2004: 81–82)

Upon hearing this, Joseph immediately understands and explains to Pharaoh that God has sent him a coded message. The two dreams mean the same thing. The seven cows and seven ears of grain symbolized seven years. The fat cows and healthy ears stand for seven years of plenty. The emaciated cows and scorched ears symbolized seven years of drought and famine. The fact that the same message has occurred twice means that God is very serious about it. Joseph tells Pharaoh, "It means that the matter has been determined by God, and that God will soon carry it out" (Berlin and Brettler 2004: 82).

The dream interpretation opens up the doors to power to Joseph. Pharaoh heeds the warning and appoints Joseph to oversee the growing and husbanding of grain during the plentiful years, and the distributing and rationing of grain during the lean ones. The plan works wonderfully, not only preserving the kingdom and its people through difficult times but also in expanding the Pharaoh's control over the kingdom and vastly increasing his wealth, for petitioners for grain must compensate Pharaoh with goods and land. As a reward for his service, Pharaoh gives Joseph the name *Zaphenath-paneah*, meaning "God speaks, he lives" or "creator of life" (Berlin and Brettler 2004: 83). He is also given a wife, Asenath, the daughter of Poti-phera, the priest of On. In general, Joseph is described as rising to such heights of power—with the title of vizier—that only Pharaoh stands above him. His power is such that when famine hits, the Pharaoh tells the Egyptians, "Go to Joseph; whatever he tells you, you shall do" (Berlin and Brettler 2004: 83).

Because of Joseph's foresight, people start to flock to Egypt for food during the seven years of famine. As it happens, Joseph's brothers arrive in Egypt in search of food to buy. After some scenes of testing and family drama, Joseph reveals his identity to them, and they reconcile. The Israelites resettle from Canaan to Egypt. Before embarking from Canaan, God makes a promise to Jacob *in a dream* that he will bring his people out of Egypt in the future—a reference to the Exodus and to God's command of the entire historical narrative: present, past, and future.

Conflict in Canaan

A closer look at the Joseph narrative generates many questions that cannot be parried by referring to the emotional or psychological sophistication of the characters but which ultimately point to a deeper rift between the text and what I call its "prehistory," an "ur-text" that casts shadows on the codified composite. The most significant moment of narrative tension comes with young Joseph's telling his dreams to his brothers and father. How could it be that Jacob and his older sons fail to recognize Joseph's dreams as divine in origin? While the reader understands the dreams as symbolic and prophetic, Jacob and the brothers do not seem to get the message.[4] This lack of awareness is quite startling. It cuts against the coherence of both the biblical understanding of dreaming (including Jacob's understanding on other occasions) and the broader conceptualization of dreaming throughout ancient Mesopotamia and Egyptian cultures (Oppenheim 1956).

By Joseph's time, dreams have played a vital role in the lives of the Hebrew patriarchs. God communicates directly with Abram (Abraham) in Genesis 15:12–16, providing prophecy and displaying God's control over time and history. To Isaac, it seems God also appears in a dream at Beer-sheba: "That night the Lord appeared to him and said, 'I am the God of your father Abraham. Fear not, for I am with you, and I will bless you and increase your offspring for the sake of My servant Abraham'" (Berlin and Brettler 2004: 55). More directly and importantly, Jacob receives a vision and communicates directly with God as he flees his father's house after the great deception of Isaac and betrayal of Esau, the "stairway" or "ladder" dream (Berlin and Brettler 2004: 58–59). Many other places in the biblical text add to the understanding of the dream as a corridor for divine communication, for example, the subsequent dreams of the prisoners and the pharaoh in the Joseph text, the prophet Nathan's dream about David's plan to build a temple, Solomon's incubation dream at Gideon, and Daniel's interpretation of the dreams of Nebuchadnezzar.

The Hebrew Bible also contains the idea of "false" dreams—even fake dreams—and spurious interpretation. In the book of Jeremiah, God is recorded to have said:

> I have heard what the prophets say, who prophesy falsely in My name: "I had a dream, I had a dream." How long will there be in the minds of the prophets who prophesy falsehood—the prophets of their own deceitful minds—the plan to make My people forget My name, by means of the dreams which they tell each other, just as their fathers forgot My name because of Baal? (Berlin and Brettler 2004: 974)

Solomon Zeitlin argues that God's direct speech here is not slandering the prophets as liars or intentional deceivers. Rather, Zeitlin believes, the prophets are simply misinterpreting dreams—or they are mistakenly seeing prophecy in dreams that are being generated as reflections of their internal desires (Zeitlin 1975: 5–6). Despite Zeitlin's claim about the later book of Jeremiah, there is no evidence in Genesis for a conception of dreaming that is psychological, mundane, or that is an expression of an individual character's private wishes, longings, or repressed yearnings. Joseph's dreams, then, cannot be a reflection of *his* desire. Considered in this light, the failure of Jacob and the brothers to recognize the divine nature of Joseph's dreams indicates one of two things, or both. It was either (a) a denial of God's prophecy and Joseph as legitimate prophet or (b) an accusation that Joseph is acting as a false prophet, that his "dreams" were fabricated (by himself or a rival deity) to buttress his claim to leadership of the clan—a very serious accusation. Seen in this way, the seriousness of this encounter is heightened far above what is understood in the conventional reading of the Joseph story. I want to suggest that the potential conflict between Jacob and Joseph reveals itself in an analysis of the narrative framing of Joseph's dreams as concerning fundamental attributes of the faith. I will expand on these two possible motives after situating the dreams scenes in context.

The seriousness of dreaming and dreaming's connection to the divine realm is ubiquitous throughout ancient Mesopotamian and Near Eastern literature. This literature provides an important frame to the discussion of Joseph's dreams, his interpretations, and other's reactions to both. The key linkage in this literature is the relationship between a god or gods, a ruler figure, and the people as the subjects of the ruler's domain. In short, what is at stake in the world of ancient dreaming is power through the triad of god-ruler-ruled. Scott Noegel sums up the status of biblical dreaming, writing, "Like message dreams in Mesopotamian historical and literary works, biblical message dreams serve to legitimate the political, national, or military concerns of the dreamer, who is invariably someone of great importance" (2001: 56).

Around 2450 BCE, Sumerian ruler Eannatum I of Lagash commissioned the production of a stele to record and glorify his military victory over the kingdom of Umma. Known as the "Stele of Vultures" (because of the depiction of vultures carrying off the severed heads of the defeated) and currently housed in the Louvre Museum in Paris, the fragments of this pillar contain the earliest recovered record of a dream. In the dream, which exists only in fragmentary form, Ningirsu, god of war and head patron deity of Lagash, stands by Eannatum's head and blesses and sanctions the war against Umma. The message of the dream is clear—Eannatum's aggression is being done in the righteous name of Ningirsu. The expansion of the power of Lagash, the stele makes clear, is in line with the will of the gods. Noegel adds to the notion that the stele is not only an expansion of royal power. "However," he writes, "we would be mistaken if we thought of it only as royal propaganda. The stele was discovered in the temple precinct and not on the border of Lagash, suggesting that the cult of Ningirsu had considerable interest in preserving the dream account. The Ningirsu priesthood probably stood to benefit as much from sanctioning the king with Ningirsu's promise as from the campaign itself" (Noegel 2001: 46). In this early dream account, we see the interweaving of political and religious power structures, the divine will, and control of the meaning of the dream narrative.

A similar link between earthly power and the divine can be seen in the fragmentary remains of the legend of Sargon, here to even greater propagandistic effect. The Sargon legend begins with an ode to the king who preceded Sargon, Ur-Zababa. Ur-Zababa is credited with elevating the city-state of Kish to prominence. The cuneiform fragments speak of his accomplishments in grandiose terms: "to turn the house of Kic, which was like a haunted town, into a living settlement again—its king, shepherd Ur-Zababa, rose like Utu over the house of Kic" (The Sargon Legend 2019). It can be safely assumed that the inclusion of laudatory rhetoric about Ur-Zababa in what is otherwise a propagandistic piece composed to justify Sargon's rule was deliberate. Ur-Zababa most likely had a loyal following in Kish and was highly respected, perhaps even feared. Certainly, he was seen as being the earthly representative of the patron gods and most likely had people strongly loyal to him among the kingdom's priesthood as the Sargon legend gained shape in the oral traditions.

The tablets make clear that Ur-Zababa loses the favor of the gods, who, instead, promote the power of a seemingly loyal and innocent servant of the king, Sargon. The gods' abandoning of Ur-Zababa is first communicated to Sargon in a dream:

> One day, after the evening had arrived and Sargon had brought the regular deliveries to the palace, Ur-Zababa was sleeping (and dreaming) in the holy bed-chamber, his holy residence. He realized what the dream was about, but did not put into words, did not discuss it with anyone. (The Sargon Legend 2019)

The precise content of the dream is not communicated to the reader, but the gist is obvious. King Ur-Zababa learns that he will be dethroned and killed and that Sargon will replace him. Ancient readers or listeners to this story would know precisely what this meant: Ur-Zababa has lost the support of the gods, who are conveying this to him through the typical conduit of the dream. A righteous king would accept his fate and submit to the will of the gods. Not Ur-Zababa, he conceals the dream, which results in sickness:[5]

> After five or ten days had passed, king Ur-Zababa… and became frightened in his residence. Like a lion he urinated, sprinkling his legs, and the urine contained blood and pus. He was troubled, he was afraid like a fish floundering in brackish water. (The Sargon Legend 2019)

The king's concealment of the divine message is in vain; Sargon receives the same or a very similar message in a dream of his own:

> It was then that the cupbearer of Ezina's wine-house, Sargon, lay down not to sleep, but lay down to dream. In the dream, holy Inana drowned Ur-Zababa in a river of blood. The sleeping Sargon groaned and gnawed the ground. When king Ur-Zababa heard about this groaning, he was brought into the king's holy presence, Sargon was brought into the presence of Ur-Zababa (who said:) "Cupbearer, was a dream revealed to you in the night?" Sargon answered his king: "My king, this is my dream, which I will tell you about: There was a young woman, who was as high as the heavens and as broad as the earth. She was firmly set as the base of a wall. For me, she drowned you in a great river, a river of blood." (The Sargon Legend 2019)

This is a startling passage. First, Sargon receives the symbolic prophecy that the gods are conspiring to kill the king, his master. Second, the king chooses to confront Sargon, despite knowing that Sargon will corroborate what he already knows—that his days are numbered. Finally, most strikingly, Sargon reveals the truth of his dream to Ur-Zababa, knowing, of course, that the sitting king will immediately see him as an enemy and try to kill him.

This is exactly what happens. Ur-Zababa plots to kill Sargon, directly controverting the divine message and setting himself up against the gods. Even worse, the king claims that the killing of Sargon is in line with what the goddess Inana's demands. From a favored and seemingly beloved king, Ur-Zababa, by refusing the truth of the dream, has turned himself into an apostate. It is Sargon who is now arrayed on the side of the gods. They have chosen to elevate him to the position of ruler, marking him for greatness. Sargon's historical greatness ultimately comes with his military victory over the hegemonic power in ancient Sumer, King Lugal-zage-si of Uruk. Not surprisingly, the final part of the extent legend connects Ur-Zababa and Lugal-zage-si in an attempt to murder Sargon, pairing the two monarchs in the sacrilegious attempt to defy the gods by acting against the dream prophecy. Sargon's final victory over both Ur-Zababa and Lugal-zage-si and his domination of all of Babylonia have now been fully legitimized. The sequence of dreams works rhetorically and propagandistically to transform Sargon from a lowly regicide, usurper, and tyrannical conqueror into the rightful and godly heir to the throne, and imperial master of the region (Cooper and Heimpel 1983: 74; Nigro 1998: 85).

One final example of ancient Mesopotamian dreaming will help form a context for the dream narratives in the book of Genesis. The Gudea cylinders A and B, a text called "The building of Ningirsu's temple," contain an elaborate use of dreaming (Gudea Cylinders 2019). In the text, King Gudea receives a dream. The vision is so impactful that he leaves immediately to tell it to the goddess Nanshe, his dream interpreter. Nanshe explains to Gudea the meaning behind every symbolic element in the dream. The dream contains the divine command to rebuild the temple for the god Ningirsu, the E-ninnu, as well as the plans for its construction. When Gudea asks for further instructions, Ningirsu again comes to the head of the sleeper and supplies great detail about the building of the temple, a grandiose and tremendously expansive project that is sure to stretch the capacity of his domain. This is precisely the point, the directives to build the temple come from Ningirsu, the god, the patron of the city, and not directly from the Gudea, the king. The temple, then, is to be a domicile for Ningirsu, not for Gudea. The labor and resources required to construct such an opulent palace are labor and resources expended in the service of Ningirsu, not for the earthly ruler Gudea. That is not to say that the building of the temple has nothing to do with Gudea. It is Gudea who provides the vital link between the people of his realm and the gods. It is Gudea who has the responsibility to build the temple. It is Gudea who has the favor of the gods and who can entice Ningirsu to dwell in the new temple of E-ninnu, thus elevating the status of Lagash and the power of the king. The dreams in this narrative are the key elements in the rhetorical and propagandist strategy of the account—an account that is intended to justify the massive civic effort to rebuild the E-ninnu and to solidify the power position of Gudea as the link between the people and the gods (Bewer 1919: 128). The completion of the temple with the most lavish materials and elaborate detail as well as the enticement of Ningirsu to dwell there set the stage for a sweeping expansion of Gudea's authority. The building of the temple, initiated and described in dreams, represented the cornerstone of Gudea's rule.

These contextual pieces provide valuable perspective on questions about Jacob's and Joseph's brothers' reaction to Joseph's youthful dreams. On the most basic level, these examples show the magnitude of the dream experience. The dream in this context is a conduit for vital communication between the divine realm and the human realm. From the three examples, it is clear that the dream message is linked to earthly power. The gods' messages can decisively shift the political or military balance on earth. Dreams are taken quite seriously by all involved. In the cases of Sargon and Gudea, the need or requirement to share the dream with others is stressed. In Sargon, the failure to tell of the dream and the keeping of the divine message secret (or within the body) is deleterious to health. Ur-Zababa keeps the dream message hidden—he suffers. Sargon reveals, despite the fact that the revelation places him in great danger. Even greater danger would come from angering the gods by keeping the dream a private matter. There is no conception of a "private" dream in the ancient Near Eastern literature. Dreams have social significance. The dreamer is required to communicate the dream. The final important lesson gleaned from these examples (and many others) is that details matter. There is nothing extraneous in ancient dream narratives.

Applied to the dreams of the youthful Joseph, these three elements (the dream as a channel of communication between the divine and the mundane; the necessity of communicating dreams to the social/political group; the significance of detail) add complexity to the interaction between Joseph and his family. The reactions to Joseph's dreams now seem doubly curious and cannot be explained by reference to jealousy, psychology, or foolishness. After listening to Joseph, the brothers ask, "Do you mean to reign over us? Do you mean to rule over us?" When Joseph tells the dreams to his father, Jacob says, "What… is this dream you have dreamed? Are we to come, I and your mother and your brothers and bow low to you on the ground?" Since there is no precedent in the ancient literature for the brothers and Jacob to see these dreams as expressions of Joseph's desires, longings, or personal ambitions, the two possibilities I present above seem the most likely. The first possibility is that the brothers and Jacob recognize these dreams as divine in origin, as coming from God, and yet choose to act against the divine message, even without fully understanding it.[6] In this reading, Jacob and the brothers are arrayed against Joseph *and* God. The second possibility is that Jacob and the brothers view Joseph's dreams as false prophecies—and Joseph as a charlatan or heretic—akin to a magician or sorcerer.[7] In this scenario, Joseph's dreams would be false dreams, Joseph a prophet of a false god or gods, who at the very least resembles Jeremiah's "prophets who prophesy falsehood." Whatever the case may be, by placing these dreams in the context of ancient Near and Middle Eastern dreaming, it becomes clear that the conflict between Joseph and his family is much deeper and more significant than previously recognized. Jacob and Joseph, far from allies, appear to represent hostile and incompatible camps.[8]

Evidence of a deep and serious theological-political antagonism between Jacob and Joseph can be traced throughout the story. Chapter 37:12–14 tells of Jacob sending Joseph out to meet his brothers in the fields. The previous line (37:11) sets the stage. "So his brothers were wrought up at him, and his father kept the matter in mind" (Berlin and Brettler 2004: 75). The conventional narrative posits that Jacob keeps the matter of the brothers' hostility in mind in order to protect Joseph. However, this makes no sense in the way it is commonly understood—for Jacob immediately and purposefully places Joseph in grave danger: "One time when his brothers had gone to pasture their father's flock at Shechem, Israel said to Joseph, 'Your brothers are pasturing at Shechem. Come, I will send you to them'" (Berlin and Brettler 2004: 75).[9] It seems more plausible that Jacob's intent is to send Joseph into grave danger in order to test whether or not Joseph is a true or a false prophet. The fact that this scene directly follows the dream sequence is not coincidental. That Jacob, in this reading, becomes a sinister version of Abraham during the attempted sacrifice of Isaac is reinforced by the parallel between Joseph's response to Jacob, "I am ready" (Berlin and Brettler 2004: 75), and Abraham's similar response to

God when called upon to hear the divine command to sacrifice his son: "Here I am" (Berlin and Brettler 2004: 45, note 22:1–19). Joseph's mirroring of Abraham's declaration is fascinating for many reasons. First, it transforms this seemingly ordinary scene of being sent out to the field into an event with divine implications. Second, it is the sacrificial son (the Isaac) and not the sacrificing father (the Abraham) who now seems to have the divine connection, for the "I am ready," just like Abraham's "Here I am," forms a communicative bridge between the godly and the mundane. Narratively speaking, this is the moment in the story when Joseph surpasses and supplants Jacob as the agent of history. Jacob's attempt to block this transition—to deny or contravene the message of the dreams—can be compared to Ur-Zababa's attempt to defy the wishes of the gods by having Sargon killed. The implication of Jacob in Joseph's (potential) murder acts to undermine Jacob's legitimacy and to defend Joseph's eventual usurpation of power over the people.[10]

As Joseph approaches his brothers in the field, they say to each other, "Here comes that dreamer! Come now, let us kill him and throw him into one of the pits; and we can say, 'A savage beast devoured him.' We shall see what comes of his dreams" (75). The brothers' scorn for Joseph's dreams has most commonly been explained as the result of jealousy and their hatred of Jacob's favor of Joseph.[11] As shown above, in the ancient context the dream is immediately a question of divine communication (either real or false). Jacob, I contend, is testing the divine status of the dreams by sending Joseph out into the fields to meet his bloodthirsty brothers. The brothers are actively rejecting Joseph's divine status—or God's will—by planning to kill him.

Jacob's reaction to the brothers' story of Joseph's death is similarly puzzling. It is Jacob, after all, who sends Joseph into danger. Jacob is well aware of the hatred Joseph's brothers have for him. And yet, when the brothers return and present Joseph's bloody tunic, Jacob seems to immediately fall for the ruse, believing that a savage beast has torn Joseph apart: "My son's tunic!" he cries, "A savage beast devoured him! Joseph was torn by a beast" (Berlin and Brettler 2004: 76). On the surface, this seems strange. Why wouldn't Jacob suspect the brothers of foul play? Here, the possibility of a second, symbolic reading opens up. Jacob's "savage beast" is a metaphor for a false god, Joseph's death the result of having been seduced from the divine path. The reader senses, however, that it is Jacob who is now treading on religiously dubious ground. This moment of narrative confusion or tension points to the "untamable" nature of Genesis, a text that invites and perhaps requires speculative readings in violation of defined academic norms (West 2018; Carr 2000).

The consequences of the brothers' act in the text substantiate Joseph's status as a prophet. It is not surprising that when the narrative picks up with Joseph next in Egypt, the story continues, "the Lord was with Joseph, and he was a successful man" (Berlin and Brettler 2004: 78). The shift from the questionable status of Joseph to the definitive status of Joseph as prophet is remarkable and important. It allows Egyptians like Potiphar to perceive Joseph's essence, despite the fact that Joseph's brothers and Jacob—the patriarch—were either blind to it or rejected it. Still, it is curious that the Lord chooses to bless Potiphar's house and that Potiphar, despite knowing that Joseph is with the Lord, believes his conniving wife over his most trusted and valuable servant, a servant who has substantially increased his wealth.

Similar questions arise during the early Egyptian part of the Joseph story. How does Joseph become confident that he is God's mouthpiece while in prison (40:8), even though he did not seem to perceive it in Canaan? Why can Pharaoh recognize the importance of dreams (41:7) when Jacob fails to see it earlier in the narrative? Why would God reveal his plans to Pharaoh (41:28), who is not a believer in the Hebrew God? These questions result from the imposition on the text of a distinct philosophy of history, a philosophy that asserts the Hebrew God's total control over all of human activity. Individual action, individual agency, is minimized in this Egyptian section to make room for God's turning of the divine wheel of time. It is here that the case is being built for the great historical epic of the Jewish faith—the Israelites' fall into slavery and God's liberation of them and delivery (with the newly divulged Law) to the Promised Land.

Joseph is the key figure in the first act of the Moses epic. He is God's human agent, the man who assists God in controlling the historical narrative. It is curious, though, that Joseph seems to become more and more Egyptian as God's use of him as the lever of history intensifies. Joseph, the seeming heir to the patriarchal tradition, marries an Egyptian woman, despite this being against the cultural practices of his people. Not only is Joseph's wife a non-believer, she is the daughter of Poti-phera, the priest of On. Considering the care Genesis takes in finding suitable marriages for Abraham, Isaac, and Jacob from within the fold, it is striking that Joseph strays from it. To facilitate Joseph's Egyptian assimilation, Pharaoh gives him an Egyptian name: Zaphenath-paneah (God speaks; he lives or creator of life). The shift of name and marriage are downplayed in the text—but their inclusion indicates that these were parts of the story that could not be denied. The tension between this new Egyptian Joseph and the old Jacobite one is symbolized most acutely in the naming of his sons: "Joseph named the first-born Manesseh, meaning, 'God has made me forget completely my hardship and my parental home.' And the second he named Ephraim, meaning, 'God has made me fertile in the land of my affliction'" (Berlin and Brettler 2004: 83). The explicit naming of the sons supports the notion of a narrative confrontation between Jacob's world in Canaan and Joseph's Egyptian existence, thus symbolically pitting the two patriarchs against each other.

These worlds come into direct contact again during the famine. As we know from the conventional narrative, the brothers come to Egypt to petition Joseph, now vizier of Egypt, for food. Joseph recognizes them, while they do not recognize him. Joseph plays games with his brothers before eventually revealing his identity to them and calling for them to bring Jacob and the entire tribe to Egypt. The brothers and Jacob obey. But Jacob has doubts about the move, which set up the following dream:

> So Israel set out with all that was his, and he came to Beer-sheba, where he offered sacrifices to the God of his father Isaac. God called to Israel in a vision by night: "Jacob, Jacob!" He answered, "Here." And He said, "I am God, the God of your father. Fear not to go down to Egypt, for I will make you there into a great nation. I Myself will go down with you to Egypt, and I Myself will also bring you back; and Joseph's hand shall close your eyes." (Berlin and Brettler 2004: 91)

This is a striking scene for at least five reasons. First, it shifts the focus abruptly back to Jacob and his relationship to God. Second, it reminds that Jacob has a direct communicative conduit with God while Joseph's link is indirect, that of an agent (witting or unwitting) of God's designs and receiver/interpreter of God's coded messages. Third, Jacob is expressing his deep unease about leaving the holy land, an unease that stands in marked contrast to Joseph's Egyptian assimilation and transformation. Fourth, it is God who directly intervenes to unburden Jacob, blessing the move away from Canaan and into Egypt, this after stressing for so long the critical importance of residing on divine ground. Fifth, the passage is an attempt to bring Jacob and Joseph back together, to plaster over the rifts in their relationship and bring closure to the story and uniformity to the text—an attempt that eventually is brought to conclusion by Joseph's kiss on the dead Jacob's body, cited above.

Two Josephs

The tensions in the Genesis account point to the existence of another version of the Joseph story, one at odds with the basic philosophy of history presented in Genesis. The Genesis account acts as an elaborate attempt to undermine the stature of Jacob and to defend and enhance the position of Joseph, thus setting the stage for the Moses epic. The key to both the Joseph story and the Moses epic is the total omnipotence of God over history—that God is spinning the wheel of earthly affairs. Joseph and Moses are both agents of God. This is a radical departure from the deal-making ("trickster") Jacob, whose power seems at times to challenge God directly, as in the nighttime wrestling scene on the bank of the Jabbok River. In the revised version of the narrative, Joseph-the-dreamer is meant to dethrone Jacob-the-dreamer. The receiver of prophecy and interpreter of God's will replace the dreamer of the ladder, a potential challenger to the unidirectional power of God and the unapproachable divine realm. What could this spectral text be that lurks below the Joseph story? To rediscover it, I experiment with peeling away the dreams, which provide the philosophy of history behind the beginnings of the Moses epic. The following counter-narrative is a speculative one.

The story begins with the rise of Joseph as a challenger to Jacob's dominance in the Canaanite camp. Jacob's removal of Joseph from the common work of the brothers is an attempt to limit his influence among them; it is not a form of preference for him. Similarly, his "gift" of the multicolored or long-sleeve tunic is a move to differentiate and ostracize Joseph—perhaps a precursor to the inquisitional *sanbenito*.[12] Joseph responds to this (or initiates this) by taking on a faith in an opposing deity, thus challenging the underpinnings of Jacob's tribal supremacy.[13] What is perceived as false faith gets Joseph thrown out of camp and sold into slavery. Joseph's ambitions and skills as a challenger allow him to thrive for a time being in Potiphar's house, but these same characteristics eventually bring him into conflict with the master. Potiphar casts Joseph into prison out of fear of Joseph's rising power. Again, Joseph overcomes his circumstances. His intelligence and skill win him the favor of the Pharaoh—Joseph beats out the other potential dream interpreters. Upon entry into Pharaoh's court, Joseph enthusiastically adopts Egyptian modes and an Egyptian identity, shedding, as much as possible, his Israelite identity. Never once does he consider returning home or reaching out to his family; he is focused completely on the accumulation of power and influence. When famine strikes and the Israelites come to Egypt, Joseph seizes his opportunity to dominate them. Instead of providing for them in Canaan in fulfillment of their request, Joseph forces them to give up their connection to the holy land and relocate to Egypt, the infidel's domain.[14] Like all others, the Israelites in Egypt are subjected to Joseph's unscrupulous wielding of power. Joseph transforms into a tyrant, a transformation preserved in the text.

Despite the attempt to cast Joseph's rule in a positive light, the implications of Joseph's actions as vizier are clear. He uses his successful preparations for the famine to dramatically increase the wealth and power of the Pharaoh (and himself) by taking control of all flocks and farmland. In addition, and shockingly, Joseph manages to trade grain for human freedom, thus reducing the population to serfdom—to agricultural laborers bound to the land of their master, the Pharaoh. The only people spared from this radical expansion of power are the Egyptian priests. It is worth remembering that Joseph has by this time married into a priestly Egyptian family. If the notion of a divine hand is rejected and Joseph's actions are seen as those of a political man, the ruthlessness is impossible to ignore. The tribe of Jacob, having been lured into Egypt, has now been stripped of wealth and property and more or less enslaved by one of its own.

Joseph-the-provider transforms in this account into Joseph-the-enslaver. Genesis preserves this anti-Joseph diatribe. While the story of Joseph-the-tyrant has been told many times, as I note above, and has been set within the context of political power, it has not been situated as representing a wholly different religious paradigm. If the Joseph story was meant to shift the underlying theology of Genesis, with what was the story of Joseph-the-tyrant meant to contrast? What alternative vision was its diatribe attacking? To speculate about this, I suggest looking at Jacob's dream of the ladder, as it is this dream that the dreams in the Joseph epic could have been meant to supersede. The reorientation of the faith had to conquer not only Jacob as patriarch, but Jacob's dreamscape.

Dreaming Two Conceptions of Faith

A second Jacob is also lurking in the shadows of the Genesis text. To discover him, the slanderous layer added for the text's reformation as an apologia for Joseph needs to be removed. In the shadow or spectral text, Jacob is not ignorant of the divine implications of Joseph's dreams, though he sees them as representing a false god—even if this god is the eventual God of the Moses epic. Jacob's "God" is a different God. Instead of reacting to Joseph spitefully and/or jealously, Jacob sees the danger Joseph presents. The dreams, for Jacob, indicate Joseph's desire to view himself as the agent of God, to act as a prophet—albeit a false prophet. Jacob and his brothers cast Joseph out of Canaan. But Jacob is tortured by this move. The loss of Rachel's son is a high price to pay for the maintenance of the faith. The story's readers would have recognized Jacob's banishment of Joseph as the fulfillment of the aborted sacrifice of Isaac—here justified by Joseph's apostasy. Of course, Jacob has not killed Joseph. Joseph emerges when Jacob sends his sons down to Egypt to buy grain. When he initiates this mission, Jacob has no intention of moving his tribe to Egypt—the deal is purely transactional, money for grain. The failure of the sons to carry out a proper transaction (they return from their first trip with both grain and the money they had brought with them to pay for it) deeply disturbs Jacob. He does not want to be beholden to the Pharaoh. This is why he sends the sons with double the amount of money when they go for the next load of grain. He intends to pay for the new grain and the old, clearing his debt.

Joseph will not support the Israelites in Canaan, leaving Jacob with a stark choice: he can either reject Joseph's support and try to outlast the famine, or he can acquiesce to Joseph's demands and bring his people to Egypt. The Jacob of the shadow text fights to stand his ground, to stay in Canaan. But Joseph's brothers prevail and eventually, despite his grave reservations, Jacob abandons the holy land and brings his people into the heart of Joseph's tyranny. While the Genesis account takes on a heroic and celebratory character, the spectral text is a tragedy, perhaps even an apocalyptic account of the destruction of the Jacobites. With Jacob's demise, his faith is transfigured into that of Joseph and leads seamlessly into the Moses epic.

Dreams play the key role in transforming the anti-Joseph text into the redacted version of Genesis. This points to the political potency of dreams in the ancient imagination. The Genesis account of Joseph, harnessing the power of the dream, asserts what will become the dominant mode of Jewish faith. This turn represents the beginnings of the faith's crystallization into religious orthodoxy, despite the assertions of some critics that Joseph offers a cautionary story or a critique of monarchical power. In any case, the power of God is complete. The Lord reigns over the world, controls history, and creates moral structures. All events are God's events. Good happenings are God's rewards; misfortunes are God's punishments. Law is devised to ensure correct behavior and social order. Keepers of the law, priests and political leaders, are empowered to rule over the people in the name of God. Ritual is formed to lend cohesiveness to the religious group and to reinforce the social order. They serve to reify the structures of power, both in the era of Temple Judaism and later in the Rabbinical and post-Rabbinical periods. This is a faith based on institutional order, hierarchy, control, subordination, domination, inequality, and first and foremost the politics of knowledge. One is forced to submit to this divinely guided hierarchical structure—as Jacob submits by going down to Egypt—or be cast out as an apostate, a heretic, even as a non-person—like Nebuchadnezzar to be "driven away from men" and to eat "grass like cattle" (Berlin and Brettler 2004: 1650).

The shadow or spectral text points to an alternative conception of faith, perhaps even a primordial version of a lost religious tradition. The clearest traces of this can be found in Jacob's dream of the ladder.[15]

> He [Jacob] came upon a certain place and stopped there for the night, for the sun had set. Taking one of the stones of that place, he put it under his head and lay down in that place. He had a dream; a stairway was set on the ground and its top reached to the sky, and angels of God were going up and down on it.
>
> And the Lord was standing beside him and He said, "I am the Lord, the God of your father Abraham and the God of Isaac: the ground on which you are lying I will assign to you and to your offspring. Your descendants shall be as the dust of the earth; you shall spread out to the west and to the east, to the north and to the south. All the families of the earth shall bless themselves by you and your descendants. Remember, I am with you: I will protect you wherever you go and will bring you back to this land. I will not leave you until I have done what I have promised you."
>
> Jacob awoke from his sleep and said, "Surely the Lord is present in this place, and I did not know it!" Shaken, he said, "How awesome is this place! This is none other than the abode of God, and that is the gateway to heaven." Early in the morning, Jacob took the stone that he had put under his head and set it up as a pillar and poured oil on the top of it. He named the site Bethel; but previously the name of the city had been Luz.
>
> Jacob then made a vow, saying, "if God remains with me, if He protects me on this journey that I am making, and gives me bread to eat and clothes to wear, and if I return safe to my father's house—the Lord shall be my God. And this stone, which I have set up as a pillar, shall be God's abode; and of all that You give me, I will set aside a tithe for you." (Belin and Brettler 2004: 58–59)

The implications of Jacob's dream vision of the ladder present a potentially sweeping challenge to the theology of the Joseph-Moses narrative. While Joseph-Moses represents a process of God becoming distant from his human worshippers, increasingly working through figures of mundane power, Jacob's dream of the ladder moves in the opposite direction, bringing Jacob physically close to God. In the scene, Jacob willingly gives his faith directly to God, while God pledges to take care of Jacob in return. There is no intermediary between Jacob and God. But this contract between Jacob and God itself does not evoke the full radicalism of the dream. That comes in the dream vision. The vision of the ladder reveals to Jacob a crack through which he can reach an eternally coexisting metaphysical sphere beyond the realm of the ordinary universe. This vision is the type of experience usually reserved for the inhabitants of the higher dimension. No other character in the biblical narrative before or after Jacob is shown this space in such a direct way.

The only other time humans aspired to a material connection between heaven and earth was the tower of Babel, which was struck down precisely because it symbolized the power of a unified human community (Gen. 11.4–9). The verses about Babel in Genesis point to similar power dynamics to the ones found in the Jacob-Joseph epic. The people of Babel work together, seemingly in conditions of equality. Their happiness and contentment appear to be the basis of their success in raising their structure to the heavens. Moreover, the building of the structure allows humans, not God, to overcome the divide between the physical and the metaphysical zones. God's response to this communal success is to sew division, to prevent open communication, and to scatter the people, destroying the power of the community in order to make humans easier to control. The anarchic-socialistic fabric of Babel transforms into a scattering of potentially hostile and authoritarian groups.

Jacob's vision of the ladder could be seen as a reimagining of the Babel ideal. Strikingly, this vision comes to Jacob raw, unfiltered, and at a time when order is collapsing in the text. Isaac is blind. Jacob has stolen Esau's birthright and goes on the run, embarking on his journey to Laban's camp. By moving beyond or between the structures of social order and control—by fleeing into an unknown and uncontrolled space—it seems as if Jacob has opened himself up to perceiving a different vision of the faith. Only such a vision could affect as it does: "'Shaken,' he said, 'How awesome is this place! This is none other than the abode of God, and that is the gateway to heaven'" (Berlin and Brettler 2004: 59).

Unlike the ancient Mesopotamian examples of gods dwelling in temples and city-states within the territory of the ruler, thereby linking the divine, the priesthood, and the king, Jacob's "abode of God" is located *between* territories of power—along the lines of local Canaanite shrine-building. The power and sanctity of the space of the dream, the space that hosts the ladder, should not be dismissed as purely or even primarily symbolic. This space—inside the dreamscape—contains the connection between the human realm and the divine. Seen as real (within the dreamscape), the ladder presents a bridge between the zones. God and angels descend and ascend—as, one could argue, Jacob (and others) can as well. In the context of the structures of religious authority in the ancient world and, more so, in that of the institutionalization of religion in subsequent historical phases, the notion that there is inherent unity of the human and divine realms instead of division gestures toward a non-hierarchical current of faith. In this current, Jacob, God, and the angels are coequals—with faith being a non-coercive compact instead of an imposition from on high.

Though it might seem strange to read this dream as "anarchic," I would like to suggest that it fits well within the concepts I have identified as elements of a specific anarchism of the dreamscape. First, the ladder dream creates a narrative rupture as Jacob journeys from one site of power (Isaac's camp) to another (Laban's camp). Second, it shows Jacob that God's blessing does not only flow through the patriarch (in this case Isaac) but can be grasped by him directly and without mediation. Third, access to the divine does not proceed through any religious structure or representative—it is immediate and total. This contrasts starkly with the increasingly mediated nature of Israelite religion in the Moses epic, culminating in the giving of the Law to Moses and the replacement of God with God's "name" as the force that dwells among the people. Fourth, the experience of the divine is not filtered through any conceptual apparatus or ideological structures—it is an affective state of being. Jacob's "shaken" can be compared with Job's "terror," with Eve's eating of the fruit, with Frost's narrator witnessing the *shattering* of ice sheet, and with Chuang Tzu's embrace of the "transformation of things." All of these moments disrupt clear structures of order and organization and present pathways for radical critique. Fifth, the dream shows the imagined division and rigid hierarchy between the divine and the mundane as false; connections exist even if they are narrow cracks in a seemingly hermetic reality. The anarchism of the dreamscape is precisely such a "crack," a fissure in the structure of waking reality that enables escape or passage through (as I suggest in my discussion of Kafka), a destabilizing of identity (as in "After

Apple-Picking") and hierarchy (Jacob's ladder), a disordering of creation (serpent in Eden), and an undermining of language and narrative constructs that support authoritarian ideologies (as I propose in the section on Rhys).

The anarchic challenges to the religious authority of the post-Edenic and Mosaic order posed by Jacob's dream of the ladder are mirrored by the intense efforts to pull the vision back into the religious mainstream. Genesis begins this work by trying to tie the image of the ladder to prophecy and ultimately to the same philosophy of history as in the Joseph and Moses stories. The biblical redactor's attempt to encircle and limit the anarchic power of Jacob's vision by providing framing, however, does not solve the problem of the anarchic potential of the episode for many religionists. For the interpreters of the text of the "ladder dream," the *vision itself* needs to be disarmed through interpretation.

The first-century historian Josephus was one of the first to make an attempt to de-radicalize Jacob's dream. Josephus wrote his history of the Jewish people, the *Antiquities*, while serving the Flavian emperors in Rome. While his account of Jewish history stands in a tense relationship to the development of post-Temple Judaism, it does set a number of key interpretive precedents for late antiquity and beyond. Josephus presents the dream sequence in the following manner:

> Jacob then was sent by his mother to Mesopotamia to espouse the daughter of her brother Laban, Isaac consenting to the marriage in compliance with his wife's wishes. He journeyed through Canaan and, because of his hatred of the inhabitants, disdained to seek lodging with any of them, but passed the night in the open air, resting his head on some stones which he had collected; and this was the vision which appeared to him in his sleep. He thought that he saw a ladder reaching from earth to heaven, down which were descending phantoms of a nature more august than that of mortals, and above it last of all plainly visible to him was God, who called him by name and addressed him thus: "Jacob, offspring of a good sire and of a grandsire who won renown for exceeding virtue, it would beseem thee not to repine at thy present lot, but to hope for better things; for indeed an abundant and abiding store of great blessings awaiteth thee through my succour. For it was I that led Abraham hither from Mesopotamia when he was driven out by his kinsfolk and that brought thy father to prosperity;

> and no less than theirs shall be the portion that I shall bestow on thee. With courage, then, go thou on this journey too, with me for thine escort. For this marriage on which thine heart is set shall be consummated, and goodly children shall be born to thee, whose descendants shall be beyond number and shall leave their heritage to a yet greater posterity. To them do I grant dominion over this land, to them and to their children who shall fill all that the sun beholds of earth and sea. Nay, fear no danger nor be dismayed at thy multitude of toils, for it is I who am watching over all that thou shalt do both now and far more hereafter."
>
> That was what God foretold to Jacob; and he, overjoyed at these visions and promises, polished the stones whereon he lay when such great blessings were predicted, and made a vow to sacrifice upon them, should he, after gaining a livelihood, return unscathed, and to offer to God a tithe of all that he had acquired, should he come back in such fashion; he moreover held the spot in veneration and gave it the name of Bethel, which denotes in the Greek tongue "God's hearth-stone." (Josephus 1926: 135–137)

Josephus's version of the dream vision is skeptical, simplified, and rendered in terms geared toward pleasing a Greco-Roman audience (Feldman 1988). Posing as a skeptic of Jewish epiphany, Josephus qualifies Jacob's vision by saying that the patriarch "thought he saw a ladder" and that the figures were "phantoms," not angels. In Josephus's account, God stands above or on top of the ladder, and though he is "visible" to Jacob he maintains a position of separation, distance, and authority, creating a hierarchical relationship between God and Jacob. Finally, Josephus rejects the disturbance and fear caused by the dream. Instead of presenting Jacob as "shaken" by the dream, Josephus asserts that he became "overjoyed." This shift from "shaken" to "overjoyed" serves to reinforce the importance of the prophecy about material good fortune and to deemphasize Jacob's vision as the focal point of the dream.

Philo of Alexandria, writing in the decades immediately before Josephus, offers an elaborate interpretation of Jacob's dream, in which he proposes various ways to understand its imagery. In his work *On Dreams*, Philo gives four interpretations of the stairway and the movement of the angels, all of which, he believes, are simultaneously true. The first interpretation is that the stairway represents the element "air," which exists between the heaven and the earth. Souls can move up through air into the realm of spirit in order to free themselves from the physical constraints of the material body or they can move down from the realm of spirit into the physical realm if they desire to become manifest again on earth. In the second interpretation, the stairway is a symbol of the human soul. The movement upwards represents the ability of God to elevate the human soul toward the divine realm. The downward movement represents the way that the words and representatives of God accompany human souls (out of compassion) as they fall back down to earth in order to help lift them up once more. The third interpretation Philo offers has to do with the dynamics of the believer. The believer is caught in an ongoing struggle between righteousness and sinfulness—and this struggle, something moving toward God, sometimes moving away from God, is visualized in the stairway and the movement of the beings up and down it. Only at the end of days, when God comes as judge, according to Philo, does this process stop. Those high enough on the stairway, he suggests, will be saved, those on the lower steps, destroyed. The final interpretation Philo offers has to do with more mundane matters. Human affairs, he argues, are by their very nature variable and subject to swift shifts of fortune. The ups and downs on the stairway, therefore, relate to vicissitudes in the human realm—simple people becoming powerful leaders, powerful leaders reduced to slaves, the poor becoming rich, the rich poor, and so on. The dream indicates that even these seemingly senseless results of fortune are part of the divine plan.

For Philo, the core of the dream image is not the stairway itself or the angels whirling moving over it; it is the appearance of God. Like Josephus, he emphasizes the elevated nature of God in the scene.[16] He writes:

> But the dream also represented the archangel, namely the Lord himself, firmly planted on the ladder; for we must imagine that the living God stands above all things, like the charioteer of a chariot, or the pilot of a ship; that is, above bodies, and above souls, and above all creatures, and above the earth, and above the air, and above the heaven, and above all the powers of the outward senses, and above the invisible natures, in short, above all things whether visible or invisible; for having made the whole to depend upon himself, he governs it and all the vastness of nature. But let no one who hears that he was firmly planted thus suppose that any thing at

> all assists God, so as to enable him to stand firmly, but let him rather consider this fact that what is here indicated is equivalent to the assertion that the firmest position, and the bulwark, and the strength, and the steadiness of everything is the immoveable God, who stamps the character of immobility on whatever he pleases; for, in consequence of his supporting and consolidating things, those which he does combine remain firm and indestructible. (Philo 1854: 325)

For Philo, the staircase's four-fold meaning supports the connection between the vision and God's message. While the vision is about the relationship between the material and divine worlds, the message reveals God's commitment to Jacob and his descendants, foremost by making a territorial promise and linking territorial sovereignty (material) with faith (divine).

This link between territorial sovereignty and faith underlies interpretations of Jacob's dream in the Jewish legends—Louis Ginzberg's collected interpretations of and supplements to the non-legal stories of the Hebrew Bible (Ginzberg 1909). The post-biblical retelling of Jacob's dream binds it tightly to the developing religious orthodoxy of rabbinical Judaism. It emphasizes the divine control of history, including the eventual messianic redemption of the Chosen People to the detriment of the seemingly all-powerful Roman Empire (Edom). It places the Temple at the heart of the religious realm, with everything that implies. It furthers the distance between God and the human, allowing only "prayer" to ascend the stairway. Prayer, ritual, devotion, subordination, and the institutional structures of the Temple (and thus the heir to the Temple tradition, the synagogue) gain primacy over the immediate and personal.

By the nineteenth century, a sterilized version of Jacob's story arose within the world of the literate, "cultured" *Ashkenazi*. Heinrich Graetz's influential *History of the Jews* presents a portrait of Jacob and the patriarchal epoch that reflects European values. Jacob's otherworldly experiences are described merely as "wanderings" and "vicissitudes," a description that, like Josephus's, emphasizes rationality over "superstition." The central thrust of Graetz's narrative points toward establishing just ownership over the ancestral lands. The issue of ownership is buttressed by anachronistic ideological conceptions, using words like "culture," "justice," and most glaringly "intellectual advancement" (Graetz 1891: 4–6). Such a view has no place for the anarchic potential of Jacob's dream of the ladder—and no such dream appears in Graetz's account. The entire scene has been erased from his Jewish history.

The closest approaches to the anarchic potential of the original dream can be found in the treatment of the dream-state in the mystical traditions. Eitan Fishbane presents a particular interesting case in his work on the medieval Kabbalist Isaac ben Samuel of Akko. Fishbane focuses on Isaac of Akko's presentation of the cyclical process of moving between the dreaming and the waking states. It is this liminal, transitional, transitory state of being asleep but not asleep (*nim ve-lo nim*) that proves fertile for the mystic's creative imagination:

> *Nim ve-lo nim* is construed to be a time of insight and hermeneutic discovery—a state in which the mind becomes capable of heightened understanding by virtue of its position between the ordinary planes of consciousness…. Isaac of Akko drew a direct line of correlation—even causation—between the experience of rising from sleep consciousness and the hermeneutic act of "seeing the secret." (Fishbane 2009: 105–110)

For Isaac of Akko, passing through the state of "asleep but not asleep" results in a similar type of intensity of insight as Jacob experiences when he leaves the dream of the stairway and finds himself "shaken."

Ladder and Night Wrestling: A Conclusion

The politics of the dreamscape is central to the unfolding of the Jacob-Joseph epic in Genesis. Joseph's youthful dreams and his ability to interpret dreams on God's behalf while in Egypt provide the philosophy of history for a mature Israelite faith that sets the stage for the Moses epic and the legal and political structures that emerge. The dreams provide the Joseph "novella" with its narrative cohesiveness. The dream Jacob has as he travels to Egypt contributes to this cohesion, supporting the main narrative and thematic thrusts of the story: God's control over the dynamics of history, exile as prelude to the return, and hardships as tests of faith.

Jacob's dream on the road to Egypt has the additional consequence of lessening or surmounting the tensions between Jacob and Joseph, harmonizing the story of patriarchal lineage, which is then sealed with Joseph's deathbed kiss of his deceased father.

Jacob's dream of the ladder provides a striking contrast to the series of dreams in the Joseph novella. While God's speech to Jacob and their negotiation of faith fit into the mold of the basic covenants throughout Genesis, Jacob's dream vision of the ladder stands apart from all other dreams in Genesis—its meaning obscure. This obscurity of meaning continues to haunt the scholarly literature on Jacob's ladder dream, and from Philo and Josephus until today, there is no consensus about it. There is no clarity about why this dream vision would be paired with God's subsequent speech and the agreement God and Jacob reach. This chapter proposes that the dream vision reflects a different variant of faith, one that stands in deep tension with the type of faith that is developed through the dream structure in the Joseph novella, and that illuminates the traces of conflict that remain in Genesis between Jacob and Joseph. I have characterized the type of faith evoked by Jacob's dream of the ladder as anarchic as opposed to the authoritarian model of faith that emerges through Joseph's dream-texts. This anarchism combines a number of elements that set it in opposition to the priestly and monarchical structures that govern the Joseph-Moses story and eventually come to dominate ancient (and much of modern) Judaism. These anarchist elements include, first, a dislocated notion of holy space, represented by Jacob having this vision between sites of power (Isaac's settlement and Laban's camp). Jacob's vision itself reveals the inherent unity of the physical and metaphysical realms as well as their connectedness. The ladder enables movement between these seemingly discrete zones. Second, the structure of the ladder recalls the construction of the tower of Babel, a representation of human cooperation and harmony, an anarchist-socialist ideal that is eventually crushed by the authoritarian deity. Jacob's ladder, then, reveals the persistent presence of this sensibility. Third, Jacob's dream provokes an affective response, opening Jacob up to the knowledge of divine presence and the interconnectedness of the human or physical and the divine or metaphysical. This "shaking" of Jacob, the awe or fear that it engenders, like Blake's Job destabilizes the self and opens Jacob up to new knowledge. Finally, the emergence of the dreamscape disrupts the narrative flow of Jacob's story, acting as a pause or an interruption of the story, fracturing the patriarchal biography. When God finally arrives in the dreamscape, he confronts not a subordinate but an equal, which sets the stage for the peculiar negotiation in which Jacob seems to play an equal, if not a stronger, hand.

If one reading of Jacob's dream of the ladder is that the text posits Jacob's equality with God as well as a growing tension or confrontation between this anarchic potentiality and a divine force set on limiting and subordinating humankind, a similar approach might help open up one of the most confounding passages in Genesis: Jacob's nighttime wrestling match with a strange being on the bank of the Jabbok River as he returns to Canaan from Laban's camp. While the text can be read as presenting a direct confrontation between Jacob and a physical manifestation of God, subsequent interpretations of this scene have tried to remove God and replace him with lesser beings—either angels, humans, or even Jacob's own internal imaginings. It seems plausible to me that the original intent of the text was to present a struggle between Jacob and God. Jacob takes on God's seeming omnipotence directly, as God comes to earth as an attacker—a tyrannical force attempting to win Jacob's submission. Jacob defeats God by fighting him to a draw (a state of equality) and threatening to expose God to the light of day—thus humiliating him and destroying his power forever. The scene in Genesis ends with God's escape and his renaming of Jacob as Israel. This is no conclusive end—and fails to deal with the implications of God's defeat. The narrative cuts off. Night is over. Day arrives. Esau appears on the horizon.

Notes

1. I am using this term as a metaphor or symbol, not as a claim that there was a definitive earlier text. My aim is to posit the potentiality of a counterforce to the dominant narrative thrust of the Joseph epic. In this sense, the "ur-text" refers to the kind of energy that exists in the text but that is unaccounted for in the standard interpretations of the story, both

those that see the Joseph "epic" as basically self-contained and those that posit that it is an assemblage.

2. The main line of debate about Joseph-as-tyrant has to do with his actions as the deputy of the Pharaoh in terms of demanding land and livestock in return for grain (Fuller 2016: 1770–1778). I agree with Berel Lerner, who shows how subtle anti-Joseph rhetoric works in the scenes about the distribution of grain to the Egyptians (1989). This perspective provides a counterpoint to readings of Joseph, congruent with the dominant understanding of the text, as a representation or defense of monarchical politics (Carr 1996: 300–305).
3. While the traditional translation of the *ketonet passim* as "coat of many colors" has been challenged in the critical literature, I still use it here. Whether it is a coat of many colors, a long-sleeve coat or shirt, or something else, the point is that it is a distinguishing garment. For further discussion, see Koelb, who analyzes the *ketonet passim* in light of Thomas Mann's Joseph novels (1976).
4. Some scholars assert that the brothers and Jacob understand Joseph's dreams as originating from God. Scott Noegel writes, "Even Joseph's family is able to understand his enigmatic dreams," as evidence of the split between insiders' and outsiders' ability to connect to the divine message (2001: 45). The problem is that while the brothers and Jacob certainly sense the prophetic structure of the dreams, they do not explicitly attribute to the dream divine origins. Even in sophisticated political readings of Genesis, like Carr's, this failure of explicit recognition of the dreams by Jacob in the brothers is not directly addressed. Carr writes, "Within the context of this ongoing, irresistible rise of Joseph, the brothers' defiance of his dreams looks foolish…" (1996: 275).
5. The physical ramifications of concealing prophetic dream material can be seen across the ancient sources. Noegel provides a rich example from the site of Mari (2001: 48).
6. Joseph's brothers and Jacob focus exclusively on the issue of power in reaction to Joseph's dreams. While power is, of course, a large part of the dreams' implication, it is certainly not all there is. The use of the sheaves indicates a clear reference to the issue of food, famine, and provision. The dream contains the prophecy that Joseph will provide for his family in times of need, that he will feed them. This element is not recognized by Jacob or the brothers. In a similar fashion, the symbolism in the dream about the sun, moon, and eleven stars bowing to Joseph is impor-

tant. The celestial bodies and their arrangement around a point indicate a spatial reorientation—in other words a migration of the people to where Joseph is. This dream, thus, contains the prophecy concerning the migration of Jacob's people to an Egypt ruled by Joseph. As such, both dreams are about power—but they are both more specific. Jacob and the brothers fail to recognize (or at least to address) the specificity and nuance of the dreams.

7. The logical problems with this aspect of the narrative have been recognized since ancient times (Josephus 1926). The solution to the problem, however, has been to change the story and to present Jacob as explicitly recognizing the divine nature of Joseph's dreams and God's control of history (Feldman 1988: 118).
8. Interestingly, Josephus changes Jacob's reaction entirely in his *Antiquities*. He writes, "This vision he [Joseph] recounted to his father [Jacob] in the presence of his brethren, suspecting no malice on their part, and besought him to explain what it meant. Jacob was delighted with the dream: grasping in his mind what it predicted and sagely and unerringly divining its import, he rejoiced at the great things that it betokened…" (Josephus 1926: 175).
9. Gordon Wenham purports that the thought of fratricide never occurs to Jacob and that he innocently sends Joseph to check up on his brothers and the flocks: "…neither Joseph nor Jacob thought he was in danger from the brothers" (1987: 353). The parallel language between Joseph and Abraham, however, points to a different sensibility.
10. Carr is right to point to the deep tensions between the narratives and characters of Jacob and Joseph. He gestures toward Niditch's argument, which proposes that while the Joseph narrative stresses the preservation of order, the Jacob story places "greater emphasis on craftily finding one's way in an unpredictable world" (Carr 1996: 281).
11. This is the basic position of Donald Redford, who maintains that the brothers' "sudden fit of jealousy is perfectly understandable within the context of the story, and it is probably wrong to read any broader meaning into their curt question, 'are you really going to rule over us?'" (Redford 1970: 70) It seems to me that Redford can only arrive at these conclusions if the status of dreaming is not taken into full consideration, despite his recognition of its central narrative importance (1970: 70–71). When it is, the brothers' question becomes absolutely central; it is about

the nexus of power formed by the triad god—priest/patriarch—common believer.

12. The *sanbenito* was a robe or piece of cloth worn by an accused heretic during the Spanish inquisition as part of a ceremony of punishment/execution or as a way to publically mark and humiliate the wearer. It is particularly interesting that both the *sanbenito* and Joseph's coat or shirt play such a prominent role in the staging of a murder or execution.
13. David Biale, in his article on the potential origins of the divine name *El Shaddai*, points to the fluidity between Israelite or Hebrew notions of God and the surrounding religious traditions. It is quite plausible, therefore, that Joseph was attempting to redefine Israelite religiosity profoundly, causing a rupture with or among the community (1982).
14. As Thomas Mann and others have pointed out, the casting of Joseph into the "pit" becomes symbolic of his journey into Egypt, itself symbolic of a descent into the underworld (Mann 1948).
15. David Carr agrees, asserting, "The 'angel ladder' and 'gate of heaven' themes were part of a cultic theology standing behind the older Bethel story" (1996: 313).
16. Philo is working from the Greek *Septuagint*, which elevates God on top of the ladder: "And Jacob went forth from the well of the oath, and departed into Charrhan. And came to a certain place and slept there, for the sun had gone down; and he took *one* of the stones of the place, and put it at his head, and lay down to sleep in that place, and dreamed, and behold a ladder fixed on the earth, whose top reached to heaven, and the angels of God ascended and descended on it. And the Lord stood upon it, and said, I am the God of thy father Abram, and the God of Isaac; fear not, the land on which thou liest, to thee will I give it, and to thy seed" (Philo 1854: 293, emphasis in text).

References

Avioz, Michael. "Why did Joseph Kiss His Father (Genesis 50,1)? A New Proposal." *Scandinavian Journal of the Old Testament* 29.2 (2015): 241–246.

Berlin, Adele, and Marc Z. Brettler, eds. *The Jewish Study Bible*. New York: Oxford UP, 2004.

Bewer, Julius A. "Ancient Babylonian Parallels to the Prophecies of Haggai." *The American Journal of Semitic Languages and Literatures* 35.3 (1919): 128–133.

Biale, David. "The God with Breasts: El Shaddai in the Bible." *History of Religions* 21.3 (1982): 240–256.

Carr, David. "Untamable Text of an Untamable God: Genesis and Rethinking the Character of Scripture." *Interpretation: A Journal of Bible and Theology* 54.4 (2000): 347–362.

———. Reading the Fractures of Genesis: Historical and Literary Approaches. Louisville: Westminster John Knox Press, 1996.

Cooper, Jerrold S., and Wolfgang Heimpel. "The Sumerian Sargon Legend," *Journal of the American Oriental Society* 103.1 (1983) 67–82.

Feldman, Louis H. "Josephus' Portrait of Jacob." *The Jewish Quarterly Review* 79.2–3 (1988) 101–151.

Fishbane, Eitan P. *As Light before Dawn: The Inner World of a Medieval Kabbalist.* Redwood City: Stanford UP, 2009.

———. "Debt-Slavery Passages in the Tanakh as a Lens for Reading Joseph's Enslavement of the Egyptians in Genesis 47:13–26: Explorations in Canonical Hermeneutics." Biblical Theology Bulletin 46.4 (2016): 177–185.

Ginzberg, Louis. *The Legends of the Jews I: Bible times and Characters from the Creation to Jacob.* Trans. Henrietta Szold. Philadelphia: Jewish Publication Society of America, 1909.

Graetz, Heinrich. *The History of the Jews vol. 1.* Ed. Bella Löwy. Philadelphia: Jewish Publication Society, 1891.

"Gudea Cylinders A and B." The Electronic Text Corpus of Sumerian Literature. Accessed 6 March 2019. http://etcsl.orinst.ox.ac.uk/cgi-bin/etcsl.cgi?text=t.2.1.7#.

———. Josephus v. 4. Trans. H. St. J. Thackeray. London: Heinemann, 1926.

Koelb, Clayton. "Thomas Mann's 'Coat of Many Colors.'" *The German Quarterly* 49.4 (1976): 472–484.

Lerner, Berel D. "Joseph the Unrighteous." *Judaism: A Quarterly Journal of Jewish Life and Thought* 38.3 (1989): 278–281.

Levenson, Jon, "Genesis: Introduction." *The Jewish Study Bible*. Eds. Adele Berlin and Marc Z. Brettler. New York: Oxford UP, 2004. 8–11.

Mann, Thomas. *Joseph and His Brothers.* Trans. H. T. Lowe-Porter. New York: Knopf, 1948.

Nigro, Lorenzo. "The Two Steles of Sargon: Iconology and Visual Propaganda at the Beginning of Royal Akkadian Relief." *Iraq* 60 (1998): 85–102.

Noegel, Scott. "Dreams and Dream Interpreters in Mesopotamia and in the Hebrew Bible (Old Testament)." *Dreams: A Reader on the Religious, Cultural and Psychological Dimensions of Dreaming.* Ed. Kelly Bulkeley. New Hampshire: Palgrave, 2001. 45–71.

Oppenheim, A. Leo. "The Interpretation of Dreams in the Ancient Near East. With a Translation of an Assyrian Dream-Book." *Transactions of the American Philosophical Society* 46.3 (1956): 179–373.

Philo Judaeus. *The Works of Philo Judaeus vol. 2*. Trans. Charles Duke Yonge. London: Bohn, 1854.

Redford, Donald. *A Study of the Biblical Story of Joseph: (Genesis 37–50)*. Leiden: Brill, 1970.

"The Sargon Legend." The Electronic Text Corpus of Sumerian Literature. Accessed 6 March 2019. http://etcsl.orinst.ox.ac.uk/section2/tr214.htm.

Wenham, Gordon. *Genesis 16–50*. Waco: Word, 1987.

West, G. O. "Facilitating Interpretive Resilience: The Joseph Story (Genesis 37–50) as a Site of Struggle." *Acta Theologica* 26 (2018): 17–37.

Zeitlin, Solomon. "Dreams and Their Interpretation from the Biblical Period to the Tannaitic Time: An Historical Study" *The Jewish Quarterly Review* 66.1 (1975): 1–18.

4

Freud's Conquest of the Dreamscape: Dynamics of Power in *The Interpretation of Dreams* and *Dora*

Introduction

Beginning with his *The Interpretation of Dreams*, Sigmund Freud turns to dreaming] to uncover the concealed psychic etiology of mental disorders.[1] This move represents a sharp challenge to nineteenth-century European medical discourse, which presents a strong materialist view of mental illness (Gay 1988: 123).[2] Psychoanalysis's move to make dreaming legible, interpretable, and meaningful opens up for Freud a channel by which to connect the conscious with the unconscious and the somatic with the psychic, thereby enabling him to merge distinct logics of inquiry into a single, cohesive explanatory structure. Freud's investigation of the dreamscape brings together a type of scientific rationale that depends on principles, hypotheses, and empirical evidence (or the imagining of empirical evidence) with a kind of hermeneutical logic that seeks to discover the deepest recesses of meaning.[3] Freud's movement between scientific and hermeneutic modes of inquiry when discussing the scene of the dream provides him with professional authority and interpretive flexibility—much like the figure of the archeologist to whom he compares himself in his case study *Dora*.

© The Author(s), under exclusive license to Springer Nature Switzerland AG 2021

S. Rogoff, *The Politics of the Dreamscape*,
https://doi.org/10.1007/978-3-030-74796-1_4

In this chapter, I focus on Freud's reading of two dreams, the so-called specimen dream or dream of Irma's injection in *The Interpretation of Dreams* and Dora's first dream in *Fragment of an Analysis of a Case of Hysteria*, and argue that Freud's creation and analysis of the dream-text express the developing politics of the dreamscape in the emerging theory and practice of psychoanalysis. Evoking the analogy of late nineteenth-century European imperialism—a movement concurrent with the development of psychoanalysis—I discuss Freud's "colonization" of the space of the dreamscape, the transformation of this space into "territory," and the importance of this territorial construction and occupation in terms of psychoanalysis's relative position in the medical field and the position of the analyst in relation to the patient.[4] The occupation of the dreamscape sets the stage for a "civilizing process" by which the analyst attempts to assert order and control over the "sick" psyche. With the specimen dream, Freud maps the general terrain of the dreamscape, understanding it as the site of a complex multiparty contestation between psychoanalyst, patient, medical institutions and discourses, and the social norms governing the public and private spheres. In the case of Dora's first dream, Freud's weaving of scientific methods and hermeneutical analysis aspires to total occupation and control of the territory of the dreamscape and represents a fully articulated expression of the authoritarian structure of psychoanalytic dream interpretation.[5] In attempts to reanalyze *Dora*, critics of the case study have contested nearly all of Freud's conclusions without, however, calling into question the political nature of the structure of his dream analysis. As a consequence of this neglect, the search for dream meaning in contemporary culture remains anchored to professionalized psychological discourse and dependent on the relationship between scientific and hermeneutical logics—a blending that is enacted through what is often the hierarchical practice of therapy and iterated in the story or text of the case study, whether it be in the form of a written report or as an oral construct produced by the therapeutic communication.

The Dreamscape as Dark Continent

In the preface to the fifth edition of his *The Interpretation of Dreams*, Freud writes, "I have not been able to bring myself to embark upon any fundamental revision of the book, which might bring it up to the level of our present psycho-analytic views but would on the other hand destroy its historic character. I think, however, that after an existence of nearly twenty years it has accomplished its task" (2010: xxix). What does Freud imagine is the task of his book on dreams? On the one hand, the goal of the book is to assert Freud's central notion that dreams have a discernible meaning (wish-fulfillment) and that the precise nature of this meaning can be grasped through careful analysis and an understanding of the psychodynamic processes that structure the relationship between consciousness and the unconscious. Dreams, Freud argues against the prevailing wisdom of the time, are not (or not only) somatically determined and generally without meaning but are primarily the result of a complex psychological mechanism that ushers potent unconscious material (dream-thoughts) into the dreamer's consciousness in concealed or distorted form. One has to understand this process if one hopes to read or decode a dream (Freud 2010: 296). On the other hand, the task of Freud's book is to position the analysis of dreams at the center of psychoanalytical treatment—as the key tool available to the psychoanalyst to disinter the root causes of a patient's disorder. The potential of dream analysis to bring about this complex process of synthesis of the psychic and somatic transforms the patient's dreamscape into the dark (unmapped) continent of the analyst's imagination.[6] Beginning with *The Interpretation of Dreams*, the analyst's job, for Freud, is to conquer and control the dreamscape, to map, define, and occupy it, thereby flushing out the psychological infirmities or sicknesses (Freud 2010: 147). Freud's quest to colonize the dreamscape opens up a channel for the assertion of power into the heart of the therapeutic relationship.

Despite its authoritarian structure, the role of dream interpretation in Freudian analysis and the way in which Freudian ideas structure how one interacts with and reads the dreamscape became the dominant paradigm of dream interpretation in the modern era (Ferguson 1996: 3). More than that, Freud's medicalization of dreaming decisively defines the dreamscape as medical territory. Dreams, for Freud, become meaningful as manifestations of illness, as sites of negotiation between the normal and the deviant, the rational and the irrational, the civilized self and its primitive desires.[7] The explicit goal of reading dreams in Freudian analysis centers on the location and mysterious overcoming of the "lower" impulses that result in sickness and the reestablishment of normal functioning to the ego or self. More immediately, however, the reading of dreams in the analytic process aims at the expropriation of the dreamscape in order to best serve the textual demands of the analyst's written report, the case study. In this sense, psychoanalytic dream analysis has much in common with the contemporaneous development of ethnology. Early ethnographic studies utilize the subject of the analysis for theoretical and/or political ends. The peoples under ethnographic investigation become characters in the ethnographer's imaginative structure, a structure—now a text—that can be set in relation to the dominant text of civilization—the history of Western man.[8] Like the ethnographer, by purloining and restructuring a patient's dreamscapes through the application of psychoanalytic concepts and method, the analyst-as-dream-writer takes control of the dream's narrative and fixes its meaning.

Power and Authority in the Dream of Irma's Injection

The centrality of dream interpretation to the development of the power dynamics in the psychoanalytic relationship comes into focus in "Analysis of a Specimen Dream"—Freud's interpretation of his own dream about his patient "Irma" in *The Interpretation of Dreams*. It is through the analysis of this dream that Freud asserts the central thesis of the book, that dreams represent the fulfillment of a wish.[9] In this case, says Freud, the wishes being fulfilled are Freud's desire to: (a) be cleared from blame for any of his failures in Irma's treatment; (b) redirect blame onto Irma, his patient, for her refusal to yield to his ideas, thus overcoming her resistance; (c) clear himself from blame more generally as a medical practitioner; and (d) denigrate the diagnostic and practical capacities of his medical colleagues, especially those at odds with his theories. In other words, according to Freud, the central issues at stake in the dream are his authority over his patient Irma and his power and legitimacy as a medical practitioner in relation to the professional field.

Freud's emphasis on issues of power and authority in his analysis of the dream of Irma's injection elevates the importance of a successful outcome of the analytic process as a reflection of the relative merits of psychoanalytic theory. Freud is anxious about success, whether this success happens in the actual analytic process (curing the patient) or in his narrative recreation of it, in other words as a successful articulation and demonstration of the correctness of his theories. In the dream, Freud reproaches Irma, "If you still get pains, it's your own fault." He goes on to add in his analysis, "I might have said this to her in waking life, and I may actually have done so" (2010: 133). The pressure Freud directs at Irma, he confesses, is at least in part a redirection of the social and professional pressures he brings into his practice: "I was expected to produce therapeutic success" (2010: 133). The notion of success or lack thereof becomes central in Freud's analysis of the dream.[10] When describing the realization in the dream that Irma's problems were organic and not psychic, Freud concludes, "It occurred to me, in fact, that I was actually wishing that there had been a wrong diagnosis; for, if so, the blame for my lack of success would also have been got rid of" (2010: 134). For Freud, the analysis points to a concern not necessarily with being correct or incorrect about Irma—at least not in the first instance—but with being viewed as above reproach and as authoritative by his patient and by the broader community of his friends and colleagues. It is interesting in this regard that Irma, at once patient and friend, blends these two categories; implicit in Freud's analysis of his "specimen dream" is the merging of public and private life. The making-public of the private, the erasure of privacy (despite claims to the contrary), is a precondition of psychoanalysis, which from the beginning contains the prospect of transmuting the therapeutic relationship into the written case study. It is not coincidental that Freud makes clear that his "specimen dream" comes on the night after he commits Irma's case to paper.

Individual relationships in Freud's analysis of his dream of Irma's injection are presented as contested and ultimately hierarchical pairings or triads (these binary or tripartite conflicts are, of course, ubiquitous in Freud's thought). The primary relationship is between Freud and Irma. This relationship contains the most important conflict in the dream, the struggle over the diagnosis of Irma's hysteria—represented by dream-Freud's utterance "it's your own fault." Irma is then compared to and conflated with her friend—whose chief feature in the dream is recalcitrance.[11] This pairing of Irma with her friend opens up a secondary front in Freud's attack on Irma as patient, allowing him to attribute the characteristic of recalcitrance to Irma (2010: 134). Irma's assigned position deteriorates even further when Freud reads characteristics of his wife onto Irma. "She again," Freud writes about this wife, "was not one of my patients, nor should I have liked to have her as a patient, since I had noticed that she was bashful in my presence and I could not think she would make an amenable patient" (2010: 135). Despite the condensation of negative characteristics of three women into Irma, Freud speculates that at least the friend would have made a better patient, reinforcing Irma's lowly position by subordinating her first to Freud and now the friend:

> Perhaps it was that I should have *liked* to exchange her: either I felt more sympathetic toward her friend or had a higher opinion of her intelligence. For Irma seemed to me foolish because she had not accepted my solution. Her friend would have been wiser, that is to say she would have yielded sooner. (2010: 135)[12]

In other words, to be recalcitrant is to be foolish; to yield quickly (to be submissive) is to be wise. Foolishness threatens the psychoanalytic process; submission increases its chances for success—success, that is, for the analyst. The triad of Irma-friend-wife results in the condensation of negative qualities onto Irma and the subordination of Irma to an idealized perfect patient—a forthcoming and submissive woman who would yield readily to Freud's ideas.

Analysis of the medical practitioners appearing in the dream affords Freud another chance to imagine contestation and establish hierarchies. Here, it is Freud who is being represented by stand-ins and compared to others. Initially, Dr. M.'s appearance in the dream provokes feelings of insecurity in Freud. Just as quickly, Dr. M. is transformed into Freud's brother. This move allows Freud to read M. as his opponent, for "they [M. and his brother] had both rejected a certain suggestion I had recently laid before them" (2010: 136). The move from Dr. M. to the brother happens through the symbolism of a physical weakness—in this case a limp caused by the brother's arthritis. The attribution of the limp to Dr. M. marks him as old and infirm, and helps Freud overcome the insecurity Dr. M. causes by reminding Freud of the time when he (Freud) killed a patient. The dream spotlight then turns to Freud's friends and fellow physicians Otto and Leopold. Immediately, it is clear that the relationship between the two is fraught with tension and competition.[13] Freud sides with Leopold over Otto and forms the third part of this triad—using his alliance with Leopold to subordinate Otto and to challenge Dr. M. With renewed confidence borne out of the Freud-Leopold-Otto triad, Freud then makes his final and victorious assault on Dr. M., the paragon of the medical profession. In the dream, Dr. M. proposes an absurd prognosis for Irma, claiming that an infection in her shoulder will be cured through dysentery-induced purgation. Dr. M.'s prognosis shatters his legitimacy and allows Freud to vanquish him with ease. Freud's victory over Dr. M. is the symbolic victory of psychoanalysis over medical orthodoxy: "I could no longer feel any doubt...," Freud concludes, "that this part of the dream was expressing derision at physicians who are ignorant of hysteria" (2010: 139).

Freud's dream of Irma's injection displays the core dynamics related to dreams and power that structure the development of psychoanalysis from its inception. The fact that Freud focuses on these power dynamics as opposed to the many alternative ways in which he could have read his "specimen dream" points to their importance for his nascent science of dream analysis and its role in the broader psychoanalytic movement. Many readers have pointed out, quite rightly, the gaps, oversights, and blind spots in Freud's analysis, showing how Freud's analysis diverges in critical ways from his own theories.[14] The striking fact that sexuality is relatively absent from Freud's analysis indicates just how central these dynamics of power are for the structures of psychoanalytic thought. The hierarchy of analyst and patient, nakedly displayed in Freud's dream of Irma's injection, will become theorized as the therapeutic techniques mature.

The Dream as Contested Space

If it seems clear from the discussion of Freud's dream of Irma's injection that one of the primary concerns of the dream and the analysis is the articulation of a series of power dynamics, then the following question arises: what is it about the dreamscape that provokes Freud to consider it such a critical space to contest and control? Three factors are important to consider when evaluating the importance of the politics of the dreamscape to the development and coalescing of Freudian theory. First, in the context of nineteenth-century thinking the dream is a fertile yet open concept. This is clear from the first part of Freud's *The Interpretation of Dreams*, a 100-page gloss of the highlights and perceived shortcomings of the era's literature on the topic. Although the nineteenth-century literature on dreams is sizable and heterogeneous, there does not emerge—at least according to Freud—a convincing and universalizable approach to dream interpretation. As a result, the notion of a dream's meaning is largely in doubt—or dismissed. Freud is able to recover the notion of dream meaning through his imagination of the dynamic interplay between consciousness and the unconscious. The dream becomes the principal host of this interplay. Second, one of the central questions concerning the dream in the nineteenth-century literature is whether it should be considered a physical (somatic) phenomenon, a mental phenomenon, or a combination of both.[15] This ambiguity locates the dream on the border between the body and the mind—the physical and the mental—a perfect position to link physical symptoms with psychic etiologies. Finally, third, the dreamscape, reconstituted as dream-text and its corresponding analysis, provides narrative structure and expository power to the emerging literary genre of the psychoanalytic case study.

The opening chapter of *The Interpretation of Dreams* allows Freud to build a context for his dream theories. With this section, Freud compiles a literature—even establishing the very discipline of "dream studies" that the rest of the book is intent on overcoming. This tactic enables Freud to set himself within and against this literature, thereby giving his theories the qualities of synthesis and innovation. Freud believes that his analysis of the "specimen dream" accomplishes this task. As his famous opening to the book's chapter three puts it, after this analysis he has "emerge[d] upon a piece of high ground" (2010: 121).

Freud's seizure of the "high ground" of the dreamscape enables him to position dreaming precisely on the border of the psychic and the somatic. In so doing, Freud makes the dream a phenomenon of medical interest and one beyond the scope of traditional psychiatric practitioners—at once, in other words, a site of scientific investigation and hermeneutical interpretation. This position on the frontier between the psychic and the somatic (and this is a central issue of Freud's dream of Irma's injection) is precisely the space that Freud needs to occupy if he is going to demonstrate the truth of his hypotheses concerning the ways in which an individual's psychodynamics crisscross the boundary of body and mind, somatic and psychic. It is ultimately the link between these two interconnected but dissociated spheres that provides Freud with professional stature. One cannot ignore that most of Freud's therapeutic targets are the explicit physical manifestations of a patient's illness—a "nervous" cough, constipation, headaches, dizziness, shortness of breath, and so on. For psychoanalysis to prevail, interpretive hermeneutics—words—must lead to a shifting of physical forces.

Equally important for the power dynamics embedded in Freud's approach is the narrative potential of the dream. Once the dreamscape becomes a narrative, a story, a text, it opens itself up to interpretation. *The Interpretation of Dreams* outlines the basic rules governing the narrativization of the dreamscape, with the "specimen dream" as the key example or template. The first aspect of this transformation is the presentation of the dream-text, a supposedly objective account of a dream. The dream-text is given special status in the broader account by dint of it being set off typographically from the remainder of the work. In the translated versions of Freud, this typography takes the form of an italicized text, indicating that something special is being conveyed to the reader. The dream-text is distinguished in other ways as well, for example by the frequent use of dashes and ellipses. Analysis of the dream-text proceeds in an exegetical fashion, focusing on individual elements, etymological connections, and context to discover hidden meaning. Like scriptural analysis, Freud brings a box of clearly articulated exegetical tools to the dream-text, including the dichotomy of manifest and latent dream content, the mechanism of distortion that changes the latter into the former, the link between latent (hidden) content and memory, specifically early childhood memory, the pervasiveness of sexuality in the dream-thoughts, the idea of condensation or the grouping of a multiplicity of dream-thoughts around a particular manifest symbol (over-determination), the notion of a censoring or repressive mechanism that not only distorts and redirects latent thoughts but has the power to transform them into their opposite, and total, unfiltered access to a patient's thoughts in order to apply the associative method of decoding the dream. The creation and exegesis of the dream-text allow Freud to control the dreamscape, thereby advancing the status of psychoanalysis as both a traditional scientific discipline and something beyond ordinary science. This potent combination of scientific methods and imaginative interpretation allows the analyst to emerge as the conqueror of the dreamscape and the patient as a submissive, defeated, occupied indigenous inhabitant of the space—or, perhaps in the best case, as a patient in exile from both treatment and text.

The dream-text becomes a pedagogical tool and tool of power. In his analysis of the dream-text of his specimen dream, Freud makes his key theoretical intervention into medical discourse precisely at a point—the dreamscape—that was beyond the gaze of clinical medicine. From this point on, control of the dreamscape becomes a central battleground in the history of medicine, including and especially psychology, psychoanalysis, and (later) neuroscience. It is no surprise, therefore, that reformers in the psychoanalytic tradition aim to capture Freud's specimen dream in order to establish their own genesis moments.[16] Jacques Lacan, for example, seizes on Freud's dream-text of Irma's injection to propose the primacy of discourse in the construction of the unconscious—what he calls the "symbolic" (1991). For Lacan and others, legitimacy (and therefore power) in the psychoanalytic community runs through the meaning of Freud's foundational moment of dream interpretation. If his dream of Irma's injection enables Freud to create, control, and utilize the territory of the dreamscape to assert his theoretical paradigm, it also beckons future challengers to invade it and establish alternative regimes of meaning.

Dreams and Power in *Dora*

The political nature of Freud's treatment of the dreamscape emerges strongly in Freud's *Dora*, which Freud calls *A Fragment of an Analysis of a Case of Hysteria*. This is the first case study Freud wrote after *The Interpretation of Dreams*.[17] Issues of power and authority in *Dora* have been the subjects of analysis for decades. Such focus has led to multiple waves of revisionist attempts to re-analyze the case with a mix of tools drawn from Freud's later writings, feminist theory, Lacanian and other branches of psychoanalysis, literary theory, and post-structuralism. While these revisionist analyses have successfully shattered an adherence to an orthodox understanding of the case as Freud presents it, they have also reinforced some of the core principles of Freudian psychoanalysis. The three most important principles the revisionist accounts have reinforced are the faith in the sexual etiology of the neuroses (though often read in reverse or divergent ways), the prime therapeutic importance of the dialectical relationship between the patient's transference and the analyst's counter-transference—embedded, of course, in the libidinal forces flowing between them—and Freud's merging of scientific and hermeneutical modes of inquiry. Ultimately, therefore, these accounts do not fully break the authoritarian structure of Freud's original study, because their authors endeavor to assert a reinterpretation of the case by playing the role of a superseding analyst. Though the expressed desire of many of these revisions is to liberate or reclaim Dora—or (more problematically) the real-life Ida Bauer (Dora is a pseudonym)—in the end they accomplish the opposite. The revisionist author as new Freud or anti-Freud is increasingly empowered while Dora recedes into deeper abstraction. The fact that complex sets of jargon and interpretive tools are deployed to wrest Dora away from Freud adds to the dynamics of what becomes a multilayered authoritarianism. In the end, the political nature of *Dora* is reanimated as a site of contestation between various psychoanalytic and postmodern paradigms vying for power.

Freud writes in his introduction to *Dora* that he originally planned to title the work "Dreams and Hysteria," a fact pointed out by most of the revisionist authors. The draft title and the prominent role of dream analysis in the text (the interpretation of dreams takes up about fifty percent of the case study) indicate the centrality of dream interpretation in *Dora*. This is no big surprise, given that Freud wrote the case study directly after finishing *The Interpretation of Dreams*. Despite this prominence, the role of Freud's analysis of dreams in the construction of the power dynamics in the case has either been neglected or subordinated to other considerations. When subordinated, it becomes a matter of reinterpreting the dreams along the lines of new theoretical impulses, a process that leaves the basic structure of the analytical model intact. The strange aversion to the politics of Freud's interpretation of Dora's dreams in the revisionist accounts has two key results. First, it perpetuates the authoritarian politics of the dreamscape as developed in *The Interpretation of Dreams* and deployed in *Dora*. Second, it contributes to what has become the much-repeated view that Freud's analysis of Dora and his subsequent case study are failures, thus underestimating the authoritarian power of the dream interpretive process. By reframing the discussion around the politics of the dreamscape, I contend that *Dora* is better understood as an authoritarian success.

The Triumphs and Limits of the Feminist Critiques of *Dora*

Philip Rieff, in his 1962 introduction to the English translation of *Dora*, presents Freud's case study in terms of power. What made the case study provocative, Rieff thinks, is the struggle between analyst and patient:

> Interpretation involves indoctrination; the two cannot be separated in the psychoanalytic combat between therapist and patient. For the therapist is engaged in the effort to change his patient's mind by an exemplary deepening of it. In this case, Dora refused to change her mind and suddenly quit as a final act of denial against the truth of Freud's insights….Because Dora's insights are part of her illness, Freud had to hammer away at them as functions of her resistance to his insight. (Freud 1997: xi)

Rieff's disdain for the patient is mirrored by David Sachs's reflections on encountering the case study for the first time as a student of psychoanalysis in the early 1960s. "My candidate colleagues did not express compassion for Dora when she tried to offer alternative understandings of herself to Freud, because we accepted his conviction that her objections were without merit" (Sachs 2005: 47). Felix Deutsch reinforces the pro-analyst perspective in "A Footnote to Freud's 'Fragment of an Analysis of a Case of Hysteria,'" which he published in 1957 after learning about Ida Bauer's life from "an informant." "It is striking," Deutsch says, "that Dora's fate took the course Freud had predicted" (1990: 39). He concludes his short article by aiming the authority of two male analysts and another unnamed source (Freud, Deutsch, and the "informant") at the patient. Ida Bauer's death "from a cancer of the colon, which was diagnosed too late for a successful operation seemed a blessing to those who were close to her. She had been, as my informant phrased it, 'one of the most repulsive hysterics' he had ever met" (1990: 43). It is telling that for Deutsch, as for Rieff, no distance exists between the literary character Dora and the flesh and blood Ida Bauer—a grievous error that will be repeated by other critics.

Beginning in the 1970s, feminist critiques of *Dora* start to challenge the decidedly pro-Freudian reading of the case study as well as earlier reinterpretations like those by Erik Erikson. Of central importance to the feminist perspectives are the theories of Jacques Lacan, especially his analysis of *Dora* in "Intervention on Transference." In the article, Lacan stresses the importance of the relationship between analyst and patient, describing it as "constituted through a discourse," and as a "dialectical experience" (1990: 93). Lacan understands this dialectical experience in relation to issues of transference—the notion that the patient redirects libidinous energy from another sexual object (father, mother, lover, etc.) to the analyst. The analyst, according to Lacan, must be aware of the nature of the transference in order to pose a dialectical reversal and to aspire to a new development of truth. For Lacan, however, there is also an issue of transference in the other direction—a countertransference of the analyst's libidinous energy to the patient. Flows along this two-way conduit need to be mastered if the dialectical movement of the analysis is to function as it should. In *Dora*, Lacan argues, Freud fails to manage the flows of libidinous energy and thus is led astray from his role as disinterested (neutral) and rational dialectician who can provoke the patient's movement from the imaginary to the symbolic.

Lacan's emphasis on the dynamics of transference in the analytical process and his identification of several moments when it seems to him that Freud's failure to master the dynamics leads to analytical mistakes provide starting points for feminist critiques of *Dora*, namely the turning of the interpretive microscope away from Dora and onto Freud. This turn of focus trains its sight on a constellation of key issues with regard to Freud's approach—his understanding of female sexuality, his inability to escape from patriarchal social and cultural norms, and (related to the issue of norms) his reliance on Victorian literary constructs to make his case. While these impressive critiques of Freud's approach move away from strict Freudian theory—and strict Lacanianism—they often still operate in a psychoanalytic manner with psychoanalytic tools buttressed by elements of psychoanalytic theory. The mission seems to be to capture territory within the psychoanalytic tradition for a new articulation of feminism.

Freud's attempt to assert his "superior" version of the truth (as Rieff puts it) over Dora has provoked critics to reassert Dora—or in some cases the real person behind the literary creation, Ida Bauer—back into the forefront in order to re-analyze the case. The results of the re-analysis have generally taken two directions: Dora/Ida Bauer has either been portrayed as a victim of Victorian patriarchy—a woman crushed by the sexual politics of *fin-de-siècle* Viennese society, family, and the theory and practice of psychoanalysis in its orthodox Freudian form—or as a heroine, a woman who went toe-to-toe with Freud and in the end defeated him by refusing his interpretation and terminating the analysis on her terms. Maria Ramas, for example, paints the portrait of a tragically heroic Dora, a young woman who desires "to escape heterosexuality and annihilation" (1990: 168). This is not to say that feminist discussions of *Dora* are reductive. Far from it, they open up important debates about the status of femininity, homosexuality, and bisexuality for psychoanalysis while adding detailed evidence for the interweaving of sexual politics with issues of culture and class.

The critical literature on *Dora* has, however, largely neglected Freud's presentation and interpretation of Dora's dreams. In part, this is understandable. In terms of the content of the case, nothing extraordinarily new is revealed in the dream analysis that is not already covered in the preceding pages. The critical attention to issues of sexuality contributes to the general lack of attention to the dreams. As many have pointed out, *Dora* is a transitional text between Freud's work on dreams and the development of his theories of sexuality.

Still, the dreams do come up in ways that reinforce the key concerns of the authors. For example, psychoanalyst Erik Erikson argues that Dora's first dream, the dream of the jewelry box, represents a crisis of adolescent identity formation rather than a disguised sexual wish, thus asserting his notions of identity over the Freudian view of ego as well as a host of other competing revisionist theories (1990: 50–51). Maria Ramas is more explicit in her reassessment of Freud's interpretation of Dora's dreams. "A reconsideration of this latent content," she writes, "even as Freud influenced it, reveals other possibilities. It is not difficult to find in Ida Bauer's two dreams the crystallization of her oedipal struggle: disavowal of the 'primal scene' and the breakthrough of repressed lesbian desire" (1990: 165). Ramas draws this into a contextual argument. "At the deepest level of the meaning in the dream," she writes, "Ida's father is represented as the enforcer of the (hetero)sexual laws and fantasies of Ida's Bauer's culture" (1990: 168). Madelon Sprengnether follows a similar path when critiquing Freud's use of the dream-texts:

> The interpretation of Dora's two dreams serves at least two functions, that of oedipal camouflage for a preoedipal fantasy based on the figure of the nurse and that of revenge. It is the combination of these two elements that accounts, I believe, for the coercive quality of Freud's interpretations and for the uneasy tone of the narrative. In his relentless pursuit of heterosexual interpretation of Dora's desire, Freud often substitutes his own train of associations for hers, a tactic that reveals the extent to which he idealizes the figure of Herr K. in order to blame Dora for her refusal. On an interpretive level, he subjects her to a process of defloration, impregnation, and parturition in an aggressively oedipal fashion, at the same time that he invalidates her rejection by naming it hysteria. (1990: 263)

Rather than concluding with Dora's sexuality, Sprengnether is more interested in analyzing Freud, but her conclusions are still interesting in relation to her critique of his interpretation of Dora's dreams. She writes:

> Freud's own anxieties and confusions regarding the nonreproductively oriented nature of female sexuality, although not unusual for the time, provide, however, an insuperable barrier to a noncoercive representation not only of heterosexual intercourse but also of any kind of adult sexual encounter. What he repeatedly misses is the other clue tantalizingly offered in his choice of a name for Dora, a clue that haunts and eludes him throughout his distraught narrative—the vision of sexual relations as open to vulnerability and to risk. If the indeterminacy of sex roles, like the indeterminacy of narrative form, represents a state of not being in control, then it is no surprise that Freud is unable to imagine love as something not taken but given. (1990: 271)

These critiques, and many others (Rose 1990; Gearhart 1990) of Freud's interpretation of Dora's dreams, make lasting and important contributions by challenging not only the specific arguments Freud makes in the case study but, more broadly, Freudian theories of sexuality and the art of the psychoanalytic process. The re-analyses of Dora's dreams have been useful in both of these critical projects. And yet, while these critiques offer—at times radically—divergent political positions from the normative patriarchal position occupied by Freud, they leave the basic structures of power in place. The analyst—now the critic who stands beyond the original coupling of Freud/Dora—still speaks with the authoritative voice. Concepts are deployed that drive the hermeneutic process often without questioning or fully overcoming the foundational merging of hermeneutical and scientific modes of inquiry. Perhaps most glaringly, there is a constant and deeply troubling elision between information that is considered evidentiary and the recognition of the information's fictiveness within the narrative construction.[18] The critics' struggle to separate Freud's character Dora from the historical flesh-and-blood Ida Bauer is only the most obvious manifestation of this problem. While various political agendas are advanced by the critical literature, the political structure of the case—the "combat," as Rieff puts it, over meaning—remains unchallenged.

Toril Moi offers a way to make the transition from the contest over meaning to the dismantling of the structures of power. The central issue for Moi is not that Freud gets the sexual dynamics of the case wrong (though she certainly believes this) but that he aims for a type of total or complete understanding of his patient. Freud wants to know everything—and in knowing everything, he can claim complete power. Moi writes of Freud:

> First, because he himself desires total knowledge: his aim is nothing less than the *complete elucidation* of Dora, despite his insistence on the fragmentary nature of the material...But such a desire for total, absolute knowledge exposes a fundamental assumption in Freud's epistemology. Knowledge for Freud is a finished, closed whole. Possession of knowledge means possession of power. Freud, the doctor, is curiously proud of his hermeneutical capacities. (1990: 194)

Moi links this insight to sexual politics. "Freud's epistemology," she writes, "is clearly phallocentric. The male is the bearer of knowledge; he alone has the power to penetrate woman and text; woman's role is to let herself be penetrated by such truth" (1990: 198). For Moi, this epistemological trap is one of the greatest limitations to Freud's thinking. She asserts, "It is politically important, however, to point out that this pathological division of knowledge into masculine totality and feminine fragment is completely mystifying and mythological" (1990: 198). The irony that Moi is able to convey the mythological nature of Freud's epistemology only by applying Freudian concepts like castration anxiety, countertransference, unconscious wish, repression of desire, and so on is not lost on her:

> The attack upon phallocentrism must come from within, since there can be no "outside," no space where true femininity, untainted by patriarchy, can be kept intact for us to discover. We can only destroy the mythical and mystifying constructions of patriarchy by using its own weapons. We have no others. (1990: 198)

While Moi might be right that Freud's patriarchy can be strongly challenged from within the psychoanalytic tradition, the nature of power at work in Freudian interpretation—and specifically in Freudian dream interpretation—requires a step beyond psychoanalytic concepts. The quest for wholeness in Freud's interpretation of Dora's first dream, I argue, is not first and foremost psychological, sexual, and patriarchal—it is spatial/colonial, textual, and authoritarian.

Dora's First Dream

Moi and others have pointed out how concerned Freud is with issues of completeness and incompleteness in his analysis of Dora. This is most clearly indicated by his inclusion of the word "fragment" in the title: "fragment of an analysis." The title can refer either to Freud's analysis of Dora in their analytic relationship or to his analysis of the results of that analysis in the case study he presents. This distinction is important. While Freud might have felt anxiety about the incompleteness of the text he is presenting, the opposite can also be asserted. Freud is boasting of his ability to take the fragments presented to him in the analysis and to create a whole out of them. It expresses not only anxiety, then, but also confidence:

> In the face of the incompleteness of my analytic results, I had no choice but to follow the example of those discoverers whose good fortune it is to bring to the light of day after their long burial the priceless though mutilated relics of antiquity. I have restored what is missing, taking the best models known to me from other analyses; but like a conscientious archaeologist I have not omitted to mention in each case where the authentic parts end and my constructions begin. (Freud 1997: 7)

Many critics, Moi included, productively analyze this passage using psychoanalytic concepts. This diverts attention from the question of how, precisely, Freud works as an archaeologist in the text. The metaphor is useful on a number of levels. First, as Freud points out, the archaeologist (at least the nineteenth century one) attempts to create a sense of wholeness out of fragments. To do this, the archaeologist utilizes a complex body of historical, geographic, and material knowledge: in other words, a combination of interpretive hermeneutics and "scientific" inquiry. But there is another important piece—the archaeologist in Freud's imagination is also an explorer of distant lands. He has gone far from home—to the Near or Middle East, East Asia, Africa, and so on—and has located, dug out, and brought back archaeological material. In this sense, the archaeologist is the companion of the colonizer and ethnographer. The archaeologist is not only supposed to be a possessor of a type of complete knowledge that allows for the reassembly of an ancient object; he is also a conqueror of space. When the reassembled object is displayed—and there must be display—the viewer of the object is meant to see, feel, and possess the authenticity of the foreign domain. Even if the object is in large part fabrication, the viewer's belief in the conquest of the foreign space imbues the object with authenticity. Had the archaeologist never stepped foot in those distant regions, had he simply applied his knowledge to generate a possible likeness of an ancient object, the mythos would be shattered, and the audience would reject the thing as fake. Halfway through *Dora*, Freud confronts just this issue. He wants to assemble a complete object, but he has not yet traveled into distant realms—the realm of Dora's deep unconscious. In order to achieve completeness, Freud must conquer the dreamscape—for it is only through the dream that those "mutilated relics" can become whole.

At first glance, it seems strange that Freud would break off halfway through his story to dedicate most of the rest of the case study to Dora's dreams. What makes it particularly puzzling is that he has already arrived at his major conclusions before he begins the investigation of the dreams. Freud has already "discovered" that the primary cause of Dora's illness is the suppression of her natural libidinous desire for Herr K., which is achieved by the conjuring up and subsequent repression of her earlier love of her father. As a secondary cause, Freud images Dora having "masculine" or "gynaecophilic currents of feeling" for Frau K. (1997: 55). The move into the dreamscape offers Freud two important possibilities. First, it presents the pathway for Freud to unfasten the analysis from the timeframe of Dora's adolescence and young adulthood, and to move it back into her early childhood. Second, and related to the first, it creates the space—the exhibition space—for Freud to assemble all the pieces, to imagine the whole, a whole that connects past and present symptoms with their multitude of perceived causes. The application of an array of analytic tools—scientific and hermeneutic—to achieve this assemblage strengthens Freud's position immeasurably. Outside the dream, Freud appears a frustrated combatant. Inside the dream-text, he is the master.

Freud attempts to make a smooth transition into his analysis of Dora's first dream, but the move instead performs the *deus ex machina* function of allowing him to shift the terms of the study from the present-day or recent past into the depths of Dora's childhood. Freud opens the section on the first dream by saying, "Just at a moment when there was a prospect that the material that was coming up for analysis would throw light upon an obscure point in Dora's childhood, she reported that a few nights earlier she had once again had a dream which she had already dreamt in exactly the same way on many previous occasions" (1997: 56). After spending the next few pages remaking the case for Dora's repressed sexual attraction to Herr K., and meeting the same resistance from Dora he had faced all along, Freud pivots to the past. This pivot allows Freud to open up multiple fronts against Dora by incorporating in the analysis a fresh set of psychoanalytic concepts concerning the role of childhood sexual dynamics in the formation of one's mature psyche, including in cases of so-called hysteria. Equally as important, Freud is able to move away from a presentation of the case based on a relatively strict adherence to the material provided by the analytic conversation in order to give free reign to his own hermeneutical maneuvers.

The move into Dora's childhood is a vital element of Freud's strategy for total elucidation of the dream. "A regularly formed dream stands," Freud writes, "…upon two legs, one of which is in contact with the main and current exciting cause, and the other with some momentous occurrence in the years of childhood. The dream sets up the connection between those two factors—the event during childhood and the event of the present day—and it endeavors to re-shape the present upon the model of the remote past" (1997: 63). This logic propels Freud into the most hermeneutically sophisticated and convoluted section of the case study, the discussion of the meaning of the jewel-case in the dream-text.

Freud has already asserted that the jewel-case symbolizes the female genitals. On the superficial level, according to Freud, the dream represents a scenario in which Dora's "jewel-case" is being threatened and her father is protecting it, a scenario in parallel with Freud's previous interpretation of Dora's Oedipal reaction to her supposed sexual stimulation by Herr K. This scenario points to Freud's secondary theory that Dora is not first and foremost afraid of Herr K. asserting himself sexually onto her, but that she fears the temptation she feels within herself to "yield to him." "In short," Freud tells her, "these efforts prove once more how deeply you love him" (1997: 63). Dora, as she has done earlier when Freud has advanced this theory, refuses to validate it. It is at this point of resistance that Freud makes his move into the past.

To fully grasp the shift in tactics from a relatively straight-forward and easy to follow discussion to the type of intense hermeneutic probing that merges Freud's theories, wild interpretive associations, elements of the analytic material, and impulses from Dora into an overwhelming *tour de force* of speculation, it is important to follow in detail how Freud builds his case. He begins with a string of tenuous connections that comes out of folk wisdom—the notion that the "fire" in the dream-text relates to matches, that matches relate to the prohibition of children playing with matches, and that this prohibition conjures a fear in children that if they play with matches, they will wet their beds. Through this circuitous route, Freud is able to make the claim that when the dream speaks of "fire" it is at the same time conveying its opposite, water or wetness:

> But I notice that the antithesis of water and fire has been extremely useful to you in the dream. Your mother wanted to save the jewel-case so that it should not be *burnt*; while in the dream-thoughts it is a question of the "jewel-case" not being *wetted*. But fire is not only used as the contrary of water, it also serves directly to represent love (as in the phrase "to be *consumed* with love"). So that from "fire" one set of rails runs by way of this symbolic meaning to thoughts of love; while the other set runs by way of the contrary "water," and, after sending off a branch line which provides another connection with "love" (for love also makes things wet), leads in a different direction. (1997: 64)

The "different direction" is that of masturbation through the way station of bed-wetting. The masturbation "set of rails" opens up fertile ground for Freud. On the most superficial level, it allows him to make the connection between Dora's vaginal discharge and her masturbation. This connection then opens the door to exploring links between masturbation, discharge, and the secrets about venereal disease that swirled through Dora's family—her father's syphilis and her mother's vaginal discharge and abdominal pains. Still on what we might call the rail of masturbation, Freud posits that Dora's deep antipathy toward physicians (and thus toward him) stems from her impulse to conceal her vaginal discharge in order to prevent an examining doctor from finding out that she wets the bed, which in turn would point toward masturbation. This shame eventually causes Dora to suppress her desire to masturbate—and it is this first act of sexual suppression that provokes the hysterical symptom (and here we see an analysis based on a scientific mode) in this case her "nervous asthma." Why does it result in this particular symptom? Freud is able to make the move to the "primal scene," a scene in which a child is exposed to parents having sex:

> Dora's symptomatic acts and certain other signs gave me good reasons for supposing that the child, whose bedroom had been next door to her parents', had overheard her father in his wife's room at night and had heard him (he was always short of breath) breathing hard during their coitus. Children, in such circumstances, divine something sexual in the uncanny sounds that reach their ears. (1997: 71)

Freud is able at this point to assert the basic sexual nature of Dora's (physical) hysterical symptoms by referring to his expertise—in other words by bringing in non-theoretical, empirical material that does not depend on hermeneutical logic:

> I maintained years ago that the dyspnoea and palpitations that occur in hysteria and anxiety-neurosis are only detached fragments of the act of copulation; and in many cases, as in Dora's, I have been able to trace back the symptom of dyspnoea or nervous asthma to the same exciting cause—to the patient's having overheard sexual intercourse taking place between adults. The sympathetic excitement which may be supposed to have occurred in Dora on such an occasion may very easily have made the child's

sexuality veer round and have replaced her inclination to masturbation by an inclination to morbid anxiety. (1997: 72)

By continuing down the "rail of wetness," Freud expands the discussion to include another of Dora's symptoms: her nervous cough or "catarrh." The word "catarrh" becomes for Freud a "switchword," a term that forges the connection between the origins of the hysterical reaction and the symptom that comes to house the hysterical response. In this case, the catarrh or build-up of mucus connects the cough with thoughts of vaginal discharge, and the vaginal discharge, as we have already seen, is connected to both venereal disease and to masturbation—and through masturbation to sexual desire. This web of connections moves Freud to assume the voice of Dora's unconscious: "I am my father's daughter, I have a catarrh, just as he has. He has made me ill, just as he has made Mother ill. It is from him that I have got my evil passions, which are now punished by illness" (1997: 74). These imaginary unconscious thoughts then cement the chain of associations between the hysterical symptom and hysterical thoughts—all of which are tied back through "wetness" to the word "fire" in the dream:

> We will now attempt to put together the various determinants that we have found for Dora's attacks of coughing and hoarseness. In the lowest stratum we must assume the presence of a real and organically determined irritation of the throat—which acted like a grain of sand around which an oyster forms a pearl. This irritation was susceptible to fixation, because it concerned a part of the body which in Dora had to a high degree retained its significance as an erotogenic zone. And the irritation was consequently well fitted to give expression to excited states of the libido. It was brought to fixation by what was probably its first psychological wrapping—her sympathetic imitation of her father—and by her subsequent self-reproaches on account of her "catarrh." The same group of symptoms, moreover, showed itself capable of representing her relations with Herr K.; it could express her regret at his absence and her wish to make him a better wife. After a part of her libido had once more turned towards her father, the symptom obtained what was perhaps its last meaning; it came to represent sexual intercourse with her father by means of Dora's identifying herself with Frau K. (1997: 74–75)

In the above passage, Freud has brought together a host of diverse modes of inquiry into a salient explanation of Dora's cough. The cough becomes more than just an expression or physical manifestation of a hysterical thought; it becomes a story, a history embedded in the subtext of the dream-text, a history that creates a foundation for the dream-thoughts.

The discussion of the "catarrh" as cough leads Freud into his analysis of Dora's genital catarrh. Freud moves immediately to connect the genital catarrh to the notion of disgust, which in turn connects to the feeling of disgust Dora experiences in reaction to Herr K. earlier in the case study. The central element of this disgust is the wetness, which is, as we have seen, rooted in the dream-text coded as "fire." "The pride taken by a woman in the appearance of their genitals," writes Freud, "is quite a special feature of their vanity; and disorders of the genitals which they think calculated to inspire feelings of repugnance or even disgust have an incredible power of humiliating them, of lowering their self-esteem, and of making them irritable, sensitive, and distrustful. An abnormal secretion of mucous membrane of the vagina is looked upon as a source of disgust" (1997: 75). This disgust is key for Freud, because it helps him imagine the end station on the rail of wetness. The rail of fire leads to Dora's love of Herr K. and her suppression of that love by conjuring her father out of fear of succumbing to it. On the rail of wetness, however, the love of her father and thus the love of Herr K. is "wet" because all sexual relations for Dora contain what Freud sees as the hysterical element of disgust. The disgust causes Dora "the tendency to a repudiation of sexuality which was already present in her and was based upon the story of her childhood" (1997: 80).

Freud amplifies the equation of wetness with a disgust and fear of sex by relating Dora's dream to her family history, specifically to her mother. The wetness of sex comes not only through Dora's sexual stimulation but also by being wetted by male semen "*in the form of drops*" (1997: 82, italics in text). The word "drops" then calls to Dora's mind the memory of her mother requesting pearl "drops" from her father—thus connecting the ideas of father, mother, and drops. "Wet," then, read through the parental relationship with its history of venereal disease, also comes to mean dirty. In the dream-text, the drops become jewelry. The "jewel" of the composite word "jewel-case" contains this whole web of associations.

Finally, Freud brings the two rails of "fire" and "wetness" together. It is the fire of love for Herr K. that provokes Dora into transforming the "drops" into the "case"—the dirtied into the immaculate. The "jewel-box" as genitals, as both immaculate and the receptacle of the drops—as sullied—becomes the symbol of Dora's entire neurotic persona, a symbol "calculated both to betray and to conceal the sexual thoughts that lie behind the dream" (1997: 83). With this, Freud arrives at the conclusion of the hermeneutic process. He has constructed a whole from the fragments:

> "Mother's jewel-case" was therefore introduced in two places in the dream; and this element replaced all mention of Dora's infantile jealousy, of the drops (that is, of the sexual wetness), of being dirtied by the discharge, and, on the other hand, of her present thoughts connected with the temptation—the thoughts which were urging her to reciprocate the man's love, and which depicted the sexual situation (alike desirable and menacing) that lay before her. The element of "jewel-case" was more than any other a product of condensation and displacement, and a compromise between contrary mental currents. The multiplicity of its origin—both from infantile and contemporary sources—is no doubt pointed to by its double appearance in the content of the dream. (1997: 83–84)

It would be ridiculous to claim that, however full this analysis of the dream is, it achieves completeness. There are certainly paths not followed, parts unexplored, and alternative interpretations available. Many of the critics take up these alternatives. Yet, the fullness of Freud's interpretation of this dream is politically meaningful. It allows him to bring together a wide array of investigative tools and strategies—everything from his dream theories to his notions of childhood sexual development to material generated by the analytic relationship to "common" sense and folk wisdom. In other words, we see a blending of theory, culture(s), and individual(s) into a composite structure, a synthesis that carries with it a logical force strong enough to overcome the questionable nature of its creation. A glance at the "rail of wetness" captures the strangeness of Freud's trajectory. An example of a chain of associations Freud makes could run as follows: fire/water/wetness/bed-wetting/masturbation/

catarrh/nervous asthma/primal scene/morbid anxiety/cough/vaginal discharge/drops/dirtied/jewelry /immaculate/jewel-case. The movement from one link in the chain to the next and the mode of inquiry required to make such concatenations become less important than the composite structure.

Freud's analysis of Dora's first dream is the heart of the case study. It compresses the entirety of his interpretation of the case into an exposition of a single dream element, the jewel-case, using Freud's full set of analytic tools. In the analysis of the dream, Freud's theory of dreams is blended with his emerging theories of sexuality, allowing him to move from present to past, past into present, thus forging a psychodynamic history of the patient. Dora's physical symptoms and their related "neurotic" thoughts are woven into the dream-text and, as a consequence, with each other. It is noteworthy that although in the rest of the work Freud is usually quite ready to talk about Dora's resistance to his ideas—even at times in response to elements of this dream interpretation—at the end of the analysis of the first dream Dora remains silent. Her silence—or rather her disappearance from the text—implies a victory by the analyst over the patient's recalcitrance. Freud makes a number of comments to tidy up the discussion—but does so in a calm, confident tone.

Many critics claim that Dora's terminating of her analysis with Freud after he interprets a second dream indicates that the analysis has failed. Janet Malcolm takes this notion of failure even further, asserting that it is not only the analysis that failed but the entire genre of the case study (1990: 321). The notion of "failure" is so pervasive in discussions of *Dora* that it has become a commonplace assumption. As I have shown, however, the accomplishments of Freud's analysis of the first dream tell a different story—one of the assertion of wholeness and analytic success.

Conclusion

Freud's psychoanalytic dream interpretation reflects important features of other nineteenth-century modes of inquiry. Like archaeology, Freudian dream theory imagines that some sort of complete or whole object can emerge from the fragmentary. The analyst-as-archeologist is tasked with setting out into wild or foreign realms (the dreamscape) in order to bring back the raw material to construct an "authentic" display—the fully articulated dream interpretation. Like nineteenth or early twentieth century ethnography, Freudian dream theory assumes a hierarchical relationship between the primitive/savage and the civilized, between nature and culture, and between the irrational and reason. Ethnography, like archeology, aspired to wholeness—the complete mapping of the "other's" society, culture, geography, and history, a mapping that went together with the actual cartographic work of imperialism throughout the world. An aspiration to wholeness—the whole object, the whole people, the whole geography—dominates the spirit of the age of Freud and is reflected in a type of hermeneutic quest to capture the whole meaning of a text, a classic example of which is Julius Wellhausen's attempt to prove the origins and existence of the four discrete authorial voices that eventually were redacted into the Pentateuch—the so-called documentary hypothesis. Wellhausen, reaching beyond the text and into speculative regions of the past, sought to explain every moment of illogic and textual rupture, and by so doing to make the text whole again: whole as a synthesis, an assemblage of pieces—not the ontological or imaginary whole of medieval scholasticism or protestant (or rabbinical) dogmatism.

For Freud, the dreamscape is vital space to occupy because it offers the possibility of wholeness. It is the staging ground for the assemblage of the total person, merging psychology with physiology, the unconscious with consciousness, and past and present. To produce such a merging requires the deployment of a diverse set of modes of inquiry. Using these tools, Freud transforms the dreamscape into the dream-text, thereby taking possession of the oneiric space and enabling him to use it to serve his interests. As we can see, issues of power and authority were at the very heart of Freud's development of his theory of dreams.

This concept of wholeness or total analysis of the dream does not imply that Freud denies the partial or fragmentary nature of his interpretations. The most poignant example of this recognition comes in *The Interpretation of Dreams* when Freud posits the existence of what he calls the dream's navel. The first appearance of the concept of the navel comes as Freud discusses the convergence of Irma, Irma's friend, and Freud's wife in his analysis of the "specimen dream." Freud adds the following footnote:

> I had a feeling that the interpretation of this part of the dream was not carried far enough to make it possible to follow the whole of its concealed meaning. If I had pursued my comparison between the three women, it could have taken me far afield.—There is at least one spot in every dream at which it is unplumbable—a navel, as it were, that is its point of contact with the unknown. (2010: 135)

Later in *The Interpretation of Dreams*, Freud returns to the concept of the dream's navel:

> There is often a passage in even the most thoroughly interpreted dream which has to be left obscure; this is because we become aware during the work of interpretation that at that point there is a tangle of dreams thoughts which cannot be unraveled and which moreover adds nothing to our knowledge of the content of the dream. This is the dream's navel, the spot where it reaches down into the unknown. The dream-thoughts to which we are led by interpretation cannot, from the nature of things, have any definitive endings; they are bound to branch out in every direction into the intricate network of our world of thought. It is at some point where this meshwork is particularly close that the dream-wish grows up, like a mushroom out of its mycelium. (2010: 528)

The idea of the navel seems to offer a way beyond wholeness and a denial of the finality of hermeneutical investigation. Is the navel, then, an emancipatory or even anarchic concept—one that denies the authority of interpretive regimes? In terms of the broader construct of Freud's theory, the answer seems to be negative. Freud fails to return to the concept of the navel in his subsequent psychoanalytic work, including in his interpretation of Dora's first dream. There is no navel identified in Freud's investigation of the dream-image of the jewel-box. Beyond this neglect of the concept, Freud explicitly deemphasizes the navel's importance for the work of analysis. The navel, the "tangle of dream thoughts," Freud says, "adds nothing to our knowledge of the content of the dream." Beyond Freud, the navel seems to be something of a trap. Its sheer mysteriousness invites exploration, the same type of mapping impulse that motivates Freud's conquest of the dreamscape in the first place. Perhaps more significantly, Freud's notion of the navel cannot be separated from the broader Freudian system of psychodynamics with its understanding of the mechanisms of dreaming.

On the other hand, if the concept of the navel could be detached from Freudian theory and understood as the contact point between the known and the unknown, the knowable and the unknowable, the legible and the illegible, in other words if that which is illegible and unknowable can somehow be permitted to remain illegible and unknowable, an opening might exist to posit anti-authoritarian conceptions of the dreamscape and even the dream-text or text in general. In the two chapters that follow, I chart the divergent pathways in modernism for the narrativization of the dreamscape. The dominant modernist mode, represented by Philip Roth and Carl Jung, seeks to banish or write out the dream's unknowable center or "navel" in the service of narrative, thematic, and systemic integration. The other path, exemplified by Jean Rhys and Franz Kafka, attempts to preserve the illegible and unknowable dreamscape as a site of radical critique.

Notes

1. A version of a section of this chapter appears as an article in *Legibility in the Age of Signs and Machines*. See Rogoff (2018).
2. In his *Autobiographical Study*, Freud reflects on the importance of dream interpretation to the development of his topographical mapping of the psyche and its relation to dominant medical discourse: "With the help of the method of free association and of the closely related art of interpretation, psychoanalysis succeeded in achieving one thing which appeared to be of no practical importance but which in fact necessarily led to a fresh attitude and a fresh scale of values in scientific thought. It became possible to prove that dreams have a meaning and to discover it. In classical antiquity great importance was attached to dreams as foretelling the future; but modern science would have nothing to do with them, it handed them over to superstition, declaring them to be purely 'somatic' processes—a kind of spasm occurring in the mind that is otherwise asleep...But by disregarding the excommunication pronounced upon dreams, by treating them as unexplained neurotic symptoms, as delusional or obsessional ideas, by neglecting their apparent content and by

making their separate component images into subjects of free association, psychoanalysis arrived at a different conclusion" (Freud 1952: 81–82).

3. The dual nature of Freud's epistemological approach has been discussed by numerous authors, including Paul Ricoeur, who makes the distinction between Freud's positivist "energetics" and his interpretive "hermeneutics of suspicion" (Bernstein 2013: 132), Richard Rorty, who claims that Freud was both a "natural scientist" and a "practitioner of hermeneutics" (1980: 185), and Peter Loewenberg. The latter emphasizes what he sees as Freud's hermeneutic innovations, writing, with almost triumphant optimism: "Psychoanalysis reduces the lies, disguises, and illusions of consciousness, makes defenses conscious, presents volition and options where previously there was only compulsion, and demystifies idealizations" (qtd. in Brooks and Woloch 2000: 100). Loewenberg's faith in Freudian hermeneutics leaves little room for an exploration of power dynamics. He writes, "Hermeneutics allows the analysand, upon reworking early childhood and present traumas, to make his or her own the meaning that was previously alien to him. The proof Freud seeks for the analyst's offered 'construction' is a hermeneutic proof—the analysand's verification by the production of new corroborative material. The analysand's confirmation is not taken at face value. Only the context of the self-formative analytic process has confirming power: 'The "Yes" has no value unless it is followed by indirect confirmations, unless the patient, immediately after his "Yes," produces new memories which complete and extend the construction'" (Brooks and Woloch 2000: 101). Ricoeur, significantly, sees dream interpretation as key to the development of psychoanalytic method: "It was in the work of dream interpretation…that the Freudian method was forged" (1970: 66).
4. Connections between psychoanalysis, colonialism, imperialism, and modernism have been made repeatedly. These studies focus largely on how Freudian theory adopts the language of colonial discourse, foremost in Freud's notions of the primitive, the hierarchy of reason and irrationality, and his treatment of superstition and religion (Frosh 2013; Khanna 2003; Brickman 2002, 2003; Valentine 2000).
5. In *The Triumph of the Therapeutic* (2006), Philip Rieff makes the distinction between "therapeutic systems," like religions, which operate in an authoritarian manner in relation to the individual, and Freud's "analytic

attitude," which provides the morally neutral and perhaps even "subversive" alternative of "self control" (Freud 1997: 28–29). Such a dichotomy, made in defense of psychoanalysis in the moment of the collapse of its hegemonic position, would soon be challenged by the poststructuralist analysis of the discursive construction of selfhood.

6. In the *Question of Lay Analysis*, Freud explicitly uses the notion of "dark continent" to describe the sexual life of adult women (Freud 1953: 211). Ranjana Khanna connects Freud's use of the term to the context of African exploration and specifically to Stanley's autobiographical *Through the Dark Continent*, concluding, "The metaphor of the dark continent, then, signals a similarity between these nineteenth-century narratives: psychoanalytic, archaeological, and colonial explorations" (2003: 52).
7. The centrality of colonial or imperial concepts in Freud's thought and language is demonstrated by Celia Brickman, who writes, "Freud's use of the idea of primitivity, which correlated the infantile stages of the development of the contemporary European psyche with the early stages in the psychological evolution of humanity, made use of this legacy of European theorizing about so-called primitive peoples, drawing on its culmination in the social evolutionism of the nineteenth century" (2003: 17).
8. Edward Said argues that in the nineteenth century a firm imaginative boundary was fixed between the West and the non-West. He writes, "With the rise of ethnography…there is a codification of difference, and various evolutionary schemes going from primitive to subject races, and finally to superior or civilized peoples…Such commonly used categories as the primitive, savage, degenerate, natural, unnatural also belong here" (1994: 130).
9. Freud goes on to nuance his thesis, stating: "a dream is a (disguised) fulfillment of a (suppressed or repressed) wish" (2010: 183).
10. This focus on the status of the outcome—and the need to frame this status through writing—is a consistent presence in Freud's case studies.
11. Recalcitrance or resistance is a recurring presence through *The Interpretation of Dreams* (Frieden 1990: 37–44). At each stage of presenting his argument, Freud revels in the conflict between himself and his doubters. Most commonly, these doubters are his patients—and most of his patients are women. Not surprisingly, the relationship between Freud and female patients—between male analysis and female resistance—has been the subject of intense scholarly inquiry (Decker 1991; Katz 1987).

12. While in the first (and longest) analysis of the dream Freud spends most time on the triad Irma-friend-wife, later on in *The Interpretation of Dreams* he argues that the dream-Irma is a condensation of additional individuals, including his daughter. This expansion does nothing to change the central point here, and, in fact, reinforces and deepens it; Irma is *reduced* through the act of analytic condensation.
13. Freud develops this notion of competition when he postulates that Leopold and Otto represented competing circles of colleagues. The "Otto Group," for Freud, was comprised of those "who did not understand me, who sided against me," while Leopold represented "the group of ideas attached to my friend in Berlin [Wilhelm Fliess], who *did* understand me, who would take my side…. point by point, I called up a friend against an opponent" (2010: 312).
14. Alternate readings of Freud's "specimen dream" based on an elaboration of the neglected sexual threads proliferate in the literature on Freud, especially from within the psychoanalytic traditions (Sprengnether 2003; Lotto 2001).
15. A clear representation of this somatic/psychic dilemma occurs in Henri Bergson's 1901 essay "The World of Dreams." Bergson concludes, "When this union of memory and sensation is effected, we have a dream" (1958: 39).
16. Erik Erikson captures the sense of the revolutionary act of re-reading Freud's specimen dream, stating, "To reinterpret the dream means to reinterpret the dreamer" (1954: 7).
17. Dora was written in 1900, but Freud delayed publication until 1905.
18. Perhaps the most interesting and sophisticated moment of this elision can be found in Susan Katz, "Speaking out against the 'Taking Cure': Unmarried Women in Freud's Early Case Studies." Katz writes, "Dora is a fiction for Freud before her appearance in his text; consequently, throughout the case history Freud's characterization of Dora wrestles with Dora's independent personality. This struggle between Dora herself and Freud's ideal for her is experienced by the reader as narrative tension, an irresolution despite the firm narrative closure. The tension arises from Dora's intractability—her insistence on preserving her self—despite Freud's medical skill and literary talent. Dora's voice breaks the sound barrier of the text, as her accusations of falseness and treachery reverberate beyond the postscript" (1987: 321).

References

Bergson, Henri. *The World of Dreams*. Trans. Wade Baskin. New York: Philosophical Library, 1958.

Bernstein, Richard J. "Ricœur's Freud." *Études Ricoeuriennes/Ricoeur Studies* 4.1 (2013): 130–139.

Brickman, Celia. "Primitivity, Race, and Religion in Psychoanalysis." *The Journal of Religion* 82.1 (2002): 53–74.

———. Aboriginal Populations in the Mind: Race and Primitivity in Psychoanalysis. New York: Columbia UP, 2003.

Brooks, Peter, and Alex Woloch. *Whose Freud?: The Place of Psychoanalysis in Contemporary Culture*. New Haven: Yale UP, 2000.

Decker, Hannah S. *Freud, Dora, and Vienna 1900*. New York: Free Press, 1991.

Deutsch, Felix. "A Footnote to Freud's 'Fragment of an Analysis of a Case of Hysteria.' In *Dora's Case: Freud—Hysteria—Feminism*. Eds. Charles Bernheimer and Claire Kahane. New York: Columbia UP, 1990. 35–43.

Erikson, Erik. "Reality and Actuality: An Address." *In Dora's Case: Freud—Hysteria—Feminism*. Eds. Charles Bernheimer and Claire Kahane. New York: Columbia UP, 1990. 44–55.

———. "The Dream Specimen of Psychoanalysis." Journal of the American Psychoanalytic Association 2. (1954): 5–56.

Ferguson, Harvie. *The Lure of Dreams: Sigmund Freud and the Construction of Modernity*. London: Routledge, 1996.

Frieden, Ken. *Freud's Dream of Interpretation*. Albany: SUNY P, 1990.

Freud, Sigmund. *The Interpretation of Dreams*. Trans. James Strachey. New York: Basic Books, 2010.

———. Dora: An Analysis of a Case of Hysteria. Trans. James Strachey. New York: Touchstone, 1997.

———. The Standard Edition of the Complete Psychological Works of Sigmund Freud, vol. 20. Trans. James Strachey. London: Hogarth, 1953.

———. An Autobiographical Study. Trans. James Strachey. New York: Norton, 1952.

Frosh, Stephen. "Psychoanalysis, Colonialism, Racism." *Journal of Theoretical and Philosophical Psychology* 33.3 (2013): 141–154.

Gay, Peter. *Freud: A Life for our Time*. New York: Norton, 1988.

Gearhart, Suzanne. "The Scene of Psychoanalysis: The Unanswered Questions of Dora." In *Dora's Case: Freud—Hysteria—Feminism*. Eds. Charles Bernheimer and Claire Kahane. New York: Columbia UP, 1990. 105–127.

Katz, Susan. "Speaking Out Against the 'Talking Cure': Unmarried Women in Freud's Early Case Studies." *Women's Studies* 13.4 (1987): 297–324.

Khanna, Ranjana. *Dark Continents: Psychoanalysis and Colonialism*. Durham: Duke UP, 2003.

Lacan, Jacques. *The Seminar of Jacques Lacan: The Ego in Freud's Theory and in the Technique of Psychoanalysis, 1954–1955, vol. II*. Trans. Sylvana Tomaselli. New York: Norton, 1991.

———. "Intervention on Transference." In Dora's Case: Freud—Hysteria—Feminism. Eds. Charles Bernheimer and Claire Kahane. New York: Columbia UP, 1990. 92–104.

Lotto, David. "Freud's Struggle with Misogyny: Homosexuality and Guilt in the Dream of Irma's Injection." *Journal of the American Psychoanalytic Association* 49.4 (2001): 1289–1313.

Malcolm, Janet. "Reflections: J'appelle un chat un chat." In *Dora's Case: Freud—Hysteria—Feminism*. Eds. Charles Bernheimer and Claire Kahane. New York: Columbia UP, 1990. 305–325.

Moi, Toril. "Representation of Patriarchy: Sexuality and Epistemology in Freud's Dora." In *Dora's Case: Freud—Hysteria—Feminism*. Eds. Charles Bernheimer and Claire Kahane. New York: Columbia UP, 1990. 181–199.

Ramas, Maria. "Freud's Dora, Dora's Hysteria." In *Dora's Case: Freud—Hysteria—Feminism*. Eds. Charles Bernheimer and Claire Kahane. New York: Columbia UP, 1990. 149–180.

Ricœur, Paul. *Freud and Philosophy: An Essay on Interpretation*. Trans. Denis Savage. New Haven: Yale UP, 1970.

Rieff, Philip. *The Triumph of the Therapeutic: Uses of Faith after Freud*. Wilmington: ISI Books, 2006.

Rogoff, Seth. "Freud's Conquest of the Dreamscape: Legibility and Power in Freud's Specimen Dream." *Legibility in the Age of Signs and Machines*. Eds. Pepita Hesselberth, Janna Houwen, Esther Peeren, and Ruby de Vos. Leiden: Brill, 2018. 51–66.

Rorty, Richard. "Freud, Morality, and Hermeneutics." *New Literary History* 12.1 (1980): 177–185.

Rose, Jacqueline. "Dora: Fragment of an Analysis." In *Dora's Case: Freud—Hysteria—Feminism*. Eds. Charles Bernheimer and Claire Kahane. New York: Columbia UP, 1990. 128–148.

Sachs, David M. "Reflections on Freud's Dora Case After 48 Years." *Psychoanalytic Inquiry* 25.1 (2005): 45–53.

Said, Edward. *Culture and Imperialism*. London: Vintage, 1994.

Sprengnether, Madelon. "Enforcing Oedipus: Freud and Dora." In *Dora's Case: Freud—Hysteria—Feminism*. Eds. Charles Bernheimer and Claire Kahane. New York: Columbia UP, 1990. 254–275.

———. "Mouth to Mouth: Freud, Irma, and the Dream of Psychoanalysis." American Imago 60.3 (2003): 259–284.

Valentine, Kylie. "Interdisciplinarities of Origin: Modernism, Psychoanalysis and Imperialism." *Colloquy: Text Theory Critique* 4 (2000): n. pag.

5

Dream-Texts Integrating and Disintegrating: Philip Roth's *Goodbye Columbus*, Carl Jung's "Individual Dream Symbolism in Relation to Alchemy," and Jean Rhys's *Good Morning, Midnight*

Introduction

The formation of the dream-text as a representation of the dreamscape is a political act, one infused with the dynamics of power on both macro- and micro-levels. As I describe in the previous chapter on Freud, the assertion of regimes of power into what then becomes the conquered *territory* of the dream is critical to the development of psychoanalytic dream analysis and to psychoanalysis in general. A key moment in the conquest of the dreamscape, exemplified by the case of Dora's first dream (the dream of the jewel-box), is the expropriation of the dreamscape as narrative dream-text. This imbues the dream-text with special status, which invites exegetical attention. In other words, the dream-text already contains its interpretation—or at least the promise of interpretation—even if the interpretation remains implicit. In Freudian theory, the dream-text has an integrative function; it merges the event of the dream with an understanding or situating of that event, the field of the dream with the landscape of "reality," and the dream-I with the dreamer-I, thereby proposing the psychological subject.

© The Author(s), under exclusive license to Springer Nature Switzerland AG 2021

S. Rogoff, *The Politics of the Dreamscape*,
https://doi.org/10.1007/978-3-030-74796-1_5

Jean Rhys's *Good Morning, Midnight* (1939) contains a single seemingly clearly delineated dream-text, what I call the "Exhibition dream," which most critics consider of central interpretive importance for determining meaning in the novel. However, this focus on the delineated dream-text in the sense of Freud's "specimen dream" or Dora's dream of the jewel-box obscures two important textual features. First, the "Exhibition dream" is not, actually, clearly delineated but emerges out of and back into the narrative in a paratactic way consistent with the rest of the novel, making it more consistent with the type of blending seen in Frost's "After Apple-Picking." As such, the status of the "Exhibition dream" as dream-text is unstable. Second, and more importantly, a focus on the "Exhibition dream" diverts attention from considering the novel as a whole as a dream-text, though in ways fundamentally at odds with the Freudian version of the concept. While the Freudian dream-text is integrative, the dream-text of *Good Morning, Midnight* trembles on the cusp of disintegration, falling apart into emptiness, scattered pieces, and a total lack of coherence. This tremble of disintegration gestures toward the type of primordial chaos I have discussed in relation to the serpent as representative of the "deep" in the Garden of Eden, and to the potential for the radical fracturing of selfhood and "reality" I identified in Robert Frost's "After Apple-Picking." The result of this tendency toward disintegration is not only a resistance to fixed meaning but the radical impossibility of both interpretation and meaning—making *Good Morning, Midnight* what one might call an anti-dream-text and Sasha Jensen, the novel's narrator, the anti-Dora. If this is true from inside the text, from outside it seems that the radical rejection of interpretation and meaning points, instead of forward to interpretation, backward to a primordial, pre-textual state of existence, that is, to the shadowy world of the dreamscape itself.

In the previous chapter on Freud, I argue that the translation of a dreamscape into a dream-text in Freud's psychoanalytic system contains a number of structural hierarchies, most importantly, the assertion of the power of the analyst over the patient and the claim of primacy for the psychoanalytic method over competing interpretive paradigms. In my analysis of Dora's jewel-box dream, I demonstrated that a core authoritarian impulse of Freudian dream analysis is the notion of total explication or wholeness, which conforms to patterns of late nineteenth century quests for completeness prominent across the European scientific and academic spectrum. Freud's composition of Dora's first dream, together with his interpretation (the two cannot be separated), forms an integrative whole that is meant to be hermetic. The result is a bewildering and convoluted web of related symbols and meanings. This structure, then, replaces the dreamscape as the fully formed dream-text.

Before getting to Rhys's *Good Morning, Midnight*, this chapter discusses two additional dream-texts in order to analyze strategic uses of the dream-text as an integrative force beyond the model of Freudian integration. It is this instrumentalization of the dream-text that I argue Rhys's novel first purports to follow with the "Exhibition dream" and then undermines with the disintegrative thrust of the work as a whole. In doing so, *Good Morning, Midnight* challenges the dominant and authoritarian model of Freudian and other types of dream interpretation, and asserts a counter-position, the emancipatory possibilities of disintegration. The two dream-texts I discuss below are Neil Klugman's "Island dream" from Philip Roth's novella *Goodbye, Columbus* (1959) and the sequence of dream reports from Carl Jung's "Individual Dream Symbolism in Relation to Alchemy" (1944; revised 1952). With Roth, my aim is to show how the integrative functions of the dream-text were deployed in popular literature (Roth's collection won the National Book Award in 1959). Carl Jung's piece on dreams and alchemy, on the other hand, represents one of the most sophisticated and complex uses of the dream-text in the quest for wholeness or totality in post-Freudian modernism (Pietikainen 2000: 529).

The "Island Dream" in Roth's *Goodbye, Columbus*

In *Goodbye, Columbus*, Philip Roth introduces Neil Klugman, a lower-middle-class Jew a few years out of college who lives with his aunt and uncle in the increasingly economically distressed New Jersey city of Newark. Neil, the novella's narrator, is bright, a former philosophy major (though the *klug* or clever/smart of Klugman seems meant both sincerely and ironically), and now works as a reference librarian in Newark's Public Library, a job that offers little promise of elevating him beyond his current socio-economic station. One summer, Neil successfully pursues a Radcliffe student, Brenda Patimkin, whom he meets while accompanying his well-to-do cousin Doris to a suburban country club, where Doris is a member. The Patimkins are wealthy; the father is a "self-made man," who landed lucrative defense department contracts during the Second World War and in so doing transformed his small operation selling kitchen and bathroom sinks into a major distribution business. As a result, Mr. Patimkin made it out of Newark, and the Patimkins became part of a flight of newly created middle- and upper-middle-class families out of US cities and into the burgeoning suburbs (Rome 2001). This dualism, the weakening and increasingly impoverished city and the strengthening and increasingly wealthy suburb, forms the backdrop for *Goodbye, Columbus* and branches off into related other dualisms: rich/poor, Jew/goy (or non-Jew), black/white, deep/superficial, spiritual/material, the preservation of cultural identity/assimilation into a homogeneous American (white, Christian) middle class.

As the summer passes, Neil and Brenda start having sex. They spend their time together always in the suburbs, never in the city, and Neil becomes a frequent guest at the Patimkin house. Toward the end of the summer, Brenda invites Neil to spend his vacation there. Though Neil is officially stationed in the guest room next door to Brenda's brother Ron, he spends his nights with Brenda in her room having sex and then retreating back to his quarters at dawn. During one such dawn, before breaking away from Brenda, Neil has the following dream, the "Island dream":

> One morning near sneaking-away time I had a dream and when I awakened from it, there was just enough dawn coming into the room for me to see the color of Brenda's hair. I touched her in her sleep, for the dream had unsettled me: it had taken place on a ship, an old sailing ship like those you see in pirate movies. With me on the ship was the little colored kid from the library—I was the captain and he my mate, and we were the only crew members. For a while it was a pleasant dream; we were anchored in the harbor of an island in the Pacific and it was very sunny. Upon the beach

> there were beautiful bare-breasted Negresses, and none of them moved; but suddenly we were moving, our ship, out of the harbor, and the Negresses moved slowly down to the shore and began throwing leis at us and say "Goodbye, Columbus ... goodbye, Columbus ... goodbye..." and though we did not want to go, the little boy and I, the boat was moving and there was nothing we could do about it, and he shouted at me that it was my fault and I shouted it was his for not having a library card, but we were wasting our breath, for we were further and further from the island, and soon the natives were nothing at all. Space was all out of proportion in the dream, and things were sized and squared in no way I'd ever seen before, and I think it was that more than anything else that steered me into consciousness. (1969: 52–53)

Neil's dream-text draws together key thematic and narrative elements of the overall story he is telling, and in so doing sets up interpretive structures for the work as a whole—both the story up to that point (the dream comes at the novella's mid-point—like in Blake's *Job* and Freud's *Dora*) and the entire novella.

The "little colored kid from the library" refers to a boy (age unclear), who earlier in the summer comes into the Newark Public Library and asks to look at art books. Neil directs him upstairs and later finds the boy engrossed in a collection of reproductions of paintings by the French artist Paul Gauguin. The boy starts to come to the library often after that first day, and each time he goes straight for the art stacks to leaf through the Gauguin prints. Neil takes a particular interest in the boy and especially in the boy's passion for the Gauguin prints, at one point claiming, "Over the next week and a half there seemed to be only two people in my life: Brenda and the little colored kid who liked Gauguin" (Roth 1969: 33–34).

The island in Neil's dream is a reference to the Pacific island of Tahiti, where Gauguin painted his famous depictions of a life of "primitive" pleasure and simplicity. Noteworthy here is the contrast the boy draws between his life in Newark and a fantasy inspired by the Gauguin paintings. When Neil is sent by his suspicious boss to check on what the boy is doing, the boy says to him, "These people, man, they sure does look cool. They ain't no yelling or shouting here, you can just see it." After showing Neil a print of "three native women standing knee-high in a rose colored stream," the boy exclaims, "Man…that's the fuckin life." The boy then asks Neil if the painter, Gauguin, is white or colored. When Neil tells him Gauguin is white, the boy adds, "I knew that. He don't *take* pictures like no colored men would…" (Roth 1969: 26). Neil immediately takes up the paradisiacal space of Tahiti as symbolic of suburban life. Directly after this discussion with the boy in the library, he muses, "I sat at the Information Desk thinking about Brenda and reminding myself that that evening I would have to get gas before I started up to Short Hills, which I could see now, in my mind's eye, at dusk, rose-colored, like a Gauguin stream" (Roth 1969: 27). Immediately, then, we have the integration of the boy's fantasy with Neil's, both of which are recalled by the dream-text's island.

Prominent in the dream-text are the "beautiful bare-breasted Negresses," representatives of the female characters in Gauguin's paintings. For the boy, they represent a life of pleasure and relaxation impossible in Newark. The calm—even "silent"—life of pleasure on Tahiti contrasts with the intensity of Newark life on just about every level; and it is this contrast, representing an alternative existence for the boy, which fuels his escapism and draws him to the book each day. For Neil, too, loudness or lack thereof has spatial significance. The loquaciousness of his Newark relatives contrasts with the relative quiet of the Patimkin dinner table.

The words "Goodbye, Columbus" refer to a record being played by Brenda's brother Ron. Ron was a high school basketball standout and went to play college basketball at Ohio State University, located in Columbus, Ohio. The record is an audio yearbook of his senior year at Ohio state and offers a stark reminder of how seamlessly the Patimkins have molded themselves into the white Christian suburban class. The cognitive dissonance of the Tahitian woman (the boy's fantasy) singing "Goodbye, Columbus" (Neil's fantasy) is easily overcome in the dream-text.

In the dream-text, Neil reproaches the boy for "not having a library card." One day, while Neil is working at the reference desk, a man tries to check out the boy's favorite book of Gauguin prints. Neil refuses the man's request, saying that the book has a hold on it by another patron.

The man, unhappily, leaves the library only to return later in the summer with the same demand. Neil again lies, saying the book is still out and tells the man that he will contact him by phone once it comes back in. The man is indignant. Neil feels some impulse to protect the boy. Later that day, he approaches the boy and tells him to get a library card and to check out the book of Gauguin prints, otherwise someone else will check it out. The boy is incredulous for many reasons. He does not want to bring the book home in fear that it might be destroyed there and likes coming to the library to escape the scene at home. The book has not left the library all summer, and the boy doubts there is much demand for it. Finally, the boy is suspicious of Neil's motivations, thinking that Neil, like others at the library, simply wants to get rid of him. As Neil reports, "'Man,' [the boy] said, squinting at me, 'why don't you want me to come round here'" (Roth 1969: 43).

The dream-text's motifs can be easily interpreted in the context in the novella. The "pirate"-like ship is a symbol for the city of Newark. Late 1950s Newark and its suburbs, the setting of novella, are critically important for Neil, and he constantly talks about the changes he is witnessing in the city and the surrounding areas between his generation and that of his parents. For Neil, one change is most noteworthy: Jews are leaving Newark behind for life in the suburbs. The Jewish character of the city is weakening, and the subculture of urban Newark Jewry is disappearing as a consequence of postwar prosperity and the strong drive toward assimilation. The American urban salad, an interweaving of identifiably different ethno-religious groups, is transforming into a suburban American stew, a homogenous blend of cultural uniformity or conformity built primarily around material expressions: house, lawn, car, clothes. As a result, those left in the urban centers like Newark are increasingly distant and less comprehensible to those in the new suburban culture. The failure of understanding between Neil and his aunt Gladys concerning Neil's vacation in the suburbs captures this cultural divide.

The pirate ship is an apt metaphor. The city, like the pirate ship, seems like something antiquated, an anachronism. It is culturally misplaced, failing to relate to more conventional (suburban) society—the society on shore. This distance between ship and shore—between Newark and its "other" (a vague fantasy for the boy, the suburbs for Neil)—can only (and must inevitably) widen. There is no force that can bring them back together—and indeed if such a reconnection could be imagined, it would be a threatening or imperious one, one of attack (pirates storming the port). On the other hand, such an attack is bound to occur as a result of the pull of cultural homogenization and the ubiquitous image of the suburban middle-class lifestyle as the symbol of the American dream. Neil captures both the separation of city and suburbs and the pull or lure of the latter when he reflects on Newark during a drive to Mr. Patimkin's warehouse in the city:

> Patimkin Kitchen and Bathroom Sink was in the heart of the Negro section of Newark…The neighborhood had changed: the old Jews like my grandparents had struggled and died, and their offspring had struggled and prospered, and moved further and further west, toward the edge of Newark, then out of it, and up the slope of the Orange Mountains, until they had reached the crest and started down the other side, pouring into Gentile territory as the Scotch-Irish had poured through the Cumberland Gap. Now, in fact, the Negroes were making the same migration, following in the steps of the Jews, and those who remained in the Third Ward lived the most squalid of lives and dreamed in their fetid mattresses of the piny smell of Georgia nights. (Roth 1969: 64)

Newark, even for Neil, is the place for those who cannot or will not escape, for those who won't follow the beaten path of migration. In the eyes of John McKee, Neil's colleague at the library, the poor blacks remaining in the city create the living conditions they deserve. While expressing his nervousness to Neil that the little black boy will mess up the art books, McKee says, "There is touching…and there is touching. Someone should check up on him [the boy]. You know the way they treat the housing projects we give to them…. They threw *beer* bottles, those big ones, on the *lawn*. They're taking over the city" (Roth 1969: 25, italics in text).

Newark, the pirate ship, is coded as poor and black, black, of course, being the color of the pirate flag. The racial element of this transformation is clearly on Neil's mind throughout the story and appears as one of the primary impulses in the dream. The fear of being coded as black, of having Newark's blackness stain Neil's whiteness, resounds throughout the novella. Neil first encounters Brenda when she asks him to hold her glasses while she swims at the country club pool, casting Neil in a subservient or "black" role right away (Roth 1969: 2). Neil calls Brenda in the evening on the telephone, reminding her that he held her glasses by the pool. She asks him what he looks like and Neil responds that he is "dark." Immediately, Brenda asks, "Are you a Negro?" (Roth 1969: 5). When Neil and Brenda meet later at night, Brenda asks what Neil's cousin Doris looks like. When Neil again uses the term "dark," Brenda again thinks about Doris being black—though Neil cuts her off before she can say it. For Neil, his association with the urban world of Newark, together with what this implies about his socio-economic status, codes him—or at least he imagines it does—as black or at least as containing blackness. When asked to babysit Brenda's little sister Julie one night at the Patimkin house in Short Hills, Neil muses that he "felt like Carlota," the Patimkins' black maid (Roth 1969: 28).

The figure of the urban Jew as "black" is not only a product of Neil's paranoid imagination; rather, it is informed by a long history of racial thinking. European racial-political thinking had linked the racial types of Jew and black together, a link that carried into American society during the waves of Jewish immigration in the late nineteenth century until the First World War.[1] The "stain" of blackness imagined by Neil both in the dream and in the novella as a whole contrasts with the whitening of Jewish suburbia. The coding of black Jews and white Jews—Newark Jews and suburban Jews—becomes a means of describing culturally "authentic" Jews (like Aunt Gladys) and a new class of country club Jewish WASPS. Critics of the story often locate its central conflict precisely here: between the authentic, rooted old-world American Jews and the conformist, assimilated suburban Jews (France 2008). This narrative fits into a broader narrative of American suburbanization, conformity, and the superficiality (emptiness) of the quest for material prosperity, especially through consumer culture (Jackson 1985). In the critical literature on the story, the issue of race relations is marginalized, and yet, as we have seen in the above analysis, it forms the center of the dream-text. In other words, Roth's novella is not only a critique of a new kind of Jewish suburban life, it is also (and centrally) a portrait of the emerging dynamics of the new American metropolitan territory, foremost its shifting racial dynamics.

In Neil's mind, racial categories (or at least racial terminology) are more fluid than in Brenda's. Jewish Americans in the post-Second World War world had been by and large accepted into the white American establishment, especially if they were willing to shed the more overt aspects of their ethnicity and to blend in (like the Patimkins) (Sundquist 2009: 20). The same opportunities were not available to black Americans. Later in the story, days after the dream, Neil is asked to pick up some things at Mr. Patimkin's office in Newark, still the home of his distribution center. At the warehouse, Neil encounters Ron overseeing a group of black workers unloading a truck of sinks. The workmen all want to take a lunch break at the same time, but Ron is pushing for them to take breaks in shifts. Mr. Patimkin, managing in an older style, overrules his son and allows the men to eat lunch together, telling Ron, "No fancy deals here … we all go to lunch at once" (Roth 1969: 67). After Ron leaves, Mr. Patimkin talks with Neil; and the two bond, at least superficially, over shared roots in Jewish Newark. Brenda's father goes so far as to favorably compare Neil to his children, calling them *goyim*, or non-Jews. But this is no straightforward insult, for they are *goyim* because they can be *goyim*, that is, because he has succeeded in business to such an extent that his kids are now part of upper-middle-class American (WASP) society. While Mr. Patimkin feels nostalgia for Neil's world, and still has one foot in it, he does not want it for his children. Quite self-consciously, he has broken this link with the past. Nonetheless, he remains a transitional figure—both an upright member of the Short Hills community and a man who purports to understand his black workers. Neil, too, is a transitional figure; he is together with the black boy on the ship, yet he is the captain.

The dream-text represents the fading away, for Neil and the black boy, of the idealized community, foreshadowing later plot developments in the novel: the boy's loss of the Gauguin book to a library card holder and Neil's loss of Brenda. In the dream, the boat is in a Tahitian harbor, which represents the boy's fantasy of a peaceful, safe, and relaxed realm. The women sing "Goodbye, Columbus," which represents the suburban country club world in which Neil is living during his summer vacation.

Both of these worlds prove ultimately unreachable. As the boat drifts away, the women move down to the shore and throw lais, an invitation to return extended precisely at the point return becomes impossible. This is the false promise—a symbol of the one offered by the seeming sanctuary of the "public" library (which is also a place of power and surveillance) and the one offered by Brenda when alluding to the possibility of marrying Neil. Neil's fantasy of living in the upper-middle-class world of Short Hills appears as fantastical as the boy's daydream of living in Tahiti. They are both mirages, forms of escapism.

Despite Neil's fear of Newark imprinting its "stain" of blackness on him, in the dream he knows that he is the captain and the boy his first mate, meaning that there is a hierarchical relationship between them, an allusion to hierarchical conceptions of race in Newark and suburbia. This hierarchy contains tension and conflict. The boy might be subordinate in rank, but he does not act in a subordinate way, and proceeds to cast the first words of blame—to threaten mutiny. Neil returns the blame, condemning the boy for not operating properly within institutional regulations (the library card) and thus somehow sabotaging their joint enterprise. They are not a crew working together; they are combatants, who are made hostile not necessarily out of hatred of one another but by shared circumstances, frustrations, suspicions, and fears. Disappointment and disillusionment are projected onto each other rather than onto the idealized world that recedes from them.

The "Island dream" acts as an integrative force both narratively and thematically. From a narrative perspective, the dream traces the arc of Neil's relationship with Brenda. The dream marks Brenda as an object of desire, like Gauguin's Tahitian women. The visual subtext of Gauguin's scenes is a history of (sexual) longing for a "primitive" native by an outsider—similar to the view Neil has of Brenda (Welten 2015: 3). Like Gauguin's women, Brenda is placed in a seemingly utopian context, which further conflates Gauguin's Pacific with suburban Short Hills (Knapp 1989: 57). In addition, the dream-text shows that even at the height of Neil and Brenda's mid-summer love affair, and only hours after sex, Neil dramatizes the relationship's demise. Though he fears outwardly from the beginning of the summer affair that Brenda will break it off or that Brenda's world will reject him, deeper down he sees these worlds as incompatible—as fundamentally separate with Neil on one side, Brenda on the other (just as in the dream-text). His jaunt in the suburbs, the dream-text tells us, is like the little boy's thumbing through Gauguin reproductions in the library, a combination of wishful thinking and willful obliviousness to reality. The narrative unfolds precisely as foretold in the dream-text. Brenda leaves Short Hills in the fall to begin the next semester at Radcliffe in Boston. Neil goes to visit her, only to discover that Brenda's mother has found her diaphragm and that both she and Mr. Patimkin have demanded an end to her relationship with Neil. Neil believes that Brenda left the offending sexual apparatus in a discoverable spot in order to precipitate the ending of the relationship, hence supporting his initial belief (confirmed in the dream-text) of fundamental incompatibility or separateness.

While the narrative integration catalyzed by the dream-text is powerful and proves determinative, the thematic integration is even more critical and points to the use of the dream-text to define and limit meaning, to reify categories and identities, and to block anarchic tendencies or potentialities. A core element of thematic integration achieved by the dream-text is the substantiation of the dichotomous and antagonistic categories of the Jewish urban and suburban social classes. This is primarily represented in the dream-text by the pirate ship/shore dichotomy and the fact that the ship is pulling away from the island, stressing inevitable (and passive) divergence despite the desires on either side. The notion of divergence or separateness is posed in its most dogmatic form at the end of *Goodbye, Columbus*. Brenda has checked herself and Neil into a hotel under the pretense that they are a married couple, a trick she learned, she divulges, from having read Mary McCarthy. In the hotel room, the charade of marriage disintegrates when Brenda informs Neil of the diaphragm incident. Brenda shares with Neil the letters she has received from her parents. Her father's letter makes clear that the family, as Neil imagines, has always seen him as belonging to a class apart: "Of course," Mr. Patimkin writes to Brenda, "I can't say We weren't all surprised because from the beginning I was nice to him and Thought he would appreciate the nice vacation we supplied for him." He goes on to add, "As for your mistake it takes Two to make a mistake and now that you will be away at school and from him and what you got involved in you will probably do all right I have every faith you will" (Roth 1969: 91). Neil quickly jumps on this line of reasoning and presses Brenda to admit that she sabotaged the relationship: "Goddamit," he says to her, "I understand more than you think. I understand why the hell you left that thing lying around, don't you? Can't you put two and two together?" (Roth 1969: 96). Neil's insistence on the inherent nature of the socio-cultural class division loops back to the novella's beginning: the country club (Roth 1969: 1), a suburban phonebook never used by Neil's aunt Gladys (Roth 1969: 3), Radcliffe (Roth 1969: 7), Brenda's nose job (Roth 1969: 9), Patimkin's Volkswagen (Roth 1969: 17), and Brenda's comment that "money is a waste" for her mother because, "She doesn't even know how to enjoy it. She still thinks we live in Newark" (Roth 1969: 18). From beginning to end, the socio-cultural dichotomy is clear: an urban, authentic Jewish subculture confronts a rising, whitening, "American" suburban Jewish class, one deeply conformist, materialistic, and unmoored from its ethic roots.

The force of this integrative quality can be seen by looking at scholarly responses to the text, which accept the basic framework of analysis given by the novella. A poignant example of this is the following conclusion by Patrick Silvey: "Neil has been rejected, but as readers we are meant to understand that this may not be such a terrible thing. He may not have gained the status of the Patimkins' high-class American materialism, but he has retained his identity as a Jewish outsider" (2014: 64). Randall Wilhelm likewise stresses the fundamental disconnect between Neil's world and Brenda's and connects this disconnect to the dream-text:

> While Neil may be able not to look closely at Gauguin plates in an art book, when Gauguin enters his dreams he slowly begins to take notice, even though he successfully represses the knowledge until later in the story. In fact, it is on Neil's second "voyage" in the story, his trip to Boston to meet Brenda during the Jewish holidays, that the dream becomes literally "true," and he has a final moment of clearing vision. Critics have discussed the ending of "Goodbye, Columbus" in varying terms, from blaming Neil to blaming Brenda to blaming both of the ill-suited lovers for their various shortcomings. Whichever position is taken, Brenda's attachment to the material goods that her parents provide over Neil's love is obvious, and it is

> this repugnant worship of all things material that finally opens Neil's eyes as to the true nature of his "Polynesian maiden." (2014: 55)

Both Silvey and Wilhelm fall into the integrative trap set by *Goodbye, Columbus*. The convergence of the novella, read through the dream-text, produces rigid categories and fixed identities that determine meaning. The clear victim of this paradigm is Brenda—rendered by both Roth and Roth scholars like Sanford Pinsker as the vacuous and materialistic "Jewish American Princess" (JAP). Pinsker writes, "Brenda Patimkin is fated to be forever the ur-JAP, a Jewish American Princess, the archetype for Jewish Bitch Goddesses to follow" (Pinsker 1984: 266).[2]

Equally rigid is the presentation of a second major thematic element proposed by the dream-text: the relationship between the little black boy and Neil. This relationship is marked by two components that exist in tension with one another: First, Neil and the black boy are presented as reflections of each other's socio-cultural circumstances, in other words the convergence of poor Jews and blacks in 1950s Newark, defined, in many cases, precisely in relation to the immediate other. However, and this is the second point, these neighbors are antagonists. As reflections, Neil and the black boy confront each other as categories—Neil is a lower-middle-class Newark Jew; the black boy is symbolic of the impoverished migratory black urban class. In the dream-text, as in the novella as a whole, these barriers of categorization are repeatedly reinforced with no attempt to get beyond them. There is no recognition either in the dream-text or in the novella that the thematization of such a reflection is highly questionable, for there are substantial differences between Neil's circumstances and those of the boy. Neil is college educated. He is, whether he fully accepts it or not, part of the new American "white" culture, which has been expanded to include Jews. While he continues to live in Newark, other relatives, his cousin Doris and her parents, live in Short Hills and belong to the same country club as the Patimkins. If Neal rejects the suburbs, he does so for cultural/intellectual reasons and not because they are structurally closed to him, despite what he imagines at the end of the novel. Undeterred by these fundamental differences, scholars have echoed the case for Neil's closeness to the black experience. Silvey, for example, writes, "The fact that Neil would feel like the Patimkins' African American maid makes it clear that he is very aware that his social class is likely much closer to Carlota's than it is to the Patimkins'" (2014: 63).

Despite the potentially caring (albeit hierarchical) parent-child relationship that develops between Neil and the black boy, clear divisions and derivative antagonisms persist between them. In contrast to Neil's fading ethnicity, the black boy still talks with a strong southern accent, indicating that his family belongs to a migrant generation. The boy is afraid to take the library book home, indicating a threatening or violent environment there. He consistently talks of the great calm in the Gauguin painting in contrast to the noisy circumstances at home. While Neil can enjoy a romp in Short Hills, the boy has no hope of making it to his paradise, Tahiti. The boy refuses Neil's plea that he should get a library card, because he fears institutions and the people who work in them, Neil included. Workers in the library harass and distrust him. So suspicious is he of the white people around him that he cannot recognize an ally (or potential ally) in Neil, probably for good reason. The boy senses that Neil is on the side of authoritarian power. As antagonists, Neil and the black boy fail to overcome rigid and formulaic categories and identity constructs. Neither is one able to make an empathic leap and recognize the singularity of the other. For the boy, Neil remains a threatening representative of power. For Neil, despite—or perhaps accentuated by—his own feelings of kinship with the black experience, the boy can only be a victim of urban black society, a victim (as Neil imagines himself) of Newark. While Neil takes pride in his paternal "protection" of the boy's access to the book of Gauguin prints, such an act is insignificant given the challenges the boy faces in his everyday life. The dream-text (echoing the novella) presents this antagonism as structural—just as Neil's separateness from Brenda is structural. However, the structural nature of the division between Neil and the black boy (like that between Neil and Brenda) can only be maintained if the social categories and resultant identities traced upon them remain intact.

The dream-text in *Goodbye, Columbus* integrates narrative and thematic elements to produce a coherent interpretation or meaning. The dream-text powers the case study, in this case Roth's analysis of the impact of the rise of American suburbia to a culturally hegemonic position. Alan France sums up the basic outcome:

> With growing interest in the historicity of literature and the continuing preoccupation with the 1960s, perhaps it is time to dust off a neglected-if minor-American classic, Philip Roth's novella *Goodbye, Columbus.* This work occupies the historically anomalous calm at the end of the post-war era but before the student revolt of the following decade. It is thus an excellent introduction to the problems of cultural identity and authenticity at the heart of that revolt, which was a treason not of young Klugmans but of young Patimkins. *Goodbye, Columbus* can help today's students see the poverty of a culture idealizing commodity satisfactions, one that continues to bulldoze ethnic and religious traditions to build the shopping malls and entertainment worlds of mass consumption. (2008: 83)

France is correct to point out the anti-establishment, anti-conformist perspective of Roth's novella. The novella acts to challenge authority (in this case that of "mainstream" white suburban society) by inverting authoritarian hierarchies. Unfortunately, this strategy leaves intact the basic authoritarian structures—rigid definitions of class and race, as well as fixed and derivative identities. Perhaps most critically, the strategy of inversion retains the integrative approach to determining meaning, which drains the dream-text of its potential to challenge, subvert, or otherwise disintegrate narratives and themes in order to destabilize fixed entities and thus challenge interpretive claims.

Goodbye, Columbus demonstrates the use of the dream-text in support of narrative and thematic cohesion. In the following section, I develop this notion of the dream-text as an integrative strategy in relation to Carl Jung's "Individual Dream Symbolism in Relation to Alchemy." This text, comprised of a series of dream-texts and commentaries, expands this integrative strategy to include additional dimensions, moving from the narrative and thematic level to the fields of psychodynamics and cultural/religious systems and history. Jung's case study is one of the most developed works of integrative dream theory, encompassing the text, the individual, and the world.

Carl Jung's "Individual Dream Symbolism in Relation to Alchemy"

In his "General Aspects of Dream Psychology," Carl Jung sums up his basic critique of the Freudian view of dreams. He writes, "The interpretation of dreams as infantile wish-fulfillments or as finalistic 'arrangements' subserving an infantile striving for power is much too narrow and fails to do justice to the essential nature of dreams. A dream, like every element in the psychic structure, is a product of the total psyche" (2010: 63). Freud's basic mistake, according to Jung, was that he remained focused exclusively on the relationship between consciousness and the personal unconscious, the essence of Freudian psychodynamics. Though the goal of the Freudian approach was the establishment of as harmonious a whole as possible, this Freudian whole remained by definition fundamentally partial from Jung's point of view. Its partiality stemmed from its failure to move beyond the individual's personal psychological position and history to consider what Jung termed the "collective unconscious." Only by fusing the personal with the collective could the whole psychological essence of an individual be comprehended—or at least posited.

Dreams, for Jung, offer a unique window into the process of creating wholeness, a process Jung terms "individuation." In his "Individual Dream Symbolism in Relation to Alchemy" (1944; revised 1952), Jung endeavors to construct a coherent narrative of this process of individuation by arranging and interpreting a series of dream-texts. The resultant "novella" serves to radicalize the authoritarian tendencies of Freudian theory. The hierarchy between analyst and patient is magnified such that the patient loses any identifying features as a real human being, appearing only as a pronoun and without any discernible physical or personal characteristics. In addition, Jung's interpretation not only employs the combination of scientific and hermeneutical approaches utilized by Freud, but it adds another layer of "expertise"—a deep and seemingly comprehensive academic knowledge of historical and religious traditions. These layers of specialized knowledge work together with the dream-text to promote both narrative and thematic integration. At the end of the article, Jung believes that he has succeeded in presenting the quest for individuation through the integration of the persona and the collective unconscious. He feels no compulsion to show the reader that his theories are correct, for example by mentioning their relationship to the life or psychological health of the patient. Rather, he asserts, matter-of-factly, the correctness of the case as the prerogative of the expert.

That the dream-text takes on an integrative function for Jung reflects his broader conception of the integrative dynamics of the process of individuation. The importance of the individuation process in Jungian theory cannot be overstated. It is a process that contains not only the personal and immediate social circumstances of a human being, but brings together the entirety of the world's intellectual, cultural, and artistic legacy. Jung writes:

> All these moments in the individual's life, when the universal laws of human fate break in upon the purposes, expectations, and opinions of the personal consciousness, are stations along the road of the individuation process. This process is, in effect, the spontaneous realization of the whole man. The ego-conscious personality is only a part of the whole man, and its life does not yet represent his total life. The more he is merely "I," the more he splits himself off from the collective man, of whom he is also a part, and may even find himself in opposition to him. But *since everything living strives for wholeness*, the inevitable one-sidedness of our conscious life is continually being corrected and compensated by the universal human being in us, whose goal is the ultimate integration of conscious and unconscious, or better, the assimilation of the ego to the wider personality. (2010: 78, italics mine)

For Jung, the process of the collective unconscious demanding compensation for what is lacking in the individual's consciousness or what crystalizes as the individual's social "persona" takes place ceaselessly. However, because it is unconscious and, moreover, because it is not generated by the individual's unconscious (like Freudian wishes) the dynamics of the compensatory mechanisms retreat into the very depths of the psyche. Shocks to the psyche or the "false wrappings of the persona" (Jung 1972: 123) can seem to the Jungian subject sudden and inexplicable. Jung's way into this invisible process of individuation is through the arrangement and analysis of the dream-text: "Dreams are the voice of the Unknown, that ever threatens with new schemes, new dangers, sacrifices, warfare and other troublesome things" (Jung 1938: 21). And again, "...my experience is in favor of the probability that dreams are the visible links in a chain of unconscious events" (1938: 38).

To understand an individual in the truest sense of the term, according to Jung, means being able to grasp the ways in which the "persona" or socially aware ego is confronted with impulses from what Jung sees as a universal and ubiquitous psychic reality—the collective unconscious. For Jung, the role of psychology is precisely to find the points of tension, friction, resistance, or rebellion at which the collective unconscious puts pressure on the persona. Gaining access to the collective unconscious, however, is tricky. About the influence of the collective unconscious on the psyche, Jung writes, "We find we are moving in a dark interior world that is vastly more difficult to understand than the psychology of the persona, which is accessible to everyone" (1972: 123). Jung believes to have found a spotlight into this "dark interior" in the form of archetypal images that appear in dreams, what he refers to at the beginning of "Individual Dream Symbolism" as "mandala symbolism"—the circular mandala standing in for the totality of the self, positing the ever-present relationship between a circle's center and its circumference (2010: 115–116).

Jung's "Individual Dream Symbolism in Relation to Alchemy" demonstrates the way an analysis of dreams illuminates the dynamics between persona and the collective unconscious, ultimately driving toward differentiation and individuation of the self, or to put it another way, toward self-realization. To accomplish this goal, Jung takes what he considers a "coherent series" of dreams provided by a patient, claiming that the patient (and not Jung) is the "author" of the dream-texts, despite the presence of Jung's strong editorial hand. From the outset, Jung's methodology is confounding. He proposes the existence of an "author" of the dream-texts as the subject of the investigation of the individuating process that can be traced through around 400 dreams. At the same time, he excises every trace of identifying information and most of the immediate personal context, which was key to Freud's analysis of Dora's dream of the jewel-box and, indeed, in all of Freud's case studies.

Two strategies underpin Jung's article on dream symbolism. First, he is intent to show the dynamics of the process of individuation through the dreams as a sort of visual diary or graphic novel. As such, the series of dream-texts Jung presents has a strong narrative thrust or plot. The plot structure can be summed up as containing the following basic components: initiating psychic dilemma, challenge, reaction, and crisis, eventually leading to resolution. These components do not occur only once but repeat with shifting intensities. This repetition and intensification create the narrative force of Jung's account, and together they are meant to dramatize the process of individuation. Second, Jung builds his analysis on the basis of a highly esoteric body of knowledge, ranging from (among many others) ancient Chinese and Hindu traditions to medieval Christianity, Kabbalah, and European alchemy. Meant to display the trans-historical and ubiquitous nature of the imagery of the collective unconscious, Jung's account also acts to radically circumscribe the zone of legitimate dream interpretation by necessitating that it relates to the traditional archetypes he identifies.

The narrative structure of Jung's account is built on a confrontation between the collective unconscious and the persona, a conflict in which, in order to compensate for deficiencies or imbalances in the conscious persona, the unconscious forces its way into the psyche with psychic demands. In the subject's first dream-text, he "puts on a stranger's hat instead of his own" (Jung 2010: 121). This act, for Jung, captures the beginning of the psychic drama: "As a general result of the exchange of hats we may expect a development similar to that in *The Golem*: an emergence of the unconscious. The unconscious with its figures is already standing like a shadow behind the dreamer and pushing its way into consciousness" (2010: 122). In the second dream, the collective unconscious begins to emerge or to force its way into confrontation with consciousness. In this dream, the dreamer blocks "the light from those who stand behind him, namely the unconscious components of his personality" (2010: 122). Such a blockage seems not to be able to hold, for in the third vision the dream narrative has its first major point of confrontation, the first manifestation of psychic conflict. The dream-text reads: "*By the sea shore. The Sea breaks into the land, flooding everything. Then the dreamer is sitting on a lonely island*" (2010: 112, italics in text). Jung interprets:

> The sea is the symbol of the collective unconscious, because unfathomed depths lie concealed beneath its reflecting surface. Those who stand behind, the shadowy personifications of the unconscious, have burst into the terra firma of consciousness like a flood. Such invasions have something uncanny about them because they are irrational and incomprehensible to the person concerned. They bring about momentous alteration of his personality since they immediately constitute a painful personal secret which alienates and isolates him from his surroundings. (2010: 122–123)

The "invasion" of the unconscious and the resultant feelings of isolation and even insanity provoke the first counteraction by the consciousness in an attempt to defend the persona. In dream #4, the dreamer is enticed by a "throng of vague female forms" but cannot engage with them until he is able to "get away from Father" (2010: 123). The appearance of the counterforce of the "Father" directly after the proposition of the "unfathomed depths" of the collective unconscious sets the stage for Jung to articulate in broad terms the quest for individuation:

> The father, the embodiment of the traditional spirit as expressed in religion or a general philosophy of life, is standing in his way. He imprisons the dreamer in the world of the conscious mind and its values. The traditional masculine world with its intellectualism and rationalism is felt to be an impediment, from which we must conclude that the unconscious, now approaching him, stands in direct opposition to the tendencies of the conscious mind and that the dreamer, despite this opposition, is already favourably disposed toward the unconscious. For this reason the latter should not be subordinated to the rationalistic judgments of consciousness; it ought rather to be an experience *sui generis*. Naturally it is not easy for the intellect to accept this, because it involves at least a partial, if not a total, *sacrificium intellectus*. Furthermore, the problem this raised is very difficult for modern man to grasp; for to begin with he can only understand the unconscious as an inessential and unreal appendage of the conscious mind, and not as a special sphere of experience with laws of its own. In the course of the later dreams this conflict will appear again and again, until finally the right formula is found for the correlation of conscious and unconscious, and the personality is assigned its correct position between the two. Moreover, such a conflict cannot be solved by understanding, but only by experience. Every stage of the experience must be lived through.

> There is no feat of interpretation or any other trick by which to circumvent this difficulty, for the union of conscious and unconscious can only be achieved step by step. (2010: 124, italics in text)

This step-by-step process is not a linear one. Forward thrusts by the unconscious are defended and pushed back by consciousness. This battle between consciousness and the unconscious is staged as an intensifying dialectical conflict. Only a resolution to this conflict can achieve both narrative closure and psychic individuation; the two go hand-in-hand.

Jung's quest for narrative resolution relies on connections to a wide body of historical material, which relates to his core psychological concepts like anima, shadow, and so on. In this specific case, the most important element of the historical-symbolic language is the mandala. Jung uses the term "mandala" in order to move beyond the visualization of the self as a mundane circular form. "The term 'mandala' was chosen because this word denotes the ritual or magic circle used in Lamaism and also in Tantric yoga as a *yantra* or aid to contemplation" (2010: 169). Jung concludes that mandala symbols "signify nothing less than a psychic centre of the personality not to be identified with the ego" (2010: 172–173). In order to propose the ubiquity of the mandala symbol, Jung, in the beginning of section II of the article, provides graphic imagery including a Shri-Yantra, a Tibetan World Wheel, the Aztec "Great Calendar Stone," a fifteenth-century Swedish mural painting by Albertus Pictor, a Lamaic Vajramandala, a Mexican calendar, the gem of a Roman ring, and a plate of two dragons eating each other's tail from an eighteenth-century scientific text.

The mandala symbol, representing the wholeness of individuation, forms the foundation of Jung's analysis of the dreams. Upon this foundation, Jung stacks layers of specialized and esoteric knowledge. Though there are dozens of moments at which Jung weaves together a complex set of associations, I will present an example of the style, which I believe captures the flavor of the text. Here, Jung presents the following dream-text: "*In the sea there lies a treasure. To reach it, he has to dive through a narrow opening. This is dangerous, but down below he will find a companion. The dreamer takes the plunge into the dark and discovers a beautiful garden in the depths, symmetrically laid out, with a fountain in the centre*"

(2010: 191, italics in text). Jung's analysis of this dream is among his most integrative:

> The "treasure hard to attain" lies hidden in the ocean of the unconscious, and only the brave can reach it. I conjecture that the treasure is also the "companion," the one who goes through life at our side—in all probability a close analogy to the lonely ego who finds a mate in the self, for at first the self is the strange non-ego. This is the theme of the magical travelling companion, of whom I will give three famous examples: the disciplines on the road to Emmaus, Krishna and Arjuna in the Bhagavad Gita, Moses and El-Khidr in Sura 18 of the Koran. I conjecture further that the treasure in the sea, the companion, and the garden with the fountain are all one and the same thing: the self. For the garden is another *temenos*, and the fountain is the source of 'living water' mentioned in John 7:38, which the Moses of the Koran also sought and found, and beside it El-Khidr, "one of Our servants whom We had endowed with Our grace and wisdom" (Sura 18). And the legend has it that the ground round about El-Khidr blossomed with spring flowers, although it was desert. In Islam, the plan of the temenos with the fountain developed under the influence of early Christian architecture into the court of the mosque with the ritual wash-house in the centre (e.g., Ahmed ibn-Tulun in Cairo). We see much the same thing in our Western cloisters with the fountain in the garden. This is also the "rose garden of the philosophers," which we know from the treaties on alchemy and from many beautiful engravings....
>
> The crash to earth thus leads into the depths of the sea, into the unconscious, and the dreamer reaches the shelter of the *temenos* as a protection against the splintering of personality caused by his regression to childhood. The situation is rather like that of dream 4 and vision 5 in the first series...where the magic circle warded off the lure of the unconscious and its plurality of female forms. (The dangers of temptation approach Poliphilo in much the same way at the beginning of his *nekyia*.)
>
> The source of life is, like El-Khidr, a good companion, though it is not without its dangers, as Moses of old found to his cost, according to the Koran. It is the symbol of the life force that eternally renews itself...and of the clock that never runs down. An uncanonical saying of our Lord runs: "He who is near unto me is near unto the fire." Just as this esoteric Christ is a source of fire...so the alchemical philosophers conceive their *aqua nostra* to be *ignis* (fire). The source means not only the flow of life but its

> warmth, indeed its heat, the secret passion, whose synonyms are always fiery. The all-dissolving *aqua nostra* is the essential ingredient in the production of *lapis*. But the source is underground and therefore the way leads underneath: only down below can we find the fiery source of life. These depths constitute the natural history of man, his causal link with the world of the instinct. Unless this link be rediscovered no *lapis* and no self can come into being. (2010: 191–194)

Jung's collective unconscious, accessed mainly through dreams, represents perhaps the most ambitious of modernist attempts to achieve wholeness in a non-metaphysical sense. The above synthesis is breathtaking in its ambition, combining alchemy, Christianity, Islam, Hinduism, and other elements to unpack a single short dream-text. The monumentality of Jung's conception allows it to challenge the central Freudian principle—indeed the central principle of psychoanalysis—the power of the sexual libido. Only, it seems, an entity as vast and deep as the collective unconscious could shove aside sex as the central dynamic force for Jungian psychology.

The contest between sexual libido and collective unconscious—between Freudian psychoanalysis and Jungian depth psychology—is just one of many issues of power and authority brought up by Jung's approach to dream analysis. Like Freud, Jung's analytical strategy seeks integration. Dream analysis becomes a key tool for the establishment of narrative structure and narrative wholeness, including the presentation of new information, temporal bridges, conflicts, and resolutions. The integrative function extends beyond narrative to issues of content and meaning. For Freud, the integrative project revolves around the explication of dream symbolism in relation to current and past sexual desire. For Jung, integration means linking the personal with the collective through the history of religious and mystical expressions. Integration of this sort, while vast in its ambitions for completeness or totality, results in at least three authoritarian outcomes. First, the analyst becomes the dominant arbiter of truth, so much so that the analysand is either made into what amounts to a fictional character (Dora) or vanishes altogether (Jung's dream "author"). Second, the complexity of Jung's analytical process fosters a hierarchy much like that between a priest and a congregant. Jung, as priest, has access to universal realms while the patient (or reader) as congregant can merely receive the wisdom. If Jung's wisdom is rejected, it is done not out of disputation of Jung's evidence but by a rejection of the basic principles of belief itself. As such, Jung's approach necessitates conflict over dialogue—just as Freud's method necessitated Dora either accepting Freud's conclusions or breaking off treatment. Third, the end result of the analytical process is the proposition of a fully understood and differentiated individual, which can now be fully known.

Just as Roth's dream-text helps locate the individual amid a constellation of racial and socio-economic categories, thereby reaffirming their solidity and validity, Jung's dream analysis places the individual directly in the stream of trans-historical or ahistorical absolutes or archetypes—the central one being the binary of male/female, the male persona versus the female anima. "The persona," Jung writes, "the ideal picture of a man as he should be, is inwardly compensated by feminine weakness, and as the individual outwardly plays the strong man, so he becomes inwardly a woman, i.e., the anima, for it is the anima that reacts to the persona" (1972: 194–195). If the individuation process—the becoming whole—is built on a reconciliation of opposites, it is at the same time a powerful force of merging into the broader community, of finding a psychologically stable place in society, at once differentiated as a self and integrated into the collective. The very becoming of self, in other words, is achieved through the subsuming of the self into the totality while still remaining individual.

Jung's emphasis on the reconciliation between the individual and the collective consciousness is part of the broader Jungian search for cohesion and transcendent synthesis, both as a matter of individual psychodynamics and as a process of socio-historical transformation (Dohe 2011: 356). Jung's syntheses often depended on reductive or even mythic constructs, most famously his notion of the "Germanic," which fit squarely into the racial politics of 1930s fascism (Dohe 2011: 355). As Jung moved toward total integration and synthesis, the writer Jean Rhys pushed in the opposite direction, toward narrative fragmentation and disintegration, tapping the anarchist potential of the dreamscape for radical political expression.

The "Exhibition Dream" and the Politics of Resistance in Rhys's *Good Morning, Midnight*

It is not surprising that readers of Jean Rhys's *Good Morning, Midnight* search for coherent and cohesive meaning(s), since the work is defined by ambiguity, fracturing, and abrupt shifting—both temporally and narratively. This quest for meaning rests primarily on the ways in which the text as a whole can be interpreted through an analysis of the novel's final scene. Two main lines of interpretation result from this process. The first reads the final scene as a culmination of narrator Sasha Jensen's decline or descent toward death—the fulfillment of a death spiral. By the concluding scene, this line of reasoning goes, Sasha no longer pushes back against death but comes to terms and accepts it as fate, even willing it in the final moments when she telepathically pulls a character named René (whom she thinks of as a gigolo) back to her bed, but then invites her deathly neighbor, the commis (traveling salesman), for sexual intercourse. The second line of interpretation moves in a related but opposite direction. Here, it is asserted that in this final scene Sasha overcomes the death spiral and is reborn through a combination of the exercise of her will and the joining of two deathly figures (Sasha and the commis) in sexual union.

The attempt to integrate the novel's final, bewildering scene with the entirety of the text to form coherent meaning depends, first and foremost, on a reading of what seems like the novel's single dream-text, Sasha's "Exhibition dream." While this approach has resulted in many impressive readings of the novel—some quite extraordinary—the tactic remains within the basic Freudian or modernist mode of appropriating, defining, and limiting the dream-text. Whereas in Roth's *Goodbye, Columbus*, this strategy of interpretation through the integrative qualities of the dream-text is obvious, in *Good Morning, Midnight*, the dream-text pushes back against its instrumentalization as an integrating force. Instead of pushing toward integration, it retreats into the deeper fog of the primal dreamscape. This retreat casts doubt on all integrative solutions to the novel's meaning, no matter how skillfully constructed, allowing, I argue, for a broadening of the understanding of the notion of "dream-text" to encompass the novel in its entirety. The novel's style, then, is that of a dream-text that seeks not reification and integration, but dissolution and disintegration. The novel as a whole, in other words, is retreating back into a pre-narrative state, the disorganized and ungraspable space beyond conscious reality—or into the dreamscape.

The case for the integrative force of Sasha's "Exhibition dream" rests, primarily, on two pillars: the symbolic value of the exhibition—thought to be the Paris exhibition of 1937—and the appearance in the dream of a man wearing a white robe who claims to be Sasha's father. Both of these symbols relate to what are considered the overarching or structuring themes of the novel: sexual power and patriarchy, economic distress and/or dislocation (which is bound to gender), the harshness of urban life (also gendered), and the radicalization of politics in 1930s Europe, especially concerning the status of minority peoples amid nationalist fervor.

Unlike Neil's "Island dream," which falls at the very center and turning point of *Goodbye, Columbus* and foreshadows the arc toward denouement, Sasha Jensen's "Exhibition dream" comes in the first pages of the text. The dream-text is as follows:

> I am in the passage of a tube station in London. Many people are in front of me; many people are behind me. Everywhere there are placards printed in red letters: This Way to the Exhibition, This Way to the Exhibition. But I don't want the way to the exhibition—I want the way out. There are passages to the right and passages to the left, but no exit sign. Everywhere the fingers point and the placards read: This Way to the Exhibition.... I touch the shoulder of the man walking in front of me. I say, 'I want the way out.' But he points to the placards and his hand is made of steel. I walk along with my head bent, very ashamed, thinking: 'Just like me—always wanting to be different from other people.' The steel finger points along a long stone passage. This Way—This Way—This Way to the Exhibition....
>
> Now a little man, bearded, with a snub nose, dressed in a long white night-shirt, is talking earnestly to me. 'I am your father,' he says. 'Remember that I am your father.' But blood is streaming from a wound in his forehead. 'Murder,' he shouts, 'murder, murder.' Helplessly I watch the blood streaming. At last my voice tears itself loose from my chest. I too shout: 'Murder, murder, help, help,' and the sound fills the room. (Rhys 1999: 13)

Scholars of Rhys's work have focused quite a bit of attention on this dream-text as a key piece (perhaps *the* key piece) in their attempts to construct an integrative interpretation of the novel. While these interpretations are significant and compelling, they shy away from what is perhaps the dream-text's most radical implication—its failure as an integrative device.

The motif of "exhibition" maintains a strong presence throughout *Good Morning, Midnight*, as many scholars have discussed. Cathleen Maslen links the exhibition motif with the notion of "commodity capitalism" (2009: 127). This connection occurs along two pathways. The first connection between exhibition and capitalism is through the object for sale—the consumer commodity. This connection, for Maslen, indicates a world that has been reduced to base economic relationships. Metaphysical notions like religion or even "humanist values" find no place in a commodity-driven consumer culture (Maslen 2009: 129). The second pathway that connects exhibition with capitalism has to do with the human relationships engendered by the exhibition or market context. An exhibition as a market event proposes the existence of an exhibited object and a consumer, even if this exhibited object happens to be another human being. The notion of the human as commodity, Sasha as exhibited object, informs Maslen's reading of the novel. Sasha, for Maslen, resists and embraces the rules of commodity culture as both a consumer herself and an object of consumption of a sadistic, objectifying gaze. The motif of "exhibition" thus points to a valueless commodification of life—the very ethos of capitalist culture. For Maslen, themes of market relationships, the commodification of human beings, and the power of the gaze can be traced to the initial dream-text. "In Sasha's dream," she writes, "there is no opposing the injunction to attend the Exhibition" (2009: 127). In other words, one cannot resist being included in the process of the commodification of life. Despite the seemingly objective nature of the capitalist social construct ("The indifferent crowd propels her [Sasha] helplessly toward it [the Exhibition]"), it "is clear," for Maslen, that "in the dream the idea of the Exhibition represents a violent, coercive ethos" (2009: 127).

Like Maslen, Mary Lou Emery sees the theme of exhibition as useful for proposing an integrative interpretation of the novel. The notion of exhibition in the dream-text, for Emery, foregrounds the social and political questions that the rest of the novel raises. She asserts that "the most important elements of this novel, which it shares with *Wide Sargasso Sea* and *Voyage in the Dark*, are the inscription of social conflict within a dream-text and the protagonist's continual efforts to revise, through her visions and through internalized voices, the meaning of a life imbued with that conflict" (1990: 148). The "social conflict" to which Emery is referring has to do with the rise of political extremism in Europe in the late 1930s.

Sasha's dream-text, for Emery (as for Maslen), allows the reader to bridge and integrate the psychological and the social domains. This is especially true when it comes to the central figure that the dream-Sasha encounters in the dreamt-text, the wounded man who claims to be her father. The figure is described in the dream-text as a "little man, bearded, with a snub nose, dressed in a long white night-shirt." The white night shirt is of particular importance, because it links the dream-figure to the commis. The commis appears throughout the novel as a threatening presence. At the end of the novel, he seems to enter Sasha's room in place of René, whom Sasha has tried to lure back into her room after his attempt to rape her. Sasha decides to accept the commis and pulls the man down into her bed in what seems like a prelude to sexual intercourse. For Emery, the dream-text sets the stage for this climactic scene—indeed the final scene "realizes" the dream (1990: 170). The dream, like the final scene, "inscribes difference and disobedience, masculine wounds, accusations of murder that blur victim and perpetrator, feminine feelings of shame and guilt, and political oppositions of left and right to which there appear no alternatives" (Emery 1990: 147). The fascistic elements of the dream-text structure Emery's interpretation of the final encounter between Sasha and the commis:

> Like the order promised by fascism, [Sasha's] submission demands pain and sacrifice. It convinces Sasha of her own guilt...and makes her a willing victim of anonymous patriarchal forces in an act of literal self-sacrifice. If this final scene suggests birth, it is that of a machine with mascaraed eyes, an artificial woman like the shop dummies Sasha has cynically admired, and an automaton who dances to a debasing tune. Following the zombie

> logic of Rhys's other novels, *Good Morning, Midnight* portrays in its final scene death-in-life and the political-psychological powers that work such evil magic.
>
> In the modern European society, the "self," unified and consolidated, gains the status of the sacred. The selves of Rhys's heroines, so tenuous and pluralized already, are sacrificeable. Though they stubbornly attempt to find, assert, and protect the voices of their multiplicitous selves, they are imbued with the violence of the society around them that, feeling itself threatened, requires victims. (1990: 171)

If the final scene represents the fulfillment of the dream-text, according to Emery, both final scene and dream-text gain their full meaning by being juxtaposed to the "carnivalesque" encounter between Sasha and the Jewish Russian artist Serge, an encounter that evokes in Sasha memories of her Caribbean childhood:

> The happy ending that might have closed this novel takes place in its middle, with a glimpse of "somewhere else" in a vision of the sea and an opening door. Sasha cannot reenact the scene later because it depended upon a spontaneous community of marginalized individuals, acting in carnivalesque concert. The terrifying grey background of Sasha's vision, modern Europe on the verge of a war in which six million "marginal" individuals will be deliberately put to death, supercedes in the novel's ending the possibilities offered by its middle. The epiphany of the middle section, however, suggests the Third World modernist concept of the individual that Rhys later develops in *Wide Sargasso Sea*; in this novel of the late 1930s it becomes a means to explore the social and political limitations governing the formalism of European modernism. (Emery 1990: 171–172)

Without dismissing the cogent and imaginative interpretations of Maslen, Emery, and others, I would like to propose that the dream-text of the "Exhibition dream" resists more than it encourages interpretive integration. First, while critics generally agree that Sasha's "self" is fractured, multiple, and fragile, they assume a direct correlation between the dominant narrative voice of the novel and the dream-I. This strikes me as a mistake, as the dream-I should be treated with as much skepticism as the other iterations of Sasha's persona. Since the dream-I is at best a representation of the self, it would be better to see the unnamed "I" as a discreet character. Conclusions about this "I," therefore, should not be immediately applied to Sasha. Second, critics emphasize certain details in the dream-text while ignoring others. The placards in the dream read, "This Way to the Exhibition," but critics do not interpret why these are written specifically in "red letters"—seemingly a point of emphasis. The line, "There are passages to the right and passages to the left, but no exit sign," is taken to mean that there is no exit or that any possible egress implies an absolute political choice (the right and left standing in for political orientation). It could very well be argued, as Emery does, that the logic of the central avenue of the 1937 Paris Exhibition, which pitted the Soviet pavilion directly opposite the Nazi pavilion, informs this dream and constructs a zero-sum choice which the dream-I refuses to make, leaving her with the only possibility of following the crowd. Yet, these passages or ways out of the central stone passage lead away from the crowd—away from the masses. The passages, rather than indicating known outcomes (fascism, communism, etc.), could point to all that is unknown, in other words to a regress into the disorganized, chaotic dreamscape. While heading straight forward is the conformist (fascist?) choice, the passages beckon the non-conformist. Notably, nobody takes any of these paths. While the dream-I is read as Sasha, it seems just as plausible that every member of the crowd is a Sasha duplicate, compounding dream-Sasha's inability to triumph over herself with an act of will. Dream-Sasha claims to "want the way out" instead of the way to the exhibition. Critics assume that the "way out" is a self-evident statement. Rather, the "way out" seems entirely murky—the "way out" to where, exactly? Together with the unknown passageways, the "way out" points to spaces that exist beyond the area presented by the dream-text, indicating a rich zone of dream space beyond that which has been captured by the dream-text. Third, the man in the dream-text is not easily reconciled with the commis, despite the commonality of their dress (white night shirt). The dream-man is little, bearded, and has a snub nose, while the commis has a "bird-like face." What is more, the commis is not always dressed in the white gown, but alternates between the "famous white one" and "a blue one with black spots" (Rhys 1999: 14). The man in the dream-text claims to be Sasha's father, a statement that strikes the dream-Sasha, and thus the reader, as dubious. The moment of doubt coincides with a startling shift in the dialogue, as the man begins to shout "murder," causing dream-Sasha to also shout "murder" and thus to mix up or confuse who is the victim of the violence and who is the perpetrator, as many critics have observed. The interpretive possibilities here seem limitless—and I tend to think that this might be the point. The simultaneous screams of "murder" catch the reader in a reflexive trap, creating an interpretive vortex. If this moment of the simultaneous "murder" screams is not interpreted, not assigned a meaning, its noise hovers eerily over the dream as a kind of sonic fog. Indeed, the dream-Sasha seems to indicate as much when she says that "the sound fills the room." It is unclear how the scene of the dream moves from stone passageway to room, but it appears as if the sound might have had a catalytic effect in this transition.

By pushing back against or resisting interpretation of the dream-text, the spatial and sensory richness of the dream opens up, gesturing back to the original dreamscape that has been translated and circumscribed. This becomes more evident at the borders—the entry and exit points—of the dream-text. Critics assume that the "Exhibition dream" is announced by the following line: "I take some more luminal, put the light out and sleep at once" (Rhys 1999: 13). The veracity of this statement, however, should give one pause. First, it is impossible to determine oneself when one has fallen asleep and entered into dream, so Sasha's clear line of demarcation must be doubted. On the previous page, Sasha is in bed and reports, "I can't sleep. Rolling from side to side…." (Rhys 1999: 12). The inclusion of the ellipsis here indicates some sort of temporal, mental, or spatial shift, the type of shift that we find typically in the flow of a dream-text. The shift, for example, from the tube station passage to the encounter with the bearded man in the white robe is occasioned by an ellipsis. After "rolling from side to side," Sasha experiences a chaotic string of memories and impressions:

> Was it in 1923 or 1924 that we lived round the corner, in the Rue Victor-Cousin, and Enno bought me that Cossack cap and the imitation astrakhan coat? It was then that I started calling myself Sasha. I thought it might change my luck if I changed my name. Did it bring me any luck, I wonder—calling myself Sasha?

> Was it in 1926 or 1927?
>
> I put the light on. The bottle of Evian on the bedtable, the tube of luminal, the two books, the clock ticking on the ledge, the red curtains....
>
> I see Sidonie carefully looking round for an hotel just like this one. She imagines that it's my atmosphere. God, it's an insult when you come to think about it! More dark rooms, more red curtains....
>
> But one mustn't put everything on the same plane. That's her great phrase. And one mustn't put everything on the same plane, either. Of course not. And this is my plane.... Quatrième a gauche, and mind you don't trip over the hole in the carpet. That's me.
>
> There are some black specks on the wall. I stare at them, certain they are moving. Well, I ought to be able to ignore a few bugs by this time. 'Il ne faut pas mettre tout sur le meme plan....'
>
> I get up and look closely. Only splashes of dirt. It's not the time of year for bugs, anyway. (Rhys 1999: 12–13, ellipses in text)

The mnemonic intrusions, hallucinations, shift of languages, and temporal shifts create an ambiguous borderland between wakefulness and dream. The phrase "more dark rooms," for example, evokes the opening line of the novel when Sasha's hotel room speaks to her with personified voice. "'Quite like old times,' the room says. 'Yes? No?'" (Rhys 1999: 9) The eerie, disembodied voice of the space sets the tone for the disjointed and multi-vocal narrative. Similar anxieties and motifs that appear in the dream-text pervade this first section, heightening its surreal quality. When describing the location of the hotel, Sasha narrates: "The street outside is narrow, cobble-stoned, going sharply uphill and ending in a flight of steps. What they call an impasse" (Rhys 1999: 9). There are obvious parallels to the dream-text here—the stone, the unidirectional quality of the way, the notion of no way out or impasse, and the general anxiety that accompanies the scene.

Line breaks and ellipses contribute to the narrative disorientation that precedes what critics consider the formal dream-text. At the end of the novel's opening, Sasha reports, "I have been here five days. I have decided on a place to eat in at midday, a place to eat in at night, a place to have my drink in after dinner. I have arranged my little life" (Rhys 1999: 9). No sooner is this relatively confident narration concluded than a line break decisively signals a profound shift in scene and mood. The story of what Sasha claims to be the previous night's events gestures toward nightmare. She is in a café or bar after dinner when a woman starts up a conversation with her. Shortly after, the woman's friend, an American, comes in and buys Sasha a brandy-and-soda. Sasha begins to cry, claiming that the outburst has been caused by "something I remembered" (Rhys 1999: 10). In reaction, "the dark woman sat up very straight and threw her chest out" (Rhys 1999: 10). The woman reproaches Sasha for her indiscretion. Sasha flees the scene and rushes to the bathroom or lavabo. Once there, the disjuncture builds:

> I stayed there, staring at myself in the glass. What do I want to cry about? … On the contrary, it's when I am quite like this, when I have had a couple of extra drinks and am quite sane, that I realize how lucky I am. Saved, rescued, fished-up, out of the deep, dark river, dry clothes, hair shampooed and set. Nobody would know I have ever been in it. Except, of course, that there always remains something. Yes, there always remains something.… Never mind, here I am, sane and dry, with my place to hide in. What more do I want?…. I'm a bit of an automaton, but sane, surely—dry, cold and sane. Now I have forgotten about dark streets, dark rivers, the pain, the struggle and the drowning.…Mind you, I'm not talking about the struggle when you are strong and a good swimmer and there are willing and eager friends on the bank waiting to pull you out at the first sign of distress. I mean the real thing. You jump in with no willing and eager friends around, and when you sink you sink to the accompaniment of loud laughter. (Rhys 1999: 10)

The multiple "reflections" in this sequence act to shatter linearity and verisimilitude, and to amplify the sense of ambiguity. The ambiguity comes primarily from either inexact language or language that indicates its opposite or that loses meaning altogether. Sasha is "quite like this"—though the "this" has no discernible meaning, even when qualified by the information that she has had a couple of drinks. She is "quite sane," another nonsensical formulation. She is "lucky," though of course the reader is aware that she has retreated, for no apparent reason, to the bathroom in tears. "Yes, there remains something," Sasha tells us, but it is impossible to determine the nature of this "something." The attempt to add clarity only enhances the ungraspable nature of the sensibility. Sasha says she is "dry and sane," though she is clearly not dry in the sense of sober and her face is full of tears, another form of wetness. How, then, precisely, is Sasha dry? The rhetorical question of what more she could want propels her deeper into a startlingly disintegrating state of mind: "I'm a bit of an automaton, but sane, surely—dry, cold and sane. Now I have forgotten about dark streets, dark rivers, the pain, the struggle and the drowning…." (Rhys 1999: 10). The claim of having forgotten the very aspects/thoughts/images that are being articulated stokes the narrative tension and fosters the surreal quality of the moment. The internal inconsistencies resound: How does "an automaton" feel pain? The contrasts between dry/wet and sanity/suffering are irreconcilable. The "loud laughter" breaks the spiral of disintegration and allows Sasha to transition to a safer space:

> Lavabos….What about a monograph on lavabos—toilets—ladies? …. A London lavabo in black and white marble, fifteen women in a queue, each clutching her penny, not a bold spirit daring to dash out of her turn past the stern-faced attendant. That's what I call discipline…. The lavabo in Florence and the very pretty, fascinatingly-dressed girl who rushes in, hugged and kissed the old dame tenderly and fed her with cakes out of a paper bag. The dancer-daughter? … That cosy little Paris lavabo, where the attendant peddled drugs—something to heal a wounded heart. (Rhys 1999: 11)

This discourse on lavabos—or on a potential book on international toilets—works as a pathway into a new scene. Sasha goes back upstairs and finds the dark woman and the American man gone. The waiter seems not to recognize her. Sasha describes his face as "blank"—again enhancing the dream-like quality of this memory. The blankness of the face immediately fades into Sasha's present moment, "I lie awake, thinking about it…." By now, this claim of being awake should be encountered with skepticism. As in the preceding scenes, with terms like "sane," "dry," and "lucky," the description of being "awake" is just as likely to indicate being not awake. In any case, Sasha falls immediately into another memory sequence that is meant to provide the rationale for her being in Paris. Sasha is in London and meets her friend Sidonie after returning from a walk. The walk itself seems as much dream-like as real: "I had just come in from my little health-stroll round Mecklenburgh Square and along the Gray's Inn Road. I had looked at this, I had looked at that, I had looked at the people passing in the street and at a shop-window full of artificial limbs" (Rhys 1999: 11). When Sasha returns, Sidonie tells her that she needs a change and should go to Paris to buy some new clothes. Sidonie offers to find her a room and to give Sasha money for the hotel and shopping. "I had not seen this woman for months and then she swooped down on me….Well, here I am. When you've been made very cold and very sane you've also been made very passive (Why worry, why worry?)" (Rhys 1999: 12). This thought leads to yet another statement about sleep: "I can't sleep. Rolling from side to side…." (Rhys 1999: 12). The return to the issue of sleep/non-sleep adds to the ambiguity of Sasha's state of being—in effect merging the zones or spaces of sleep and wakefulness, or at least creating a porous and indeterminable border between them. The intensity of this ambiguity then serves to heighten the images encountered in the scene immediately preceding the text of the "Exhibition dream." Specific images and phrases in what could be called the moment of dream-incubation point to the existence of the dream/wakefulness borderland. They include "the tube of luminal," "the clock ticking on the ledge," "the red curtains," "more dark rooms, more red curtains….," "black specks on the wall," and "only splashes of dirt" (Rhys 1999: 12–13).

The movement from the dream-text into wakefulness—the dream exit—also presents a moment of profound ambiguity and reinforces the notion that a clear demarcation of a formal dream-text is not possible. In the dream-text, dream-Sasha shouts "Murder, murder, help, help" and reports that the "sound fills the room." It is not possible to determine which room, precisely, this sound is filling. The strongest connection to the notion of "room" at this point in the novel is to the personified "room" of the opening line, the creepy voice of Sasha's hotel room. If the scream of murder is filling this room, either the dream scene has shifted perilously close to Sasha, overtaking her reality, or the screams themselves carry over into wakefulness. Either way, the sound of the screams forms a sonic connection to the next moment. Sasha says, "I wake up and a man in the street outside is singing a waltz from *Les Saltimbanques*" (Rhys 1999: 13). The scream and the singing create a mixed soundscape for the movement from dream to wakefulness—though it is left unclear exactly how they relate temporally. Moreover, the assertion "I wake up" is as unreliable as the earlier parallel statements "I can't sleep" and "I…sleep at once." The words of the street musician's song seem to cascade into Sasha's consciousness, offering the ironic counterpoint to her sense of isolation, abandonment, and hopelessness—and a stark, though comical, juxtaposition to her shouts of murder: "'C'est l'amour qui flotte dans l'air a la ronde,' he sings" (Rhys 1999: 13). The dream-like quality of this performance denies conclusion to the dream-text and leaves unresolved the relationship between the dreamscape and the subsequent narrative. This irresolution disrupts the narrative coherence of the dream-text and problematizes the search for meaning as a cohesive whole. The breakdown of the dream-text's borders serves to rupture its integrative potential.

The breakdown of the borders of the dream-text and the opening up of ambiguous borderlands—both on the periphery of the dream-text and within the dream-text itself—disrupt attempts at integrating interpretations of the dream-text with broader interpretations of the novel as a whole. What is more, these borderlands gesture toward un-narrated spaces or chaotic (in the sense of un-formed) moments: the passageways to the right and left, the transition between tunnel and room, the comingling of the screams, the relationship between the scream and the street musician, and so on. I want to suggest that this disintegration of the dream-text opens up the possibility to expand the definition of the dream-text in *Good Morning, Midnight* beyond the narrow confines of the "Exhibition dream" to include the entire novel. Like the "Exhibition dream," however, the novel-as-dream-text should not be considered a hermetic unity. Rather, the novel, like the "Exhibition dream," continuously pushes beyond its boundaries into ambiguous borderlands, like those between wakefulness and sleep, dream and reality, memory and delusion/illusion, past and present, chaos and creation. This deep ambiguity has radical implications, going beyond critiques of mass society, capitalism, and the gender politics of 1930s Western Europe.

Critics are in general agreement that *Good Morning, Midnight* is a response to the political authoritarianism sweeping Europe in the 1930s. In her book on Rhys, Elaine Savory writes: "The mid to late 1930s saw a crisis within European humanism as fascism triumphed in Spain and then in Germany. Fascism, with its emphasis on authoritarianism and conformity was the polar opposite of Rhys's idiosyncratic anarchism" (2008: 128). In a footnote to this statement, Savory says: "I use the term anarchism here because it best describes Rhys's individualistic resistance to centralized authority of all kinds" (2008: 276). Helen Carr, too, cites Rhys's opposition to fascism as the main political thrust of *Good Morning, Midnight*. Rhys, Carr writes, "is describing the febrile nightmarish world of Europe on the eve of the Second World War, with its anti-Semitism, its racism, its class-machinery, its nationalistic posturing. Rhys' writing demonstrates in fictional form Robert Young's terrifying proposition that the Holocaust was not an aberration: 'Fascism was simply colonialism brought home'" (2012: 53). Yanoula Athanassakis similarly sees Rhys's novel as a response to European power dynamics in the 1930s:

> Rhys's female protagonists in general participate in a pointed refusal to comply with networks of power outside of their control. Their movement signals an implicit critique of unjust hegemonic structures (patriarchal and colonial) and foreshadows recent developments in postcolonial feminist studies. Sasha Jensen does not *reverse* the bildungsroman process, but Rhys forcibly deconstructs and questions hegemonic forms of selfhood. Sasha (much like the other three female protagonists in the series of four post-WWI novels) is in many ways reduced to a shadow of her former self and the very statelessness she feels potentially allows a new discourse on what it means to be a racialized and sexualized subject circa 1939 in England. (2016: 14–15)

While critics are in general agreement about the political orientation of *Good Morning, Midnight*, there is some divergence about the novel's strategies of resistance—and about what, specifically, is being resisted most fervently, and how the resistance operates. For Emery, a main locus of resistance can be found in the style or formal aspects of the novel, what she calls the novel's "paradox of style" and defines as the "power to effect new discoveries in the midst of crisis and the threat it presents of empty but controlling form…" (1990: 163). The paradox demonstrates itself in two formal components that "create a complex and contradictory style…." The first component, Emery argues, is that

> Rhys presents Sasha in varying degrees of split consciousness. Isolating and fracturing Sasha's perceptions, this strategy begins with abrupt shifts from first-person narration to direct interior monologues and back again.... The narrative fracturing of time and voice portrays Sasha at her most desperate moments... These abrupt shifts from present to past portray her struggles to revive, through memory, an identity now violently disordered. (1990: 163–164)

The second component works in the reverse direction. According to Emery, "The second formal strategy, which perhaps builds on this fragmentation but also competes with it, is that of a poetic logic that combines, condenses, and potentially transforms Sasha's fragmented perceptions into newly unified acts and symbols" (1990: 164). Emery's interpretive construct opens up a new way to approach the novel's ambiguous ending, one which escapes the dichotomy of Sasha as either submitting to death or embracing rebirth. For Emery, the core meaning of the ending lies in its "disturbing"—perhaps shocking—ambiguity (1990: 169). On Sasha's final coupling with the commis, Emery writes: "In this scene, we might view Sasha as 'acting' but no longer in the sense of bringing to her performance an interpretation. Rather, the passage bears the full ambiguity of an original *act.* Her act creates a metaphor for sexual oppression that gives formal order to her experience" (1990: 169). The notion of act as metaphor bridges the two formal strategies of fragmentation and consolidation. In Emery's account, the political force of *Good Morning, Midnight* coalesces in the social, psychological, and political ambiguity of the marginalized. In 1930s Europe, the marginalized, nationless, jobless outsider—an impossible position—represents the antithesis to state power and social domination.

Even if the above interpretations of *Good Morning, Midnight* are valid—and I think they are—the question remains: what are, precisely, the foundational aspects of Rhys's anarchism or her resistance to power? Savory's idea of "Rhys's idiosyncratic anarchism" as an "individualistic" anarchism points in a potential direction, though as demonstrated by Emery, the "individual" of this individualistic anarchism is a complex, fractured, fragmented, and fundamentally ungraspable entity. Furthermore, as other critics point out, the individual can even be a site of powerlessness, unable to escape traumatized subjectivity (Linett 2005). I would like to propose a different type of "idiosyncratic anarchism" at work in *Good Morning, Midnight*, one evoked by the disintegrating quality of the novel-as-dream-text. Though the entire novel can be read as a disintegrating dream-text, that is as a dream-text collapsing back into a primordial dreamscape, the following analysis focuses on two key sections of the book that contain the most radical examples of narrative disintegration: Sasha's "birth scene" and the concluding scene of Sasha's violent confrontation with René and her seeming encounter with the commis.

Good Morning, Midnight as Disintegrating Dream-Text

Before turning to the two specific parts of the novel, it is important to establish a relationship between the form of the novel and the genre of the dream-text. The dream-text as a model for certain strains of literary modernism can be seen in works ranging from Strindberg's *A Dream Play* (1902) to Schnitzler's *Dream Story* (1926) to Joyce's *Finnegans Wake* (1939). While the form of the dream-text is often announced or framed, by the 1930s it had become pervasive enough to be presented without this formal setting-off. This accounts for the difference, for example, between the use of dream-text in Schnitzler's "Dream Story" and that in *Finnegans Wake* but does not mean that the setting-off of dream-text as a text-within-the-text disappears, as seen in Roth's *Goodbye, Columbus* and in the presentation of the "Exhibition dream" in *Good Morning, Midnight*. As I hope to have demonstrated above, however, Rhys explores the relationship between the discrete dream-text in the Freudian or Jungian sense of a separate object for investigative interrogation and the text as a whole, merging or blending textual layers so as to question or even obliterate their independence; ultimately, they are not only related but indistinguishable. Rhys's borderless dream-text of the "Exhibition dream" allows the central formal principles of dream-texts to seep out into the novel. In this sense, it is relevant that the "Exhibition dream" comes at the beginning of the novel and not in the middle (as in Freud, Roth, Blake, etc.), where narrative conventions typically dictate a curving of the narrative arc toward climax and resolution.

On a formal level, *Good Morning, Midnight* displays key features of the dream-text. Like Freud, Rhys makes frequent use of ellipses—the central typographic indicator of dream writing. In the novel's first three pages, for example, there are over ten ellipses. These ellipses do not have a recognizable and/or consistent function. They are meant as visual ruptures in the story's flow, indicative of the disjointed and dissociated nature of dreaming. Beyond the use of ellipses, the dream-text style shows itself throughout the novel in a number of other ways, which include temporal ruptures, the blending of memory and contemporaneity, the eruption of strange/out-of-context imagery, illogical or surreal associations or descriptions, linguistic confusion or loss of speech/voice, sudden spikes of anxiety or emotion, and a lack of conclusion or internal coherence of scenes. These elements can be seen by taking a close look at the section of the novel that includes Sasha's "birth scene" and ends with the shocking death of Sasha's baby (Rhys 1999: 57–61).

The scene opens in the present tense, that is, with the purportedly current temporal setting of the novel, though coming after a section break the precise temporal positioning is impossible to determine: "I get up into the room. I bolt the door. I lie down on the bed with my face in the pillow. Now I can rest before I go out again. What do I care about anything when I can lie on the bed and pull the past over me like a blanket? Back, back, back…." (Rhys 1999: 57). This seems to indicate the beginning of a memory. And yet, it is also seemingly a prelude to sleep and the coming of a dream. The reader cannot be sure, for the first ellipsis is immediately followed by a second: "…I had just come up the stairs and I had to go down them again" (Rhys 1999: 57). The shift into the past tense indicates flashback, though whether this is memory or dream remains obscure, asserting the essential borderlessness between the concepts. Nonetheless, the subsequent stream-of-consciousness makes clear that Sasha is presenting the story around the birth and death of her son. This story begins, as the novel begins, with the focus on the room. A disembodied voice speaks to Sasha: "No, no, your room's not ready. You must come back, come back. Come back between five and six" (Rhys

1999: 57). When Sasha learns that it will be over six hours until her room is ready, the voice tries to calm her, "'Courage, courage, ma petite dame,' she says, 'Everything will go well'" (Rhys 1999: 57). It is interesting to note here the move back into the present tense. In any case, after this interaction with the disembodied voice, the narrative speeds up dramatically and, as in the prelude to the memory, finds Sasha in bed on the border between sleep and wakefulness:

> I go down the stairs again, clutching the banisters, step by step.
>
> I stop a taxi. The man looks at me and hesitates. Perhaps he is afraid I may have the baby in his nice new taxi. What a thing to happen!
>
> No danger at all, I want to say. Hours and hours and hours yet, she says.
>
> I get back to the hotel and climb upstairs to my room. This is a hard thing to do. Has anybody ever had to do this before? Of course, lots of people—poor people. Oh, I see, of course, poor people....Still, it is a hard thing to do, walking around when you're like this. And half-past five is a long time off—centuries of time.
>
> When I climb the stairs again I am not seeing so well.
>
> "Courage, my little lady. Your room is ready now."
>
> A room, a bed where I can lie down. Now the worst is surely over. But the long night, the interminable night.... (Rhys 1999: 57–58)

Again, as with the "back, back, back....," the "interminable night...." presents an opening into the dreamscape, or in this case into another tier or realm of an already unfolding dreamscape, a dreamscape within a dreamscape, indicating that dream/memory contains a vortex-like force. The "interminable night...." shifts the scene as someone repeats the use of the word "courage," though it is unclear if it is the same person. As the scene unfolds, the ambiguity grows:

> "Courage, courage," she says. "All will be well. All is going beautifully."
>
> This is a funny house. There are people having babies all over the place. Anyhow, at least two are having babies.
>
> "Jesus, Jesus," says one woman. "Mother, Mother," says another.
>
> I do not speak. How long is it before I speak?
>
> "Chloroform, chloroform," I say when I speak. Of course I would. What nonsense! There is no doctor to give chloroform here. This is a place for

> poor people. Besides, she doesn't approve of chloroform. No Jesus, no Mother, and no chloroform either....
>
> What then?
>
> This.
>
> Always?
>
> Yes, always.
>
> She comes and wipes my forehead. She speaks to me in a language that is no language. But I understand it.
>
> Back, back, back.... This has happened many times.
>
> What are you? I am an instrument, something to be made us of....
>
> She darts from one room to another, encouraging, soothing, reproaching. "Now, you're not trying. Courage, courage." Speaking her old, old language of words that are not words.
>
> A rum life, which you come to think of it. I'd hate to live it. However, to her it's just life.... (Rhys 1999: 58–59)

Fragmentary thought, distant voices, unrecognizable language, repetitions, vague or even spectral figures, longings, and anxieties pervade this memory/dreamscape of Sasha's delivery of her child. The final ellipsis trails off, presumably, into the moment of birth—seemingly an unrecoverable experience that cannot be represented directly in dream/memory form. This circumambulation and thus absence of the core moment draw attention to the narrative's incompleteness. The incompleteness is radical, because it serves to call into question or deny the narrative coherence of the scene. The birth narrative, emphasized by Sasha's evocation of the Jesus/Mary relationship, dissolves into various types of ambiguity.

The post-delivery narrative is structured around an anxiety loop with Sasha lamenting her inability to sleep caused by rising anxiety about the fate or future of her child. The section emphasizes the blurred boundary between dream and wakefulness. Sasha begins, once again moving from the present tense to the past after a line break, "Afterwards I couldn't sleep. I would sleep for an hour or two, and then wake up and think about money, money, money for my son; money, money...." (Rhys 1999: 59). The word "money" acts in a similar way to the image of the apple in Frost's "After Apple-Picking." It is an endless and repeating intrusion into the narrator's consciousness, interrupting her train of thought, pushing against other images, and undermining narrative development. Money and sleep or "can't sleep" form the two axial points for a revolving circle of anxiety:

> Do I love him? Poor little devil, I don't know if I love him.
>
> But the thought that they will crush him because we have no money—that is torture.
>
> Money, money for my son, my beautiful son….
>
> I can't sleep. My breasts dry up, my mouth is dry. I can't sleep. Money, money…. (Rhys 1999: 59)

The memory/dreamscape fluctuates between moments in which it gestures toward narrative and others when narrative flow is ruptured by static concepts (money, sleep). At these points, the trajectory halts and the narrative disintegrates into phrases, words, punctuation—or even into nothingness, blankness in the form of ellipses and gaps between the paragraphs. One such narrative gap covers the seemingly un-representable moment of birth. The next spatial gap in the text comes after the repetition of "money" quoted above. Following this gap, the unnamed character exclaims:

> "Why!" she says. "Can't you sleep? This will never do."
>
> She probably knows why I can't sleep. I bet some of the others here can't either. Worrying about the same thing. (This is not *a* child; this is *my* child. Money, money….)
>
> "Well, why can't you sleep?" she says. "Does he cry, this young man?"
>
> "No, he hardly cries at all. Is it a bad sign, that he doesn't cry?"
>
> "Why no, not at all. A beautiful, beautiful baby…. But why can't you sleep?" (Rhys 1999: 59)

The unnamed woman starts to materialize out of the shadows, gaps, or blankness of the scene as Sasha describes her eyes: "She has slanting eyes, very clear. I like people with slanting eyes. I can still give myself up to people I like. (Tell me what to do. Have you a solution? Tell me what to do.)" (Rhys 1999: 59). The woman comforts Sasha, though with a confidence and calmness that betray a dubious, nightmarish quality:

> She pats me on the shoulder and says: "You're worrying about nothing at all. Everything will come right for you. I'll send you in a tisane of orange-flower water, and tonight you must sleep, sleep…."
>
> I can't feed this unfortunate baby. He is taken out and given Nestlé's milk. So, I can sleep…. (Rhys 1999: 59–60)

Though the woman has come into the foreground a bit more and now possesses at least a single material characteristic (slanted eyes), she remains mostly invisible and, more importantly, has taken on sinister attributes. She tries to assuage Sasha's well-founded anxiety about her baby, foreshadowing her role not only as midwife, but also as handmaiden of death. She administers to Sasha a seemingly helpful potion, which could very well have narcotic effects; it seems likely that the infusion is spiked with a sleep-inducing agent. Then she takes Sasha's baby away from her.

The sinister quality of the midwife increases after another line-break when Sasha describes her process of dressing the physical manifestations of pregnancy and birth with the goal of "fixing" Sasha so she appears never to have carried or delivered a child—both a real and a symbolic erasure. The process is successful: "When she takes [the bandages] off there is not one line, not one wrinkle, not one crease" (Rhys 1999: 61). This is a radically dissociative moment when Sasha's body is manipulated to conceal its past and its scars. Another line break precedes the concluding moment of the scene. Sasha reports:

> And five weeks afterward there I am, with not one line, not one wrinkle, not one crease.
>
> And there he is, lying with a ticket tied round his wrist because he died in a hospital. And there I am looking down on him, without one line, without one wrinkle, without one crease…. (Rhys 1999: 61)

The report of the death of Sasha's baby ends with an ellipsis and then a section break, shifting the narrative to Sasha's visit to the hairdresser. While the elliptical and fragmented structure of the birth memory/dream section emphasizes incompletion and open-endedness, the use of section breaks as bookends sets it apart as a discrete sub-entity. The section creates a confused and blurred reality. All physical or bodily impact from the action in the section vanishes in the transition from hospital morgue to hair salon. The slanted-eyed woman has disappeared, still nameless. Sasha's body has regained its pre-birth appearance as if the birth never happened. Scars, wrinkles, creases in flesh have disappeared. The child has died, his body gone. Like a dreamscape, the section leaves only mental, psychological, or emotional traces as the scene emerges into the "reality" of the hair salon, though it is more accurate to say that the narrative jumps from one dream-text to the next without any attempt to harmonize or justify the transition.

If the goal of the modernist dream-text is to lay a foundation for interpretation, I see the function of Rhys's birth memory/dream-text moving in the opposite direction and pointing to radical possibilities in line with the kind of anarchist conception of politics I outline in my discussions of Chuang Tzu's "transformation of things" and *hundun* and the post-Edenic origins of the dreamscape. First, this section, like the novel as a whole, is defined by rupture. The first transition from the seeming present to the memory/dream sets the stage for the scene with its two consecutive ellipses separated by a line break. These gaps in the text point to the ambiguous and unknowable relationship between dream/memory and wakefulness/reality. At the same time, the movement from one state to another lacks framing, which points to the fluidity of states of mind (and bodies). Reality, memory, dream, and perhaps even delusion/illusion exist on the same plane, fundamentally undermining hierarchical notions of being. The ruptures also serve to create a temporal mishmash in which past and present become indistinguishable, as if memory and reality, dream and wakefulness, exist in a one-dimensional, flat (perhaps cubist) structure. This flattening of the temporal dimension disrupts the linearity of narrative storytelling, which adds resistance to interpretations. Second, in contrast to the reconsolidation of selfhood in Frost's "After Apple-Picking," the characters in the birth scene resist fixed identities. They are spectral figures that depend, at times quite literally, on the existence of the other for any sort of definition or recognition. This is the case between Sasha and the slanted-eyed midwife, who spoke an "old language of words that are not words" but is nevertheless understood. A positive view of this relationship is emphasized by Deborah Kelly Kloepfer, who states: "Rhys makes explicit connection between maternity and a kind of language that is not language, not the symbolic but the rhythm, intonation, gesture, the sound of words detached from signification, words not words, old, old, back, back, thrusting into some primordial space, but it is this 'language,' as opposed to any other, that Sasha, as the material body, finally, 'understands'" (1989: 81–82). Kloepfer's insightful analysis gestures to the regressive quality of the dream-text that I emphasized in my discussion of the Garden of Eden narrative: the tendency of the dream-text to experience slippage back into the less defined dreamscape, itself bordering on pre-creation chaos. On the other hand, Kloepfer considers the relationship between the midwife and Sasha to be harmonious, whereas it contains at least an equal share of sinister darkness and quite a bit of tension. It is this dual nature of the relationship—harmony and tension—that keeps it suspended in a zone of un-interpretability. In general, the encounter between these spectral characters intensifies the chaotic movement of the scene as it lurches from rupture to rupture. The baby is the most enigmatic. He is silent and won't eat, then vanishes and reappears as a corpse. His basic inscrutability in both life and death echoes throughout the scene (and the rest of the novel) like a pulse of nausea, which can never be overcome. The silent baby becomes the paragon of the identity-less individual, the selfless self. Though he has no discernible selfhood, he is still clearly a subject. As such, he becomes a site of a multitude of intersecting projections, including the dominant one, the discourse on poverty, while still maintaining his position outside of the other characters' discursive constructs.

Rather than an anarchism as "individualistic resistance to centralized authority of all kinds," as Savory puts it, I want to suggest that *Good Morning, Midnight* expresses an even more radical form of anarchism. Individuals break into fragments of selfhood, speech falls into the vortex of silence, physical surroundings vanish and partially reemerge into amorphous and unstable places, and the temporal logic of narrative is obliterated. The borders or boundaries between people, spaces, and events are porous or even, at times, non-existent. The entirety of the text is defined by an intense and multi-layered ambiguity that opens up radical doubt without providing interpretive foundations. As such, *Good Morning, Midnight* does not assert a counter-structure to the dominant political forces coursing through the novel (nationalism, patriarchy, capitalism, racism, anti-Semitism, fascism). Instead, it undermines the possibility for the building of structures through identities, spaces, and narratives that wield power and form hierarchy, and, thus, the conditions of domination.

The final scene of *Good Morning, Midnight* can be read in light of these anarchist concepts in a way that escapes the dualism of the ending's meaning as either passive capitulation/self-sacrifice/death or rebirth through a reversal of roles. The scene (keeping in mind the ambiguity of all scenes in the book) comes at the end of an evening that Sasha spends with René. The basic sequence of action is as follows: Sasha and René have taken a taxi back to Sasha's hotel. Once there, they part ways and Sasha heads upstairs to her room. In the darkness of the hallway as Sasha is trying to unlock and enter her room, René emerges and the two of them embrace. Sasha ushers him into the room and fixes drinks for both of them. The conversation quickly turns combative. Sasha tells René to go. He refuses, forcing his way onto her in order to rape her. Defending against the aggression, Sasha tells René that he should rather just take her money, at which point René stops the rape attempt and seems to rob her. He leaves. Sasha eventually inspects the envelope with her money and sees that René has not taken anything. She falls into a series of delusions or imaginings, at the end of which she begins to try to mentally pull René back to her. Her mind seizes on him, pulling him back to the hotel and up into the room. In the meantime, Sasha has undressed and unlocked and opened her door. She gets back into bed. The person she thinks is René returning comes in and shuts the door. Sasha glances up at him and sees that the figure in her room is wearing a white dressing gown, seemingly marking him as the commis. Sasha pulls the figure down into bed, seemingly in prelude to sexual intercourse. Sasha's final words, which end the novel, are "Yes – yes – yes…." (Rhys 1999: 190).

This final scene unfolds in a similar manner to the birth scene discussed above and contains all the elements of what I call the form of the disintegrating dream-text. The final scene lacks definitive boundaries; its characters are spectral and interdependent; the flow is marked by temporal ruptures and gaps; it contains fantastical illusions/delusions; and its mood shifts swiftly from comedic to menacing. In this context, the residual elements (white robe, luminal, painting of the banjo player, etc.), which could provide the basis for an integrative interpretation, remain encased by a thick ambiguity that prevents their conjoining into a coherent interpretive structure. The result is a shocking openness of meaning—maybe even a total lack of meaning—which then poses as the sharpest possible challenge to the dominant ideological structures of the age (capitalism, patriarchy, communism, fascism).

As with the birth scene, the final scene opens with a shift in time and place. The reader is transported into a seemingly fictional realm within the novel, though this realm contains enough particles of memory that the resultant text remains highly disorienting. There is no way to distinguish between the setting and mood of this text, for example, and that of the "Exhibition dream":

> I am in a little whitewashed room. The sun is hot outside. A man is standing with his back to me, whistling that tune and cleaning his shoes. I am wearing a black dress, very short, and heel-less slippers. My legs are bare. I am watching the expression on the man's face when he turns around. Now he ill-treats me, now he betrays me. He often brings home other women and I have to wait on them, and I don't like that. But as long as he is alive and near me I am not unhappy. If he were to die I should kill myself. (Rhys 1999: 176)

This unsettling paragraph, full of co-dependency, masochism, claustrophobia, abuse, and so on, dissolves into Sasha's thought about her "film mind: My film mind…. ('For God's sake watch out for your film-mind….')" (Rhys 1999: 176). Though the scene has vanished, the mood and tensions arising in the scene remain like a fog above the subsequent action in the text, calling into question whether the rest of the final scene, too, takes place in the "film mind." Significantly, throughout the scene, cinematic elements resound.

The sound of René's whistling connects the scene before the "film-mind" interlude with the scene that follows it. Otherwise, the connections are tenuous and could be doubted. The mere belief that the male character is definitely René should be questioned, as he is unnamed for the remainder of the text. As Sasha ascends the stairs in the hotel, the lights go out and she finds herself surrounded by darkness. "Just as I have got to my door there is a click and everything is in darkness. Impossible to get the key in" (Rhys 1999: 177). The darkness casts the reader back a few pages when Sasha explicitly imagines "blackness" and "darkness" as gaps and ruptures. She reflects: "You are walking along a road peacefully. You trip. You fall into blackness. That's the past—or perhaps the future. And you know that there is no past, no future, there is only this blackness, changing faintly, slowly, but always the same" (Rhys 1999: 172). A page later, as she reenters the stream of the narration, Sasha writes: "I heave myself out of the darkness slowly, painfully. And there I am, and there he is, the poor gigolo" (Rhys 1999: 173). Amidst her dialogue with René, Sasha interrupts the conversation to present the reader with "I want to get out of this dream" (Rhys 1999: 174). The construction of the night with René as a "dream" makes her report of it a kind of "dream-text." And yet, as seen from the multitude of breaks, gaps, ellipses, fissures, and so on the dream-text is constantly slipping into other temporal or physical spaces—or, more radically, into a kind of temporal and physical emptiness, what Sasha calls a blackness or darkness, and what could also be described as a pre-narrative state of chaos, a dissolution of all modes of order.

By stepping out of the darkness on the hotel landing outside of Sasha's room, René (or the figure who is seemingly René) reactivates the "dream-text" narrative. The moment of their kiss, immediately following the recrystallization of the scene, however, begins to dissolve narrative coherence. The embrace brings Sasha's attention to the instability of her selfhood. "We kiss each other fervently," she writes, "but already something has gone wrong. I am uneasy, half of myself somewhere else" (Rhys 1999: 177). René seems to reflect Sasha's anxiety over this splitting of self when he accuses her of acting, of playing a role. In this sense, the independent existences of Rene and Sasha are called into question. As the scene of the rape intensifies, so too does Sasha's dissolution as a whole or unified selfhood. Her voice becomes disembodied, "I lie there, thinking, 'Yes, I understand'. Thinking 'For the last time'. Thinking nothing. Listening to a high, clear, cold voice. My voice" (Rhys 1999: 183). Immediately after trying to persuade René to rob her instead of raping and robbing her, she says to herself, "Don't listen, that's not me speaking.

Don't listen. Nothing to do with me—I swear it…." (Rhys 1999: 183). After René departs Sasha splits into two discrete voices:

> When he is gone I turn over on my side and huddle up, making myself as small as possible, my knees almost touching my chin. I cry in the way that hurts right down, that hurts your heart and your stomach. Who is this crying? The same one who laughed on the landing, kissed him and was happy. This is me, this is myself, who is crying. The other—how do I know who the other is? She isn't me. (Rhys 1999: 184)

The voice of this "other" begins to assert itself. The voice is hostile to Sasha and follows René in describing Sasha's actions—indeed her entire stay in Paris—as theater, as a final performance. The inner, though foreign, voice gives way to Sasha's addressing of the banjo player in the painting she purchased from the Russian Jewish painter Serge: "I know the words to the tune you're playing. I know the words to every tune you've ever played on your bloody banjo. Well, I mustn't sing any more—there you are. Finie la chanson. The song is ended. Finished" (Rhys 1999: 185).

A break in the text ushers in a bewildering mix of voices and illusions. Elements of the narrative force themselves into the scene, not as symbolic elements but rather as part of a chaotic stew:

> A hum of voices talking, but all you hear is "Femmes, femmes, femmes, femmes…." And the noise of a train saying: "Paris, Paris, Paris, Paris…." Madame Vénus is angry and Phoebus Apollo is walking away from me down the boulevard to hide himself in la crasse. Only address: Mons P. Apollo, La Crasse…. But I know quite well that all this is hallucination, imagination. Venus is dead; Apollo is dead; even Jesus is dead. (Rhys 1999: 187)

In other words, no valid paradigm of analysis remains for Sasha or the reader. As if to emphasize the breakdown of a type of coherence achieved through the application of an interpretive perspective or system of understanding, Sasha offers the following image:

> All that is left in the world is an enormous machine, made of white steel. It has innumerable flexible arms, made of steel. Long, thin arms. At the end of each arm is an eye, the eyelashes stiff with mascara. When I look more closely I see that only some of the arms have these eyes—others have lights. The arms that carry the lights are all extraordinarily flexible and very beautiful. But the grey sky, which is the background, terrifies me.... And the arms wave to an accompaniment of music and song. Like this: "Hotcha—hotcha—hotcha...." And I know the music; I can sing the song.... (Rhys 1999: 187)

The image is followed by another gap in the text, during which the "other" voice inside of Sasha vanishes. Then, yet another voice rings out inside of Sasha, speaking to her in the second person—another fracturing: "Put your coat on and go after him. It isn't too late, it isn't too late. For the last time, for the last time...." (Rhys 1999: 187). It is unclear what this voice means by it not being "too late" or it being the "last time." Sasha then begins her process of catching him with her thoughts and reeling him back to her:

> Come back, come back, come back....
>
> This is the effort, the enormous effort, under which the human brain cracks. But not before the thing is done, not before the mountain moves.
>
> Come back, come back, come back....
>
> He hesitates. He stops. I have him. (Rhys 1999: 188)

Sasha addresses the now silent man, ordering him to return to her. In the meantime, she readies herself for his reentry, unlocking the door, stripping naked, and getting into bed. Again, however, there is a dissociative element introduced. "I get into bed. I lie there trembling, I am very tired./Not me, no. Don't worry, it's my sale cerveau that's so tired. Don't worry about that—no more sale cerveau" (Rhys 1999: 189). Moments later, Sasha says, "Now I am simple and not afraid; now I am myself" (Rhys 1999: 189). This could be seen as the culminating articulation of identity in the novel. The assertion of being oneself can, however, only be read with utter skepticism. It comes after multiple scenes of fracturing, rupture, and splitting, as well as amid a hallucinatory fantasy/nightmare. When this phantasm of René enters the room and shuts the door, Sasha refuses at first to look at him. "I lie still, with my arm over my eyes. As still as if I were dead…." (Rhys 1999: 190). The ellipsis is followed by a line break, installing a rupture before the final scene in which René seemingly transforms into the commis. It is wrong, I think, to assume that the figure entering the room before the break is the commis. It is (or could very well be) the figure of René. Somewhere in the chaos of the dreamscape, however, the transmutation takes place. The fact that the transmutation occurs without visual verification—"I don't need to look. I know"—supports the reading of this final scene as dream-text. The erotic sadomasochistic fantasy of seduction or domination by the rapist slips into another type of narrative in which Sasha gives herself to or takes the commis. Yet both narrative strains remain incomplete and shrouded in multiple layers of ambiguity. Any possible conclusion about the scene's meaning is excluded.

The radical doubt that results from Rhys's disintegrating dream-text precludes the application of first or foundational principles. The Descartian answer to doubt—the assertion of self (I think therefore I am)—is obliterated by the seemingly endless splitting and fracturing. Descartes's fear of the inability to distinguish between dream and reality takes on new life as Rhys's multi-layered and multi-perspectival text presents all impulses on the same plane. Everything—whether dream, reality, delusion, memory, imagination, hallucination—becomes part of the same text with no way to create a hierarchy of truthfulness among them. The Freudian answer to doubt is the application of psychoanalytic method—but this requires precisely the distinguishing between dream and reality through a clearly delineated dream-text, the likes of which Jung also employs. Rhys's refusal to contain the dream-text and her expansion of the dream-text throughout the narrative resist this analytic method. Rhys's attack on fixed conceptions of identity, the autonomy of selfhood, the separateness of characters, narrative coherence and logic, temporal and spatial order, the division between dream/nightmare and reality (or even between one dream and another) leaves radical doubt intact. This radical doubt stands opposed to coherence, definitions, systems, and structures of any kind—and while this, too, could be described as a "meaning," it is so in the sense of an openness to the multiplicity of meaning. Only such a radical refusal of foundations could stand against the seemingly totalistic systems of the day, whether fascism, communism, or capitalism. By opening up meaning to multiplicity, refusing coherence and the stability of definitions, and by undermining the clarity of language and communication, *Good Morning, Midnight* poses a challenge to psychoanalysis, racism, antisemitism, and first and foremost to the patriarchal formations which are contained in all of these hierarchical systems or structures of oppression. This expression of antithesis is not a positive vision, nor does it represent a new mode of existence. It is darkness, chaos, marginality, shadow—a slippage back into the dreamscape. Rhys's "serpent," the representative in the novel of the state of the primal "deep," the state of pre-creation, is the ellipsis (…) or (….)—the ultimate unknowable nature of the dreamscape is here, a Freudian navel without Freud.

Conclusion

This chapter has argued that modernist dream-texts tend to function as tools of narrative and thematic integration. Narrative and thematic constructs built around the dream-texts work to delineate and circumscribe meaning. Following Freud, these dream-texts are clearly set off from non-dream-texts and invite interpretation of their content from the vantage point of the main text's dominant system or structure. In the case of Freud, as I discuss in the previous chapter, this system is built on his general principles of psychodynamics. This chapter has presented two examples of the integrative function of dream-texts, one primarily narrative and thematic (Roth) and one primarily structural or systemic (Jung). My discussion of the "Island dream" in *Goodbye, Columbus* proposes that the integrative work of the dream-text is built on a host of identity constructs and social/racial hierarchies. While the novella can be read in diverse ways, these various "meanings" obit around a deeper core forged by these constructs and hierarchies. Roth's novella, centered on the dream-text, harnesses these identity constructs and hierarchies in the service of plot and character development, thus embedding what I would call authoritarian thinking into the fabric of the narrative.

The example of Jung's "Individual Dream Symbolism in Relation to Alchemy" picks up the argument about the use of dream analysis as psychological or philosophical systems-building. Like Freud, Jung aspires to a total understanding of the psyche and views dreaming as the key pathway for unveiling otherwise hidden aspects of the individual. The notion of "wholeness" is important for Jung in two senses. First, he understands the individual as a "whole"—one that must somehow reconcile the internal psyche or persona with what he describes as the "collective unconscious." Second, he views the collective cultural legacy of the world as a whole or system, connected by an elaborate grid of concepts that are embedded in a symbolic code. The role of the Jungian analyst becomes the mastery of this code and its application to the specific information provided by the patient, thereby joining the individual case with the collective in its unique way. In "Individual Dream Symbolism in Relation to Alchemy," the dream-texts provide both the raw material for this process of merging persona with collective conscious, thus defining the psychological dynamics of the individual, and the narrative structure for the achievement of "wholeness." I argue in this chapter that Jung's process of dream analysis is a radicalization of the authoritarian impulses of Freudian dream interpretation. For all intents and purposes, the Jungian mode erases the patient from the case study. The dream-texts are edited and arranged to serve the case's narrative and philosophical agenda. The incorporation of a vast array of knowledge about world cultures places the analyst far above the patient in terms of expertise. The analyst assigns meaning to each component in the system.

Rhys's *Good Morning, Midnight* cuts against the narrative, thematic, and systematic push toward integration and wholeness. The novel tears the dream-text out of its confined and separated/specified place in the narrative and infuses its elements into the entirety of the work, thereby dissolving both the integrity of the dream-text and opening up the whole text to dream-logic (or illogic). This infusion of the dream-text into the novel is made manifest most obviously by the work's frequent use of ellipses, line breaks, and temporal and spatial ruptures. I argue that by expanding or exploding the dream-text into the novel as a whole, Rhys creates a text of radical doubt and ambiguity, a text that refuses or slips away from all possible meanings or interpretations. Though various interpretations can be proposed, the novel remains, I argue, beyond interpretation. This "beyond," I contend, gestures beyond the dream-text to the field of the primordial, pre-textual dreamscape, to *hundun* or the "the deep." My argument that *Good Morning, Midnight* can be productively seen as a collapsing or disintegrating dream-text offers an alternative framework for reading the novel, one that builds on (and incorporates) key insights by critics like Maslen, Emory, Savory, Carr, and others, but also provides a new view of a specific anarchistic politics in Rhys's work.

One moment in the novel, it seems to me, frames the basic anarchistic impulse in *Good Morning, Midnight*, and relates directly to the "Exhibition dream" discussed above. The scene comes toward the end of the novel when Sasha is out at night with the supposed gigolo. She reveals to him that the only people with whom she has had a good connection in Paris were the two Russians. The gigolo's response to this is a xenophobic and antisemitic exclamation. Sasha reacts: "For some reason I am very vexed by this. I start wondering why I am there at all, what I am doing in this box of a restaurant, swapping dirty stories with a damned gigolo. I want to get away. I want to be out of the place" (Rhys 1999: 163). Interestingly, Sasha decides at this moment that she wants to see the Exhibition, reversing the terms of the dream-text, in which the Exhibition was "in" as opposed to the "way out." Here, the Exhibition offers the means to "get away" or to "be out of the place." Sasha and the gigolo arrive at the Exhibition, entering through the Trocadéro. Presumably, they are gazing down the corridor framed by the Nazi and Soviet pavilions, looking at the "Star of Peace." René, the gigolo, calls the star pathetic, adding, "It's vulgar, that Star of Peace" (Rhys 1999: 163). Sasha responds by saying that the building is "very fine" and narrates, "We stand on the promenade above the fountains, looking down on them. This is what I wanted—the cold fountains, the cold, rainbow lights on the water…." (Rhys 1999: 164). René cuts in again, "It's mesquin," he says, "your Star of Peace" (Rhys 1999: 164). The Star of Peace acts as a site of projected longing for Sasha here, a glimmer of hope framed by the daunting and massive Nazi and Soviet structures. This is a romantic longing, a notion that some inherent or central goodness can keep the antagonistic totalitarian ideologies at bay. That the Star of Peace is situated where it is, that it draws Sasha to its defense, indicates the futility of this romantic choice. Inside the structures of the Exhibition, real resistance does not exist—only false hope. This non-"way out" reanimates the idea of the desire for a "way out" in the "Exhibition dream." The novel does not propose a direct response or solution to this problem: how to find the "way out" of the "exhibition" space (perhaps expanded into the entirety of Paris or even modernity/the modern metropolis) that itself plays host to fascism, Soviet communist totalitarianism, and hyper-capitalism? The "way out" crystalizes through the explosion of the dream-text into the entire fabric of the novel, tearing its temporal and spatial coherence, unsettling fixed identities, proposing/testing/exploring shifting relational dynamics between the characters (without settling on any fixed roles), undermining the coherence of language through the use of ambiguity and rupture. Rhys's anarchism of the dreamscape models an emancipatory "way out," revealing that the architecture of power is as artificial as the Exhibition's pavilions and as transitory as the crowd that gathers there. The authoritarian and hierarchical ideologies built towers that tried to outdo each other in height, a mode that can be represented as a vertical line: |. To the vertical, Rhys juxtaposes horizontal movement, the ellipsis... as anarchic act, as emancipatory "way out," a pathway opened by the dissolving dream-text back into the dis-integrated dreamscape. In the following chapter on Franz Kafka, I develop this notion of "escape" or "way out" by identifying the concept of the dreamscape in his novel *The Castle* as a rupture or tear in the hermetic order of power. This rupture exposes the imaginary or mythic quality of hierarchy and authority and provokes a sense of freedom in its purest possible form—an idea of freedom detached from any conjoined preposition (from, to, for, etc.). While scholars have defined Kafka's politics with a wide range of definitions, none has attempted to capture the politics of Kafka's work on dreams.

Notes

1. Eric Sundquist writes, "Although the Nuremberg Laws might be traced circuitously to the anti-Semitism of medieval and early modern Europe, the perversions and predatory behavior ascribed to Jews by Nazism were derived more directly from works of nineteenth-century racial science that

tended to group Jews and blacks together in their proscription of miscegenation. Jews were deemed a dangerous mongrel race, carriers of pestilence and disease, including tuberculosis and syphilis, and their propensity for hybridization, resulting in pathological 'blackness,' was said to derive from an intermixture of Negro blood or their descent from African tribes" (2009: 183). See also Goldhagen (7–15), Mosse (1985: 105–112), Gilman (1991: 99–102, 171–176). For a critical analysis of the black-Jewish thesis, see HaCohen (2018).

2. In contrast to the presentation of Brenda as a JAP by both Neil and, following Neil, most of critics of the novella, Barbara Waxman offers a more sympathetic portrait of Brenda through a psychological reading of both characters. Interestingly, though, while Waxman finds a more sympathetic Brenda in this reading, she does not fundamentally shift the terms of the debate. She writes, "And Brenda Patimkin turns out to be less the arrogant and confident 'Jewish Bitch Goddess' than the vulnerable young Jewish woman, yearning for autonomy and integrity while struggling to reclaim a place in her uncharitable mother's heart" (1988: n.p.).

References

Athanassakis, Yanoula. "The Anxiety of Racialized Sexuality in Jean Rhys." *Anthurium* 13.2 (2016): n.p.

Carr, Helen. *Jean Rhys*. Horndon: Northcote House, 2012.

Dohe, Carrie B. "Wotan and the 'Archetypal *Ergriffenheit*': Mystical Union, National Spiritual Rebirth and Culture-Creating Capacity in C. G. Jung's 'Wotan' Essay." *History of European Ideas* 37.3 (2011): 344–356.

Emery, Mary L. *Jean Rhys at "World's End": Novels of Colonial and Sexual Exile*. Austin: U of Texas P, 1990.

France, Alan W. "Roth's 'Goodbye, Columbus' and the Limits of Commodity Culture." *MELUS* 15.4 (2008): 83–89.

Gilman, Sander L. *The Jew's Body*. New York: Routledge, 1991.

HaCohen, Ran. "The 'Jewish Blackness' Thesis Revisited." *Religions* 9.7 (2018): 222+.

Jackson, Kenneth T. *Crabgrass Frontier: The Suburbanization of the United States*. New York: Oxford UP, 1985.

Jung, C. G. *Dreams*. Trans. R.F.C. Hull. Princeton: Princeton UP, 2010.

Jung, C. G. *Collected Works* Vol. 7. Trans. Gerhard Adler and R.F.C. Hull. Princeton: Princeton UP, 1972.

Jung, C. G. *Psychology and Religion*. New Haven: Yale UP, 1938.

Kloepfer, Deborah K. *The Unspeakable Mother: Forbidden Discourse in Jean Rhys and H.D.* Ithaca: Cornell UP, 1989.

Knapp, James. "Primitivism and Empire: John Synge and Paul Gauguin." *Comparative Literature* 41.1 (1989): 53–68.

Linett, Maren. "'New Words, New Everything': Fragmentation and Trauma in Jean Rhys." *Twentieth Century Literature* 51.4 (2005): 437–466.

Maslen, Cathleen. *Ferocious Things: Jean Rhys and the Politics of Women's Melancholia*. Newcastle-upon-Tyne: Cambridge Scholars Publishing, 2009.

Mosse, George. *Toward the Final Solution: A History of European Racism*. Madison: U of Wisconsin P, 1985.

Pietikainen, Petteri. "The Volk and its Unconscious: Jung, Hauer and the 'German Revolution.'" *Journal of Contemporary History* 35.4 (2000): 523–539.

Pinsker, Sanford. "Philip Roth." *Dictionary of Literary Biography 28: Twentieth-Century American-Jewish Fiction Writers*. Ed. Daniel Walden. Detroit: Gale, 1984. 264–275.

Rhys, Jean. *Good Morning, Midnight*. New York: Norton, 1999.

Rome, Adam. *The Bulldozer in the Countryside: Suburban Sprawl and the Rise of American Environmentalism*. Cambridge: Cambridge UP, 2001.

Roth, Philip. *Goodbye, Columbus and Five Short Stories*. New York: Bantam Books, 1969.

Savory, Elaine. *Jean Rhys*. Cambridge: Cambridge UP, 2008.

Silvey, Patrick. "'I'm Just Jewish…' Defining Jewish Identity in Philip Roth's 'Goodbye Columbus and 'Five Short Stories.'" *Philip Roth Studies* 10.1 (2014): 59–76.

Sundquist, Eric. *Strangers in the Land: Blacks, Jews, Post-Holocaust America*. Cambridge: Belknap Press of Harvard UP, 2009.

Waxman, Barbara. "Jewish American Princesses, Their Mothers, and Feminist Psychology: A Rereading of Roth's 'Goodbye, Columbus.'" *Studies in Jewish American Literature* 7.1 (1988): 90–104.

Welten, Ruud. "Paul Gauguin and the Complexity of the Primitivist Gaze." *Journal of Art Historiography* 12 (2015): 12+.

Wilhelm, Randall. "Seeing Paul Gauguin in Philip Roth's 'Goodbye, Columbus.'" *Philip Roth Studies* 10.2 (2014): 47–60.

6

Dreams and Power in Kafka's *The Castle*

Introduction

"Deeply lost in the night," begins Kafka's prose fragment "At Night" (1920). This sense of being "lost" points in at least two directions—it is a loss of one's bearings or one's notion of place in a physical space or territory, and it is a loss of one's self or identity. "Just as one lowers one's head to reflect, thus to be utterly lost in the night" (Kafka 1995: 436). The state of the writer bent over the desk at night (when Kafka did most of his writing) and the state of sleep during which wakefulness gives way to dream are blended, entangled in this image (Schwenger 2012: 74–76). This confluence of writing and sleeping can be seen in one of Kafka's iconic notebook drawings of a man bent down over his desk in an ambiguous position between sleep and thinking/writing/suffering. The tension of the blurred boundary between writer and dreamer persists in the fragment "At Night," "All around people are asleep. It's just play acting, an innocent self-deception, that they sleep in houses, in safe beds, under a safe roof, stretched out or curled up on mattresses, in sheets, under blankets…" (Kafka 1995: 436). In this nighttime scene, borders and boundaries are fluid, illusory; it is a kind of theater, the same type of theater that

© The Author(s), under exclusive license to Springer Nature Switzerland AG 2021

S. Rogoff, *The Politics of the Dreamscape*,
https://doi.org/10.1007/978-3-030-74796-1_6

reveals itself in one of Kafka's earlier dreams that I will describe later in this chapter in which the divisions between audience and actors have disappeared or are constantly shifting. "At Night" continues:

> …in reality, they have flocked together, as they had once upon a time and again later in a deserted region, a camp in the open, a countless number of men, an army, a people, under a cold sky on cold earth, collapsed where once they had stood, forehead pressed on the arm, face to the ground, breathing quietly. (Kafka 1995: 436)

The text has entered a new space—seemingly a dreamscape, a "deserted region," one that conjures images of a different social organization and way of life, perhaps tribal, nomadic, certainly more intense and exposed to the elements.

Peter Schwenger places his analysis of "At Night" in his chapter "Sleepless" and reads the fragment as an insomnia text rather than as a dream-text. For Schwenger, Kafka's piece expresses the following: "For if the insomniac writer has the terrible privilege of access to a knowledge that is fundamentally other, along with that comes an equally terrible responsibility: to write it" (2012: 74). While Schwenger presents an impressive and thoughtful analysis of "At Night," and while I agree with him when he characterizes the "homelessness" of the piece and its "vaguely delineated primitivism," I do not think he accounts for the movement of subjectivity in the fragment. The displacement into the "deserted region" is not symbolic but real—and such a shift of place indicates that this is not a metaphorical piece about insomnia but rather a piece about the disorienting experience of moving across the borders of sleep into the dreamscape.

Schwenger, again, reads the following passage metaphorically: "Are you watching? Are you one of the watchmen," the text continues, "you find the next one by brandishing a burning stick from the brushwood pile beside you. Why are you watching? Someone must watch, it is said. Someone must be there" (Kafka 1995: 436). For Schwenger, the writer is the watchman, a rare breed of observer who confronts what the masses cannot see and cannot handle seeing. He writes:

> Only in the watchers of the night, when anodyne sleep has failed us, do we glimpse something of the impersonal existence that bears up what we like to think of as "our" existence. This nocturnal revelation comes notably to the writer—or writers, since the speaker here is only one of a number of watchmen, scattered at distant intervals in the dark. For Kafka, his fellow watchmen would have been authors such as Hugo von Hofmannsthal or Robert Walser. Their lights are few and far between, and are unheeded by the sleepers. (2012: 75–76)

There are a number of errors in this description. First, if the "watcher" is the "writer" then the "nocturnal revelation" does not, in fact, come to him but to the narrator. While the watchman is being identified by the narrative voice as a watchman (indirectly through a question!), the addressee does not necessarily seem to understand himself as one. In addition, the "speaker" of the piece is not a watchman, but a voice questioning the figure of the watchman—the "you." The identification of the watchmen with writers—Kafka, Hofmannsthal, Walser—could be right, but if it is, these writers are not heroic observers of the human condition, but rather lost subjectivities in the wilderness, groping for contact with each other by the most inauspicious means. In contrast to this interesting but ultimately limited metaphorical reading of the fragment as being about the nocturnal revelations of the insomniac writer, I read "At Night" as concerning the disruptive, disintegrating movement over the border of wakefulness into the dreamscape. It is this movement that creates the new space, the piece's energy, and its openness to meaning. In this nomadic encampment of the dreamscape, the watchmen are nearly blinded by the darkness. They can only perceive whatever exists in the immediate surroundings of their homemade torches—all else blurs into the blackness. The watchmen, then, "watch" nothing—but at the same time "must watch," as a dream-I cannot but experience the unfolding of a dream, cannot prevent being devoured by the dreamscape. The watchmen seem not to be looking out for an enemy. The "you" is not guarding the encampment. The "you" is, rather, trying to make contact with another watchman—most likely to establish his own existence and to understand where and even who he is—a subject only defined through the encounter with an equally undefined "other."

The worlds of Kafka's stories operate as hermetic territories—even if they are defined by clashing and hierarchically arranged systems. "At Night" offers a kind of trapdoor in the system—an escape from what seems like a hermetically closed or sealed territory into a parallel zone. These trapdoors are almost nonexistent in Kafka's work—the oppressive beauty and tragicomedy of which rely precisely on the seeming completeness of their enclosure. Yet the prose fragment points to a possible way out of sealed territories—through the dream and into the "adjacent" space of the dreamscape, a dreamscape defined by its nomadism, opacity, and partiality—partiality in terms of space and subject. This movement into the dreamscape ruptures understandings of one's position in space, society, and culture—leaving identity or selfhood in tatters. For Kafka, the movement into the dreamscape, precisely because it shatters the territoriality of the hermetic "real," presents an opportunity to affirm freedom, even if it is the freedom of the watcher to grope rather helplessly by torchlight in the dark. Although this movement—which I have argued throughout this study is one into anarchic politics—is seldom realized in Kafka's work, one particularly rich example is K.'s dream in *The Castle.* By reading K.'s dream against Kafka's conception of power in *The Castle*, *The Trial*, and selected shorter works, I argue that Kafka's most radical political expression, the expression of freedom in *The Castle*'s dream scene, relies on an understanding of dream experience that is grounded in notions of disintegration, intensity, and escape.

While gesturing toward the anarchist tradition of striving for freedom from dominant socio-cultural power structures, the type of anarchism that I identify in Kafka's work is non-systematic and seemingly ephemeral. Its very smallness in the text indicates its relationship to power. Mechanisms of control, hierarchies, and oppressive systems are large and complex (often convoluted) in Kafka's work, while the countertendencies toward freedom are minuscule. I propose, however, that this smallness is part of the design of Kafka's anarchistic impulse—as the smallest hole in a tire defines the entire tire as either functional or not, the "hole," in a sense, becoming the "whole." When looking at Kafka as an anarchist, it is more generative, it seems to me, to find such a political pinprick rather than to look for a systematic expression of anarchism or a fully developed political ideology. Perhaps anarchism itself would do better to create strategic "holes" rather than to reinvent the wheel. These holes would work to destabilize the structures that systems of domination use to wield their power. The act of making these punctures opens the space for freedom.

Power in "The Judgment," "In the Penal Colony," and *The Trial*

Interpretations of the way Kafka deals with issues of power have been central to the analysis of his work. The most common ways of understanding how power functions in Kafka's work link it to modern notions of authoritarianism and totalitarianism in politics, and to the bureaucratization of society.[1] The seemingly all-encompassing nature of power in the texts is emphasized, as is the seemingly helpless plight of the individual caught in the maw of a great social, legal, or political machine. While I do not have any direct interest in overturning these interpretations or rejecting them, I would like to propose an alternative understanding of the way power functions in the novels *The Trial* and *The Castle* with reference to Kafka's short works, particularly the stories "The Judgment" and "In the Penal Colony." My central argument is that while power in Kafka's work tends to operate in seemingly hermetic zones, with nothing outside their system or reach, the structures of authority that wield power are deeply unstable and incredibly fragile—always on the verge of collapse. The drive for a hermetic system of authority appears as a symptom of this fragility and points to a kind of fatalism. Kafka's authorities are fading, weakening, vanishing—the power they have will soon be replaced by more dominant structures, which might be less overtly menacing but are nonetheless threatening in indirect ways. The central protagonists of the two novels I discuss here, Joseph K. in *The Trial* and K. in *The Castle*, are the targets of the authorities precisely because they make manifest the breakdown of a system of authority and its imminent replacement by a more powerful structure. The vigilance of the authorities in *The Trial* and *The Castle* is one of desperation, the last (though not insubstantial) gasp of a crumbling order. And yet, what will replace this order is nothing to celebrate—it is the hegemonic force of a new power: a type of rational, atomistic, rootless modernity that is present in *The Trial* and on the outskirts of *The Castle*.

The notion of a dominant yet fragile authority in Kafka's work can be traced back to the early story "The Judgment" (1912). The power dynamic in this story revolves around the relationship between Georg Bendemann, a young merchant, and his father. The father is the dominant force in the story, and Georg is attempting to break out of his father's sphere of control or, at least, his massive shadow (Pan 2000; Sokol 1977). The attempt proves futile. The father crushes Georg, who is driven to suicide by jumping from a bridge. Even as he is about to plummet to his death, Georg reaffirms his dedication to his father, "With weakening grip he was still holding on when he spied between the railings a motor-bus coming which would easily cover the noise of his fall, called in a low voice, 'Dear parents, I have always loved you, all the same'" (Kafka 1995: 88). Georg's suicide indicates that the father exercises incredible power over him, a type of all-encompassing power or authoritarianism within the family. Despite this power, however, the father is not described in the story as a typical domineering patriarch. He is physically weak, bedridden, and dependent on Georg for care. When Georg starts to change his father's clothes, he takes full measure of the latter's infirmity—and it is precisely at the moment when Georg understands his father's dependency on him that the father strikes back with the vicious attack that precipitates Georg's suicide.

Georg nurtures hope of breaking out of (or inverting) the father-son binary. The father knows this, and although he is deteriorating and does not have much time left (it seems), he understands how to destroy his son's psychological and emotional stability in order for his position of authority to continue—in this case by preventing Georg's marriage and the emergence of an independent nuclear family. On the other hand, the destruction of the son does not change the basic fact that the father is infirm, dependent, and likely dying. The destruction of Georg is as much a suicidal impulse of the father as a homicidal one. The father is not likely to thrive or even survive for long without the son. Thus, the father's destruction of Georg is the dying blow of a weakening patriarch; a combination of apparent total power (in Georg's eyes) and utter powerlessness defines the father.

"In the Penal Colony" contains a similarly fragile and fleeting authority. Like "The Judgment," "In the Penal Colony" presents two distinct loci of power—one represented by the officer and his method of execution by means of the old commandant's torture machine and the other by the new commandant of the colony and his retinue. These loci of power contain whole systems of authority and philosophies of rule, including understandings of legality, individuality, and social organization (Cumberland 2013; Tulley 2018). Two elements of the story are critical as a foregrounding to my discussion of power in *The Trial* and *The Castle*. First, the authority of the officer as the representative of the old commandant is positioned as fundamentally incompatible with the new system being constructed by the new commandant of the island. Though there is a period of tense coexistence, the implication is that at some point the struggle between the two systems needs to be resolved with one system triumphing over the other—and this seems to happen toward the end of the story. The character of the explorer or visitor to the penal colony is being used as a pawn in the contest between the officer and the new commandant. In the very presence of the explorer, who identifies almost totally with the new commandant's regime, the outcome of the struggle is clear—the officer's reign is coming to an end. Realizing this, the officer sacrifices himself in his own machine. In an inversion of "The Judgment," the "son" has killed the "father."

Despite the apparent tidy history of one regime of power asserting itself over another, the social dynamics on the island at the end of the story are not as clear as they might seem. While the old commandant's power has been broken at the level of administrative authority, his power as a system of belief has not been eradicated from the colony. The ambiguity is reflected at the end of the story when the explorer finds himself in a teahouse where the old commandant is buried beneath the floor. The implication of the explorer's discovery of the grave in the teahouse is that the apparent final defeat of the old commandant (represented by the self-sacrifice/suicide of the officer) is only one stage of the historical process envisioned by the former leader. The real, material power of the old commandant, which continued through the officer and his use of the old commandant's machine and punishment plans, has now transformed into the basis for a *potential* underground movement of dissent against the new authorities on the island, one based on messianic faith in the old commandant's future return and the ability of this faith to create and sustain a cohesive following. From primarily legal and political, the old commandant's authority has become social and cultural. The fact that the followers of the old commandant have to remain in the shadows indicates that they are a minority or perhaps a suppressed majority. The following's continued existence thus points to the tense relationship between subcultural forces and the political hegemony of the ruling class and its ideology. The two worldviews confront each other as inherent antagonists. Liberal notions of rights and a sense of historical and linear progress toward reason and "justice" define the worldview of the new commandant. Traditional notions of community and a messianic understanding of time (as cyclical and divinely ordained) underpin the worldview of the old commandant. The explorer is caught between these paradigms of authority and while almost entirely of the new mode, he cannot rid himself of a nostalgic appreciation, a longing (perhaps a desire) for the old. Paradoxically, he seems to be drawn closer to the machine and its operator, the officer, as he notices the ways in which it is breaking down by neglect.

The portrait of power becomes more complex and mysterious in the novel *The Trial*. Here, the antagonistic authorities previously represented by the father/son relationship or the relationship between the old and new commandants are translated into two systems or societies occupying the same landscape—the modern city. The two systems can be roughly defined as the system of the "bank," meaning that which follows the rules of individualist, rights-bearing, contractual society based on clear legal processes and administrative operations, and the system of the "trial," which is vague, mysterious, amorphous, clandestine, and depends on communal or interpersonal relationships—not processes. While the novel is fundamentally about the power of the second system, that of the "trial," the more powerful position is occupied by the other, the world of the "bank." The fragility or infirmity of the trial system goes a long way in explaining its vehemence and the intensity with which it tries and then executes the novel's protagonist, Joseph K. But the execution of

Joseph K. is a sign of weakness, of the trial's inability to successfully integrate him into its system. The world of the trial is marginal—it strikes at the center, at the world of the bank, from the periphery. It is a challenge that is fated for failure, but not before it destroys Joseph K.

In his illuminating discussion of Kafka as anarchist in *The Trial*, David Tulley presents the nature of the trial as one emanating from, not against, the modern state. He writes, "In presenting the court as a totalising and pervasive force in society, which individualises itself in human subjects, Kafka suggests that 'to live outside the trial' would entail a wide-ranging social transformation, the successful subversion and dismantling of the subjectifying power of the state and all forms of hegemonic power" (2018: 26). This is precisely the opposite of what Kafka indicates in the novel. To "live" outside the trial, precisely, is to live *in* the modern state with its legal and economic logic. To live "in the trial" is to submit to the forces/hierarchies of the trial society. One might be able to straddle these two zones of subjection, to move from one to the other, but there is no possibility shown in the novel of escaping hegemonic power completely.

The ostensible setting for Kafka's novel is the world of the bank. The story unfolds in a modern city, which operates (at least on the surface) by modern rules. In this bank world, clear hierarchical relationships exist between people. For example, Joseph K. holds a position in the bank hierarchy—he has subordinates and superiors; he understands quite well who is above and who below him. This bank world is governed by time, by the clock. The temporal divisions of the clock create the structure of daily life, built, of course, around the working hours. Space in the world of the bank is clean, airy, and orderly. Social relationships are governed by well-established norms of social etiquette (and deviance), including those of sexual and domestic life. The prevailing ethos of the bank world is rational and individualist—each member of society possesses rights and can exercise them in the face of challenges through clear and rational/logical/legal arguments and procedures. The spirit of the bank world is atomistic. In pursuit of individual goals and ambitions—or simply as a product of the general ethos of such a society—the individual becomes divorced from deeper community structures and traditions, even from the wider family or kinship network. In this regard, Joseph K., it seems, is totally alone.

The articulation of the values and guiding notions of the bank world only arises in reaction to its confrontation with the trial—otherwise these values would remain in the realm of common sense, habit, and norm. The narrative voice seems to enter Joseph K.'s thoughts as he processes his "arrest" at the beginning of the novel: "What authority could they represent? K. lived in a country with a legal constitution, there was a universal peace, all the laws were in force; who dared seize him in his own dwelling…" (Kafka 1992: 4). Soon after this, Joseph K. demands that the arresting authorities abide by the expected legal procedures. "But how can I be under arrest? And particularly in such a ridiculous fashion?" Faced with their refusal to answer, he continues, "Here are my papers, now show me yours, and first of all your warrant for arresting me" (Kafka 1992: 5). When the arresting parties cannot fulfill Joseph K.'s demands for procedural clarity, he reasons that the affair cannot be of great importance—events gain meaning for Joseph K. through their relationship to the established norms:

> …on the other hand, it can't be an affair of any great importance either. I argue this from the fact that though I am accused of something, I cannot recall the slightest offense that might be charged against me. But that even is of minor importance, the real question is, who accuses me? What authority is conducting these proceedings? Are you officers of the law? None of you has a uniform…. (Kafka 1992: 11)

Joseph K.'s choice of concepts is telling here. He argues his position from "fact." He talks about accusations, offenses, charges—all terms of the established legal system, in which there is always a clearly defined accuser, an authority issuing the accusation, and a set of "proceedings" through which the accused can anticipate the charge moving. In addition, officers of the legitimate authorities are clearly distinguishable from people on the street.

Joseph realizes that this "trial" stands in contrast to his experience, and when reflecting back on his arrest, compares it with his job at the bank. Bank and trial are two incommensurable entities, though Joseph K., while recognizing this, is still unable to grasp that they are totally separate and competing systems:

> … in short, if I had behaved sensibly, nothing further would have happened, all this would have been nipped in the bud. But one is so unprepared. In the Bank, for instance, I am always prepared, nothing of that kind could possibly happen to me there, I have my own attendant, the general telephone and the office telephone stand before me on my desk, people keep coming in to see me, clients and clerks, and above all, my mind is always on work and so kept on the alert, it would be an actual pleasure to me if a situation like that cropped up in the Bank. (Kafka 1992: 20)

When discussing the events with Ms. Bürstner, Joseph K. admits that he is applying a type of official language to them that might not fit. Tellingly, he has no other way of describing the situation. The language of the bank world has completely structured his thinking, despite inklings that it is inadequate to capture the deeper reality of what is going on. "I have already told you all I know," Joseph tells Bürstner, continuing, "In fact more than I know, for it was not a real Court of Inquiry. I called it that because I didn't know what else to call it. There was no interrogation at all, I was merely arrested, but it was done by a Commission" (Kafka 1992: 26). Joseph K.'s move from "Court of Inquiry" to "Commission" underscores how fully the bureaucratic language has structured his interpretation of events. Once an arrest is declared, Joseph K. constructs his response in the only way he can—by applying the rules and structures of thinking from the bank world.

The arresting parties attempt to educate Joseph K. that the trial to which he has been called cannot be understood in the typical terms of the bank world—an attempt that fails miserably. Still, the reader of the novel is provided with ample evidence that this "trial" is not a bureaucratic operation and/or the result of the impersonal crushing of the individual by the state. The trial has no connection whatsoever to either an official bureaucracy or the state. It is extra-official—beyond the realm of officialdom completely and, in fact, directly opposed to it. "Our officials, so far as I know them, and I know only the lowest grades among them," the warder who arrests Joseph K. tells him, "'never go hunting for crime in the population, but, as the Law decrees, are drawn toward the guilty and must send out us wardens. That is the Law. How could there be a mistake in that?' 'I don't know this Law,' said K. 'All the worse for you,' replied the warder. 'And it probably exists nowhere but in your own head,' said K." (Kafka 1992: 6).

The trial takes place on the periphery of the bank world—it is peripheral in that it is excluded from the domain of hegemonic power. The interrogations are scheduled (by telephone—not by official letter) for Sunday when the bank, like the whole of the official world of work, is closed. The trial informs Joseph K. that if Sunday does not work, proceedings could be held at night—again outside of the regular working hours. The first trial event occurs at a location where Joseph K. has previously never been. It is physically separate from the official world, the world of the bank. "[Joseph K.] was given the number of the house where he had to go, it was a house in an outlying suburban street where he had never been before" (Kafka 1992: 32). Interestingly, the representatives of the trial give Joseph K. no specific time for his Sunday appointment, indicating that the importance of exact time in the world of the bank does not hold in the world of the trial. Joseph K., still unable to see this distinction, reasons, "…what he was really thinking was that it would be best to go to the address at nine o'clock on Sunday morning, since that was the hour at which all the law courts started their business on weekdays" (Kafka 1992: 33). The specific building to which Joseph K. has been summoned is the precise opposite of the bank building with its bank employees. The way the novel describes the scene Joseph K. encounters there is critical for establishing this dichotomy. The street, Juliusstrasse, consists of a string of identical "high gray tenements inhabited by poor people." He sees windows "piled high with bedding," "men in shirtsleeves," "the disheveled head of a woman," "women…thronging" and "gossiping," "a barefooted man…sitting on a crate," a "sickly young girl…standing at a pump," "children… playing on the stairs" of the building, and so on (Kafka 1992: 34–35).[2] As Joseph K. continues to search for the specific room (this information has not been given to him), he takes in the full scope of the building's society:

> …almost all the doors stood open, with children running out and in. Most of the flats, too, consisted of one small single-windowed room in which cooking was going on. Many of the women were holding babies in one arm

> and working over the stove with the arm that was left free. Half-grown girls who seemed to be dressed in nothing but an apron kept busily rushing about. In all the rooms the beds were still occupied, sick people were lying in them, or men who had not wakened yet, or others who were resting there in their clothes. (Kafka 1992: 36)

Eventually, Joseph K. finds himself in a "meeting-hall," not a legal courtroom or official's chambers. It is full of a "crowd of the most variegated people…," who can stand only with "bent posture." The air is "too thick for him" (Kafka 1992: 37). The room's "fuggy atmosphere…prevented one from seeing the people at the other end" (Kafka 1992: 44–45). Unlike the orderly proceedings of a court of law, the gathering seems to Joseph K. rather like the coming together of a "political meeting," divided among itself into "factions." The clothing, too, takes him aback; most of the people "were dressed in black, in old, long, and loosely hanging Sunday coats…" (Kafka 1992: 38). Furthermore, "As far as one could make out in the dimness, dust, and reek, they seemed to be worse dressed than the people below" (Kafka 1992: 39).

The situational irony is that despite all of these observations, which clearly indicate that this trial has nothing in common with the functioning of a state or bureaucratic operation, Joseph K. still approaches it with the same tools. He applies hegemonic notions of power to a system of power that is peripheral to and arrayed against those dominant structures. The trial's first "interrogation" illustrates this clearly—and it should be said that even the term "interrogation" and nearly all of the "legalistic" terms used to describe the "trial," including the word "trial" itself, do not emanate from the "trial" but are projected on it from the outside. Indeed, the world of the "trial" as "trial" does not exist. Something is happening to Joseph K., power is being exercised over him, and to call it a "trial" in the ordinary sense of the term is almost as meaningless as naming it anything. In one of the novel's key passages, Joseph K. recognizes this definitional opacity, though (building the ironic tragicomedy) still discounting it:

> This question of yours, Sir, about my being a house painter—or rather, not a question, you simply made a statement—is typical of the whole character of this trial that is being foisted on me. You may object that it is not a trial

> at all; you are quite right, for it is only a trial if I recognize it as such. But for the moment I do recognize it, on grounds of compassion, as it were. (Kafka 1992: 40)

Despite his notion that the "trial" is pathetic and deserving of a certain type of "compassion," Joseph K. projects onto it a kind of grandiosity more fitting for the modern state. His understanding of this should not be accepted—for though K. senses that his "trial" is no trial at all, he cannot break free of the implications of the very term:

> ...there can be no doubt that behind all the actions of this court of justice, that is to say in my case, behind my arrest and today's interrogation, there is a great organization at work. An organization which not only employs corrupt warders, oafish Inspectors, and Examining Magistrates of whom the best that can be said is that they recognize their own limitations, but also has at its disposal a judiciary hierarchy of high, indeed of the highest rank, with an indispensable and numerous retinue of servants, clerks, police, and other assistants, perhaps even hangmen. I do not shrink from that word. And the significance of this great organization, gentlemen? It consists in this, that innocent persons are accused of guilt, and senseless proceedings are put in motion against them, mostly without effect, it is true, as in my own case. But considering the senselessness of the whole, how is it possible for the higher ranks to prevent gross corruption in their agents? (Kafka 1992: 45–46)

The "sense" Joseph K. is searching for is the "sense" of the hegemonic legal order. The structures of power he imagines are the mirror image of an imperial court system—with a clear hierarchy and the possibility of corruption trickling down the ladder of competence. He has not yet (and never will) become fully conscious of the two dueling and incompatible spheres of power.

The threat of hegemonic power to the subcultural world of the trial is revealed when Joseph K. returns to the scene of the first interrogation the following week and encounters the wife of the "usher." The woman quickly reveals to Joseph K. her dissatisfaction with life in the realm of the trial's society, foremost because she is being sexually harassed and repeatedly raped (this same sexual dynamic will reappear in *The Castle*).

The woman entertains notions that Joseph K., coming as he does from the bank world, could free her from her horrid predicament. "…I'll go with you," she tells him, "wherever you like, you can do with me what you please, I'll be glad if I can only get out of here for a long time, and I wish it could be forever" (Kafka 1992: 56). Joseph K. fantasizes about how taking this woman from the trial's society would be a great act of revenge for its injustice to him:

> And probably there could be no more fitting revenge on the Examining Magistrate and his henchmen than to wrest this woman from them and take her himself. Then some night the Examining Magistrate, after long and arduous labor on his lying reports about K., might come to the woman's bed and find it empty. Empty because she had gone off with K., because the woman now standing in the window, that supple, voluptuous warm body under the coarse, heavy, dark dress, belonged to K. and to K. alone. (56)

This fantasy of possession illuminates the essential threat Joseph K. poses to the world of the trial. The woman's situation highlights the internal power dynamics of the trial society (she is a plaything of male power) and represents fertility and thus the future health of the social entity. Though Joseph K. eventually loses this battle over the usher's wife, the very fact that his presence brought into the open the woman's longing exposes the fragility of the system. While Joseph K. might have lost,[3] eventually the world of the bank is bound to win as it encroaches and pushes the trial society further to the periphery of the city—and then out of it entirely. Sexual mixing will not harm the world of the bank, but it can utterly destroy the society of the trial—at least in the eyes of the trial's members.

If the bank world is governed by clear temporal dimensions, procedural operations, legal norms, contracts, rights, and so on, the world of the trial is ruled by what seems like a web of social relationships of the type impossible to untangle for a social outsider—a web that might or might not be organized by higher principles, whether legal, moral, or theological. This is demonstrated most clearly by another "accused" man Joseph K. encounters in the "offices." Joseph K. asks the man a seemingly clear or easy question, namely, "What are you waiting here for?":

> But this unexpected question confused the man, which was the more deeply embarrassing as he was obviously a man of the world who would have known how to comport himself anywhere else and would not lightly have renounced his natural superiority. Yet in this place he did not know even how to reply to a simple question and gazed at the others as if it were their duty to help him, as if no one could expect him to answer should help not be forthcoming. Then the usher stepped up and said, to reassure the man and encourage him, "This gentleman merely asked what you are waiting for. Come, give him an answer." The familiar voice of the usher had its effect: "I'm waiting—" the man started to say, but could get out no more. (Kafka 1992: 64)

Despite the trial's opacity to those on the outside of its social system, those on the inside clearly understand how it functions. This is even true of those, like Joseph K.'s uncle ("a small landowner from the country"), who are mostly of the trial world but venture now and then beyond its borders (Kafka 1992: 91). When Joseph K. tells the uncle, "The first thing to grasp…is that this is not a case before an ordinary court," the latter responds, "That's bad" (Kafka 1992: 96). But the uncle had already heard about his nephew's trial, belonging as he does to the trial society. His first advice for Joseph is for him to break with the bank world, even if temporarily, removing himself from the hegemonic power in order to integrate into the world or zone of the trial—in other words to become himself peripheral. He tells Joseph K., betraying quite an intimate understanding of the trial's processes and essence:

> Things like this don't occur suddenly, they pile up gradually, there must have been indications. Why did you never write to me? You know I would do anything for you, I'm still your guardian in a sense and till now I have been proud of it. Of course I'll do what I can to help you, only it's very difficult when the case is already under way. The best thing, at any rate, would be for you to take a short holiday and come to stay with us in the country. (Kafka 1992: 96)

The uncle's admonition of Joseph K. presents a glimpse into the society of the trial, a view that Joseph abruptly dismisses. However, the uncle's statement should be carefully studied. First, he indicates that the context of the trial is of a much longer duration than Joseph K. (and the reader) had initially assumed. The accusation is not, in fact, the beginning of the process, but more like the end—or certainly indicative of an advanced stage. The accusation did not come out of the blue, as Joseph K. imagines ("Someone must have been telling lies about Joseph K., for without having done anything wrong he was arrested one fine morning" (Kafka 1992: 1)). Rather, it had been building for a long time and providing Joseph K. with ample "indications" of it, signs that he could not see or understand. Second, the prudent move for Joseph K., according to the uncle, is to reconnect to his family. The family connection is emphasized strongly. Joseph K.'s lack of parents is seen as an element that perhaps loosened his connection to the kinship network, but the uncle is suggesting that it can be reactivated. Third, the uncle is indicating the importance of space. The countryside is beneficial because it severs Joseph K. from the world of the bank at the same time as it forces him to integrate back into the kinship sphere. That Joseph K. responds in the following fashion only emphasizes the incompatibility between his way of looking at the case and his uncle's—showing that no matter how directly he is presented with a counter-scenario to the one he imagines from his position in the bank system, he cannot see it. So subsumed is he in the realm of the hegemonic power structure that he is made blind to any currents of subcultural or subaltern forces. He says to his uncle:

> Since you tell me that the family would be involved in any scandal arising from the case—I don't see myself how that could be so, but that's beside the point—I'll submit willingly to your judgment. Only I think going to the country would be inadvisable even from your point of view, for it would look like flight and therefore guilt. Besides, though I'm more hard-pressed here, I can push the case on my own more energetically. (Kafka 1992: 97)

Joseph K. has misunderstood everything that his uncle has told him. What he sees as "beside the point" (the family's deep involvement) is actually utterly central. He thinks that the guilt is still to be decided, even though the uncle has just divulged to him that it was already quite late in the process and his guilt had, more or less, been decided on. He thinks that his case could be better managed from the city, even though the society of the city is largely to blame for his guilt.

Such errors of judgment are compounded during Joseph K.'s visit, together with his uncle, to the lawyer. Though Joseph K. learns that the lawyer has arranged for a Chief Clerk of the Court to be present, Joseph K. excuses himself from the meeting, not realizing the clerk's importance. The constellation of the lawyer, the uncle, and the clerk represents a powerful triad to advance his position in the trial, but Joseph K. cannot see it, describing the confabulation to the lawyer's nurse Leni as "old men jabbering" (Kafka 1992: 107). Joseph's avoidance of the meeting exhausts his uncle, who upbraids him:

> Joseph…how could you do it! You have damaged your case badly, which was beginning to go quite well. You hide yourself away with a filthy little trollop, who is obviously the lawyer's mistress into the bargain, and stay away for hours. You don't even seek any pretext, you conceal nothing, no, you're quite open, you simply run off to her and stay beside her. And all this time we three sit there, your uncle who is doing his best for you, the lawyer, who has to be won over to your side, above all the Chief Clerk of the Court, a man of importance, who is actually in charge of your case at its present stage. (Kafka 1992: 111)

Joseph K.'s absence from the meeting shatters the cohesiveness of his support and in effect precipitates the further polarization of his thinking vis-à-vis the process of the trial.

Leni, too, attempts to instruct Joseph K. about the workings of the trial, both directly and indirectly, but again he cannot internalize her analysis of his predicament. As Joseph K. presses her for help, she pleads with him, "Please don't ask me for names, take my warning to heart instead, and don't be so unyielding in future, you can't fight against this Court, you must confess your guilt. Make your confession at the first chance you get. Until you do that there's no possibility of getting out of their clutches, none at all…" (Kafka 1992: 108). This is a fairly stunning piece of information, one that fits precisely with the lesson of the uncle about the trial's timing: guilt has been determined and needs to be recognized for any movement in Joseph K.'s favor to occur. The movement is back into the fold of the society of the trial, one that Joseph cannot even glimpse or fathom, let alone accomplish.

Joseph K. rejects the two central lessons he has been told during his visit to the lawyer: first (and most importantly), that he should admit his guilt; second, that he should proceed with the trial through the personal and familial connections available to him. Instead, he continues to apply the values of the bank world, namely that he is innocent until the trial proves him guilty and that he must succeed procedurally and operationally in the context of the trial. It is not as though Joseph K. decides this; the discursive structures of the bank world dominate him so thoroughly that he cannot consider an alternative.

That Joseph K. is eventually executed by the trial system indicates that it is still a powerful entity, though the manner of the execution again points to marginality. Two men fetch Joseph K. They take him out of town—again to the periphery of the city. The execution scene proceeds as follows, ending the novel:

> But the hands of one of the partners were already at K.'s throat, while the other thrust the knife deep into his heart and turned it there twice. With failing eyes K. could still see the two of them immediately before him, cheek leaning against cheek, watching the final act. "Like a dog!" he said; it was as if the shame of it must outlive him. (Kafka 1992: 229)

Three elements are vital for understanding the nature of Joseph K.'s death. First, the method of killing is not one of the hegemonic power but of the marginalized group; and in this case the allusion is to the method of killing used by the ancient *sicarii*, a society of resistors charged with killing Jews in Jerusalem who collaborated with Roman power.[4] Second, the statement "like a dog" refers to the widespread belief that in the ancient world the "dog" was a common epithet for the "godless" gentile or Roman.[5] Third, Joseph K.'s killing, like those perpetrated by the *sicarii*, is meant as both individual punishment and a means of social control, as an example, in other words, of the fate of the apostate. The shame that is to "outlive" Joseph K. is the shame of leaving the social fold and aligning with the dominant power.

Power in Kafka's *The Trial* is thus represented by two antagonistic and incompatible systems. The world of the bank is hegemonic, the dominant ideology in the novel. The trial world is peripheral, marginal—forced to the edges of the city, where it occupies only the most undesirable spaces, and the countryside. It is out of sight, nearly invisible to the dominant power. Yet the very process of marginalization provokes retaliation against a former member of the trial society who has crossed the line into the zone of hegemonic power. The trial first attempts to recuperate Joseph K., but this proves impossible. He is too much a man of the bank world. The only choice left is to execute him as an apostate, but such a move only serves to underscore the weakness of the trial as a whole; a stronger system would have been able to bring Joseph K. back. While the novel is about the trial's prosecution of Joseph K., it might be more accurate to say that Joseph K. is actually the aggressor, the persecutor. He enters the zone of the trial as the explorer lands on the island of the penal colony, that is, with a fully articulated "modern" worldview that cannot countenance the violation of its core principles. Time and again, Joseph K. ridicules and prosecutes the trial using the ideological weaponry of the bank. The trial's victory is a Pyrrhic one: it might have assassinated Joseph K. as a "Roman" collaborator, but it, like the *sicarii*, will eventually be annihilated at its own "Masada"—under siege by the modern constitutional, corporate state—the new imperial power.

The trial is not an operation or a legal institution—*it is a society*, one marginalized, peripheral, and fighting for its continued existence. It is able to exist at the edge of the modern city, for now. Its vehemence stems from the perpetual siege it is under by the dominant social power, the bank world. The bank world denies it, ridicules it, presses down on it—and by the sheer force of its centripetal energy and the appeal of its enticements pulls people away from the society of the trial. The usher's wife and Leni indicate that the appeal to leave is especially prominent among women, a response to their social debasement. Power, then, is represented here as a social construct, a social mechanism. It can contain multiple structures at once, though one dominant social structure forces all others to the margins. The margins strike back at the center, at times with lethal force, but never with realistic hope of challenging the hegemony.

The basic characteristics of power in Kafka's work discussed so far set the stage for a type of resistance offered through Kafka's conception of the dreamscape. These characteristics include the hermetic quality of systems of power, a system's foundation in a set of social (including legal) and cultural norms and practices—the expression of power as performance or everyday practice, the inherent fragility (despite their apparent invulnerability) of power structures, and the tendency of one system of power to overtake, displace, or marginalize competitors—a system's intolerance. Kafka's protagonists tend to resist the structures of power from within the basic authoritarian structure. George Bendemann aims at a kind of parricide. The explorer in the penal colony supports the new commandant over the old. Joseph K., in *The Trial*, attempts to impose the logic of the bank world on the culture and society of the "trial." Whether they fail (like George or Joseph K.) or succeed (like the explorer), the basic dynamics of power remain authoritarian. Kafka, it would seem, thematizes a set of concentric circles of power with no way out. In the reading of *The Castle* that follows, I propose that the way out, the anarchic impulse in Kafka's work, is most clearly presented through his views on dreams.

Kafka and Dreams

Toward the end of his life, Kafka describes the dream as a kind of radical space or force, one that can produce, or result in, a rupture or transfiguration of waking life. The radicality of the dream experience, traceable to 1911 in his diaries, seems to have grown for him with the years. By 1919, the combination of internal and external pressures provokes a new kind of (understanding or view of) dream intensity, which carries into the early 1920s and the period when Kafka writes *The Castle*. Kafka's view of the dream as a symbolic entity and, first and foremost, a narrative construct—a story—gives way to an understanding of the dream as a boundary-crossing movement or propulsion and as a creative or even artistic *intensity*, though not primarily in a positive sense.

That dreams are a central concern for Kafka is evident from a reading of his diaries. Among his first entries is a dream-text focusing on the dancer Eduardova (Kafka 1988: 9). Even in this first recorded dream,

Kafka seems to have a sense that the boundaries of the dreamscape are fluid. The following passage straddles the line between the clearly defined dreamscape and the non-dream space, or "reality":

> The dancer Eduardova, a lover of music, travels in the tram, as everywhere else, in the company of two vigorous violinists whom she makes play often. For there is no known reason why one should not play in the tram if the playing is good, pleasing to the fellow passengers, and costs nothing; i.e., if the hat is not passed round afterwards. Of course, at first it is a little surprising and for a short while everybody finds it improper. But at full speed, in a strong breeze and on a silent street, it sounds quite nice. (Kafka 1988: 9–10)

It is textually impossible to determine whether Kafka means this paragraph as a continuation of the dream-text or as a description beyond the dream. Such a straddling is made explicit in a diary entry from 1911. It is noteworthy that Kafka perceives the dream state as being discrete from being asleep or awake. It is a third state—an entry into a distinct space:

> October 2. Sleepless night. The third in a row. I fall asleep soundly, but after an hour I wake up, as though I had laid my head in the wrong hole. I am completely awake, have the feeling that I have not slept at all or only under a thin skin, have before me anew the labour of falling asleep and feel myself rejected by sleep. And for the rest of the night, until about five, thus it remains, so that indeed I sleep but at the same time vivid dreams keep me awake. I sleep alongside myself, so to speak, while I myself must struggle with dreams. About five the last trace of sleep is exhausted, I just dream, which is more exhausting than wakefulness. In short, I spend the whole night in that state in which a healthy person finds himself for a short time before really falling asleep. When I awaken, all the dreams are gathered about me, but I am careful not to reflect on them. Toward morning I sigh into the pillow, because for this night all hope is gone. I think of those nights at the end of which I was raised out of deep sleep and awoke as though I had been folded in a nut. (Kafka 1988: 60)

In the same diary entry, Kafka connects sleep patterns to his work as a writer:

> I believe this sleeplessness comes only because I write. For no matter how little or how badly I write, I am still made sensitive by these minor shocks, feel, especially toward evening and even more in the morning, the approaching, the imminent possibility of great moments which would tear me open, which could make me capable of anything, and in the general uproar that is within me and which I have no time to command, find no rest. In the end this uproar is only a suppressed, restrained harmony, which, left free, would fill me completely, which could even widen me and yet still fill me. But now such a moment arouses only feeble hopes and does me harm, for my being does not have sufficient strength or the capacity to hold the present mixture, during the day the visible word helps me, during the night it cuts me to pieces unhindered. (Kafka 1988: 61)

The October 2 entry contains key concepts. First, Kafka makes the clear distinction between two selves—a sleeping self and a dreaming self: "at the same time vivid dreams keep me awake. I sleep alongside myself, so to speak, while I myself must struggle with dreams." While not a full dissolution of selfhood, the passages recognize that the dream-Kafka and the dreamer-Kafka are distinct beings. Yet, the doubling function of the "I" alone is not what provides the experience with its intensity. The intensity is drawn from the vague recognition of the simultaneity of sleeping and dreaming, of one self's awareness of the other across the oneiric boundary.[6] Second, Kafka attempts to preserve the intensity of the simultaneous existence of a dream-Kafka and the dreamer-Kafka by his rejection of dream interpretation: "When I awaken, all the dreams are gathered about me, but I am careful not to reflect on them." Kafka seems aware that the production of the dream-text, the interpretive story that comes from reflection, will concretize the dreamscape using dominant discursive strategies, most likely Freudian. Kafka's rejection of reflection is a rejection of the production of the dream-text in order to preserve the intensity of the experience of the dreamscape, even though this intensity seems to be difficult to handle and potentially even destructive.

In the second part of his entry about the night of October 2, Kafka makes the connection between the destruction of the unified or atomistic self and the creative process—there is "harmony," he thinks, two steps below the unified self of wakefulness and one step below the disunity of the fractured dreamscape. He writes, "…in the general uproar that is within me and which I have no time to command, find no rest. In the end this uproar is only a suppressed, restrained harmony, which, left free, would fill me completely, which could even widen me and yet still fill me." It is unclear what Kafka means by "suppressed, restrained harmony," though it is connected to the creative process of writing—perhaps it is the foundation of the artistic act. The foundation of the creative act of writing, then, is posed as an intensity of the movement in and out of the dreamscape, or at the very least it is positioned in the borderland between dream and restless nocturnal wakefulness or insomnia. The shocking results of the upwelling of the artistic intensity are twofold. First, the drive toward harmony, if "left free, would fill me completely, which could even widen me and yet still fill me." In other words, the intensity enables the self to be self-actualizing and to go beyond its shape, body, or limits. The intensity of the movement in and out of the dreamscape "widens." Second, the result of this widening and self-actualizing is fragmentation, destruction, death: "during the night," Kafka writes, "it [the mixture] cuts me to pieces unhindered." The "mixture" is all that is contained within the self—including its experiences in the dreamscape. The advance and withdrawal of the dreamscape are the major disintegrating force.

Less than two months after the night of October 2, Kafka records a dream in his diary that again poses the idea of crossing boundaries or zones:

> November 19 [1911]: Dream: In the theatre…I sit right up at the front, think I am sitting in the first now until it finally appears that it is the second. The back of the row is turned toward the stage so that one can see the auditorium comfortably, the stage only by turning….Despite the fact that when the play began many people in the first rows left, apparently to go backstage, I can see very little, for the girls left behind block the view with their large, flat hats, most of which are blue, that move back and forth along the whole length of the row….On the stage two critics sit on the floor, writing, with their backs resting against a piece of scenery….Again facing the auditorium I see that it is lit by simple paraffin lamps that are stuck up on simple chandeliers, like those in the streets, and now, of course, burn only very low. Suddenly, impure paraffin or a damaged wick is

> probably the cause, the lights spurt out of one of these lanterns and sparks pour down in a broad gush on the crowded audience that forms a mass as black as earth. Then a gentleman rises up out of this mass, walks on it toward the lamp, apparently wants to fix the lamp, but first looks up at it, remains standing near it for a short while, and, when nothing happens, returns quietly to his place in which he is swallowed up. I take him for myself and bow my face into the darkness. (Kafka 1988: 122)

While the dream recognizes the separation between the stage (the performance space) and the audience (the real), this division is immediately called into question by the narrator's positioning. He is turned to view the audience, as if the performance space is there—or also there. This reversal of the significance of the spaces is reinforced by the position of the two critics, who would normally be in the audience but who are now on stage, leaning against a piece of the stage set as if folded into the territory of the performance. Are they writing a theatrical review of the "real" from the vantage point of the stage, or even as actors? The narrator's view of the stage is blocked by the wall of blue hats, again de-emphasizing the stage as the primary site of the gaze.

The central dramatic moment in the dream-text comes with the explosion of the paraffin lamp in the auditorium among the audience. This burst of intensity precipitates two additional boundary crossings. The first is that a man rises out of the audience, which had before this been a "mass as black as earth." In other words, the man crystallizes in reaction to the lamp's explosion as a potential individual or self, distinguishable from the masses. At the end of the theater dream, the narrator "bows [his] face into the darkness." The "darkness" here is multivalent. It is the darkness of night. It is the "black earth" of the audience—the indistinguishable crowd. It is the darkness of the theater—and, connected to it, the edge of the perceivable dreamscape. The dream ends with the wrenching discomfort of two simultaneous subjects locked together but wholly other: first, the viewer of the scene and, second, the actor who emerges out of, and vanishes back into, the crowd.

Kafka's two most radical formulations of dreaming come later in the diaries. On December 5, 1919, he writes, "Again pulled through this terrible, long, narrow crack; it can only be forced through in a dream. On purpose and awake, one could certainly never do it" (Kafka 1988: 390). On February 3, 1922, Kafka, already at work on *The Castle*, writes, "Almost impossible to sleep; plagued by dreams, as if they were being scratched on me, on a stubborn material" (Kafka 1988: 411). The 1919 entry reminds of the tunnel in Jean Rhys's "Exhibition dream." The dream for Kafka in this instance could be considered a kind of tunnel, a passage through which one can pass as if through a maze, finding one's way somehow from the entry point of the dreamscape to the exit—as Aeneas enters the underworld through Cumae and exits through the gates of horn, as Alice enters the dreamscape through the rabbit hole. However, Kafka's tunnel or passageway differs from Rhys's or Virgil's or Carroll's tunnel. Here it is not a tunnel at all, but merely a "crack." The body's movement through this narrowest of cracks or fissures creates the zone of the dreamscape. It is a harrowing journey, one, as Kafka says, that he could "never do" if awake. It is only into the dreamscape that he can experience a "movement" of such raw intensity. It is this intensity—this force—that confronts the author of the creative act.

The diary entry from 1922 pushes even further into the domain of pure intensity. Here the intensity of the dreamscape prevents sleep entirely and suspends the person between wakefulness and sleep in a forbidding, hostile zone "plagued by dreams." Beyond this, the dreamscape encroaches on the other side of the dream/real divide, marking it indelibly—scarring or even defacing it—"as if they were being scratched on me, on a stubborn material" (Kafka 1988: 411). The dream here is being written on the surface of waking life, on the body as a sort of tattoo. This conjures the image of the body as a surface to be written upon, to be inscribed and thus to be animated. The awoken person seems defenseless against these re-inscriptions. As such, the passage through the dreamscape adds disfigurement to the body in an endless process of remaking it (or making it), rewriting it (or writing it)—in the same way as Kafka did with *The Castle*, a work or, better, a *literary process* with no end. Schwenger might have had this in mind when he writes, "…within the security of sleep is something that is in many ways its direct opposite. That something, of course, is the dream. And if in sleep we secure ourselves in rest, in dream we open into a restlessness without end" (2012: 80–81).

Kafka's depictions of the movement between an insomniac wakefulness and the space of the dreamscape and his representation of this movement as an intensity that makes or reconfigures the subject and the subject's body present a challenge to Freudian dream analysis, which sees dreaming as an interpretable text within the framework of a diagnostic process. Kafka was aware of Freudian dream theory, as Schwenger points out, but his choice to avoid Freudian analysis of his recorded dreams indicates that he did not feel entrapped by or perhaps even attracted to these ideas. To the contrary, in a letter to Milena Jesenská, Kafka rejects psychoanalysis, mainly because, for him, it pathologizes the very intensities that define the opening up of the dreamscape. He writes:

> …I consider the therapeutic part of psychoanalysis to be a hopeless error. All of these so-called illnesses, sad as they may appear, are matters of faith, efforts of souls in distress to find moorings in some maternal soil; thus psychoanalysis also considers the origin of religions to be nothing but what (in its opinion) causes the "illnesses" of the individual. Nowadays, of course, we generally lack a sense of religious community; the sects are countless and confined to single individuals—though perhaps it only appears so to the eye coloured by the present.
>
> Such moorings, however, which really take hold of solid ground are after all not an isolated, interchangeable property of man, rather they are pre-existing in his nature and continue to form his nature (as well as his body) in this direction. And it's here they hope to cure? (1999: 173)

While this quotation does not address Freudian dream theory, it suggests that Kafka rejects the psychoanalytic impulse to systematize and medicalize the flux of a subject's inner life, including one's dreamlife. In light of the social reading of *The Trial* above, it is noteworthy that Kafka understands individual "pathology" in terms of the individual's quest for a community of faith. Psychoanalysis, Kafka implies, is the theory of the bank world, an attempt to understand individuals as rootless and atomistic, and to cure the anachronistic or primitive desire to belong to a "religious community." The politics of "belonging" form the basic context for Kafka's novel *The Castle*, as the quintessential outsider, K., arrives in a village that does not seem to want him there and yet does not expel him.

The Castle

The Castle begins with a man's arrival in a country village late in the evening. The man, K., crosses a bridge and finds a village inn. He requests a night's lodging and receives it, only to find out shortly afterward that he is not permitted to reside, however temporarily, in the domain of the castle of Count Westwest. K. meets this exercise of power by claiming that he is the land surveyor summoned by the castle itself. While likely an act of subterfuge, the embrace of the identity of land surveyor represents a major challenge to the status quo of village life, a challenge that reverberates immediately in the novel. After K.'s (false) disclosure, an unattributed voice is heard uttering, "Land surveyor?" Moments later, the narrative voice tells that K. "watched the peasants gathering timidly and conferring, the arrival of a land surveyor was no trifling matter" (Kafka 1998: 3). The sudden presence of a self-proclaimed land surveyor in the village is a significant challenge to established authority and provokes what seems like an emergency response from the castle—a response understood by K. in the following way:

> K. listened intently. So the Castle had appointed him land surveyor. On one hand, this was unfavorable, for it showed that the Castle had all necessary information about him, had assessed the opposing forces, and was taking up the struggle with a smile. On the other hand, it was favorable, for it proved to his mind that they underestimated him and that he would enjoy greater freedom than he could have hoped for at the beginning. And if they thought they could keep him terrified all the time simply by acknowledging his surveyorship—though this was certainly a superior move on their part—then they were mistaken for he felt only a slight shudder, that was all. (Kafka 1998: 5)

K. becomes bound to the castle through his naming as land surveyor—and, in fact, he is rarely referred to as anything else throughout the novel.

By naming K., or recognizing his self-imposed function, the castle-village system attempts to reconcile itself with the challenge K. presents as a stranger, foreigner, or newcomer—in other words, as an inherently disruptive force to the delicate equilibrium that has been established among all members of this society. The strength of "castle" power, even if the castle is but a projection and remains a part of the village society, is its hermetic structure and the order it has established within this structure.[7] This is not to say that this order is fixed and unchanging—rather there are explicit references and many more hints that the power within the castle-village system is fluid—for example, in Frieda's journey from stable girl to barmaid and her eventual coupling with Klamm.

Evidence that K.'s arrival and, specifically, his naming as land surveyor cause disruption and reorientation abounds early in the novel. At Master Tanner Lasemann's house, responding to Lasemann's comment that no guests are needed in the village, K. says, "But every now and then someone is needed, such as me, the land surveyor" (Kafka 1998: 12). Lasemann cannot bring himself to refute this, despite his doubts, saying, "I don't know about that…if they summoned you, then they probably need you, this may be an exception, but we little people go by the rule, you shouldn't blame us for that" (Kafka 1998: 12–13). K.'s presence is marked as exceptional—a disruption of the norms of daily life. The next hint of the ripple effect of this disruption is the assignment of two people to work as K.'s assistants—Artur and Jeremias. Though clearly men of the village-castle, they take on the label of assistants to the land surveyor. Whether or not they are assigned to K. as a method of control seems to me less important than that they are assigned at all, further entrenching K. in his identity of land surveyor and connecting him to the web of the village-castle society.

Walter Corbella sees the type of surveillance he claims the assistants represent as fundamental to the operation of castle authority. He writes, "I maintain that Kafka's Castle operates on the basis of panoptic principles, relying on an authoritarian regime and permanent surveillance for the sake of individual discipline and social stability" (2007: 70). He continues, quite correctly, I think, "The Castle resides primarily in [the villagers'] minds, governing their thoughts and determining their behaviors, and it marks, symbolically, the site of the gaze that reaches them in any place at any moment" (2007: 72). While this is true, the discipline and the social stability Corbella sees in the novel should not be exaggerated. As I will demonstrate below, the novel shows the scars of a fairly dramatic shifting of power within the village and social flux. The authoritarian regime, as Corbella calls the castle, is actually not governed by the castle and its officials at all—it is the product of a balance of power within the village itself.

K. is right, then, when he senses that he has power in relation to the power structures of the castle-village. The first chapters demonstrate this quite clearly. K.'s arrival and self-definition succeed in maintaining his presence in the village—none dares expel the land surveyor. He receives explicit recognition from Klamm in a letter. He provokes the assignment of assistants. When he enters the taproom with Olga, his presence behind her shifts the way the peasants interact with her. While in the taproom, he attracts the attention of the peasants who are curious to learn something new from him. Such an insertion of new information, new knowledge, is a threat to the status quo of any hermetic system. Most centrally, K. breaks the relationship between Klamm and Frieda, and himself begins a relationship with Frieda, a direct challenge to the seeming hierarchy of the castle-village, which goes totally unanswered:[8] "And as though Frieda had been fortified by K.'s consent, she clenched her fist, knocked on the door, and cried: 'I'm with the surveyor. I'm with the surveyor'" (Kafka 1998: 41). Frieda breaks with Klamm and goes with K. to improve her position—most notably to escape the abuse she endures from Klamm's servants. Again, as in *The Trial*, women inside the trial or castle-village system see outsiders as potential ways to either improve their situation or to escape from the structures entirely (and, indeed, Frieda's secret dream is ultimately to escape—to "France or southern Spain").

The first day with Frieda is the high point of K.'s power in the novel—partly because his intentions to stay are not yet clear and so the castle-village system does not perceive him as a continued threat, let alone as a representative of a bigger, looming existential threat. Having left the Gentlemen's Inn with Frieda for his lodgings at the Bridge Inn, K. finds himself in a quite comfortable condition:

> Besides, it wasn't so terribly unpleasant, sitting at the table drinking the good coffee Frieda had brought, warming himself at the stove Frieda had

> stoked, having the assistants run up and down the stairs ten times in their clumsy eagerness to bring him soap, water, a comb, a mirror, and finally, since K. had softly uttered a wish that could be interpreted that way, a little glass of rum. (Kafka 1998: 45)

Though critics often focus on the ways in which the dominant castle authority controls and frustrates K., it would be more accurate to say that K., even if unwittingly at times, challenges the structures of castle-village power quite profoundly and provokes responses that reveal not the strength of the castle-village system, but its fragility—or, more accurately, that reveal both its strength in the immediate territorial sense and its fragility in the wider context.[9]

K.'s self-identification as a land surveyor creates a crisis in the castle-village system—the extent or seriousness of this crisis has not been fully appreciated in the critical literature on the novel. The arrival of a land surveyor presents at least three discrete types of threats: (1) the potential encroachment of an external state on castle-village lands—threatening precisely the territory's "sealed up" nature, as Reiner Stach calls it (2015: 443); (2) a redistribution of lands within the castle-village system; (3) shifts in interpersonal relationships in relation to this new variable. The depth of the threat of the arrival of a land surveyor emerges during K.'s meeting with the council chairman. Like the representatives of authority in "The Judgment," "In the Penal Colony," and *The Trial*, the chairman is presented as a sick, infirm man, bedridden, in this case, from illness and gout. Toward the beginning of the meeting, the chairman explains to K. why a land surveyor is not needed in the village—and in doing so points to the very threats the land surveyor represents:

> You were, as you say, taken on as a surveyor, but we don't need a surveyor. There wouldn't be the least bit of work for a person like that. The boundaries of our small holdings have been marked out, everything has been duly registered, the properties themselves rarely change hands, and whatever small boundary disputes arise, we settle ourselves. (Kafka 1998: 59)

This statement exposes the anxieties that the idea of the land surveyor raises in the castle-village system. First, a land surveyor, it seems by definition, is an outsider—there are no land surveyors in the castle-village system and thus, if one is needed, he has to be summoned from abroad. The lack of a local land surveyor indicates that property lines in the castle-village system are permanent and fixed—or, if not fixed, then determined by other means than a strict adherence to a property deed or title. Moreover, the chairman's statement that the "boundaries of our small holdings have been marked out" could indicate that the borders of the entire domain of the castle-village system are being challenged from outside. One potential way of understanding this scenario is to see the castle-village system as an aristocratic territory, one which, though nominally still dominated by the aristocratic family, has now been subsumed under the aegis of the modern state. While the aristocrat, Count Westwest, is still symbolically important for the coherence of the region's identity, the state has stripped him of any real power. It is likely that the count and his heirs have abandoned the territory entirely out of economic necessity—leaving behind the castle-village system, which regulates itself through the deployment of traditions and the web of relationships based on them. In such a situation, any breaching of the system's boundaries—any assertion of the state into the territory—would cause massive social disturbance and even social and cultural collapse. Far from being, as Michael Löwy claims, "the modern state with its bureaucratic, hierarchical apparatus, impersonal, authoritarian, and alienating," the castle or castle-village system is a territory beyond the state, a territory threatened by the state, and its assertions of power across the borders—in however seemingly insignificant ways (2004: 204).

The very idea of a land surveyor's arrival creates a political crisis in the castle-village system, revealing the system's instability and fragility. The first rift that occurs is between the castle officials and the peasants. The chairman tells K. what happened when news got out about the potential summoning of a land surveyor:

> ...every day formal hearings were held at the Gentlemen's Inn with respected members of the community. Most stood by me, but a few became suspicious, land surveying is an issue that deeply affects peasants, they scented some sort of secret deals and injustice, they also found a leader, and Sordini [a castle official] had to conclude from their presentations that if I

> had raised the matter at the local council not everyone would have opposed the summoning of a surveyor…In all this a certain Brunswick played a prominent role…. (Kafka 1998: 66–67)

The notion of the arrival of a land surveyor, in other words, results in or exacerbates factionalism in the castle-village system of a type that cannot be controlled by the castle authorities and their village representatives, again betraying that there is no inherent difference in power between them and the villagers. There are only apparent differences—as there is only an apparent Westwest, not a real one. In the debate over the issue of the land surveyor, Brunswick emerges as a powerful political force. As the chairman tells K.:

> As for Brunswick: if we could expel him from the community, virtually everyone would be happy, Lasemann not least of all. But Brunswick gained some influence at that time, he's not a speaker but a shouter, and that's good enough for some. And so I was forced to lay the matter before the council, which by the way was Brunswick's only success at first, since the council naturally decided by a large majority to have nothing to do with the surveyor. That too was years ago, but the matter still hasn't died down, partly through the conscientiousness of Sordini, who tried to probe the motives of both majority and opposition by means of the most meticulous inquiries, partly through the stupidity and ambition of Brunswick, who has various personal contacts with the authorities that he was able to bring into play thanks to his boundless imagination. (Kafka 1998: 67)

K., upon announcing himself as a land surveyor, enters into this political struggle. He is not, then, simply arrayed against the castle-village system as an outsider and opponent. Immediately, he is subsumed into intense social-political conflict—or reanimates it: "And just imagine," says the council chairman, "how disappointed I was, Surveyor, after the happy conclusion of the entire affair…when suddenly you appear and it seems as if everything is about to begin all over again" (Kafka 1998: 69). The authorities in the castle-village system cannot bring themselves to remove K. from the territory—one of the biggest puzzles of the book. Why is K. not simply expelled from the village environs and made to continue on his journey? Two reasonable answers present themselves.

First, the authorities fear that by expelling K. they will be made even more vulnerable to external interference. Second, it could be that the internal political dynamics make such an expulsion impossible. Either way, the authorities conclude that the best method of dealing with K. is to attempt to absorb him into the castle-village structure, albeit as a permanent "outsider" or "stranger," and in a role less politically problematic—that of school janitor instead of surveyor. The limits of this strategy are plain to see—most tellingly in that even after K. agrees to take on the job as school janitor, he is still mostly referred to as "surveyor."

The character of Brunswick provides a link between the two most significant political events in *The Castle*—the debate over the summoning of a land surveyor and the ruination of the Barnabas family by the castle-village complex. K. learns the saga of the Barnabas family from Olga, one of Barnabas's sisters. As Olga tells it, following a celebration in the village, a castle official made an outrageously vulgar sexual proposition to her sister Amalia, summoning her to the Gentlemen's Inn. Amalia rejected the offer, tearing the official's note into pieces and tossing them at the official's messenger. This act of defiance, so Olga says, resulted in social ostracism for Amalia and the whole family—despite the fact that no direct punishment or any word at all was issued from the castle authorities. The most prominent result of the ostracism was the loss of class status; the Barnabas family had been prominent middle-class artisans but was now reduced to penury. The father had been a master cobbler with Brunswick as his apprentice. Soon after the incident, this relationship reversed; Brunswick left the workshop to start his own shop, taking all of the clients with him. Barnabas's father lost his livelihood and eventually the family lost their house and valuable possessions, all taken by Brunswick. It seems probable that the political capital Brunswick accrued during the debate over the summoning of a land surveyor helped him achieve or solidify the professional reversal of fortunes with Barnabas's father. The actual appearance of K. in the village as land surveyor, thus, represents a new front in the power struggle between Brunswick and the Barnabas family, one that could have deep implications for the society and culture of the whole castle-village complex. It is precisely this potential that Olga senses and that motivates her to pull K. into her sphere. The alliance of the land surveyor with the Barnabas family presents a potentially powerful front against the Brunswick faction and the ideology that supports it—"castle stories," as Amalia derisively calls the entirely unsubstantiated mythology of castle life.

Contrary to much work on *The Castle*, the picture that emerges of power in the novel from my reading is not one of bureaucratic domination, robust state authoritarianism, inflexible parameters, or fixed relationships. Castle-village power is entirely social. These relationships are anything but fixed—people are constantly looking for ways to maneuver within the castle-village system. Frieda uses K. to break from Klamm and her position as the barmaid at the Gentlemen's Inn. Pepi rises from her position as chambermaid to fill Frieda's role. The landlady at the Bridge Inn exploits her relationship to the landlord to acquire the inn under favorable conditions. Brunswick succeeds in inverting the master-apprentice relationship to Barnabas's father. The Barnabas family declines from a solid middle-class existence to abject poverty. The introduction of K. as a new variable in the equation of power threatens to produce both small and large ripple effects in the system.

If power in *The Castle* is understood as social and shifting (instead of hierarchical and rigid), the vulnerability of the castle-village structure as a whole can be better grasped. K.'s arrival as land surveyor both threatens the system as a whole from beyond its borders and disrupts its internal dynamics. It could even be that, much like Joseph K.'s death presages the death of the trial world, K.'s very arrival in the village means the dissolution of a now anachronistic castle-village system. K. might be the first foreigner to cross the bridge into this strange domain, but he is likely not the last. The only response the system can muster against K. is an attempt to incorporate him into the social body. The great irony of the book is that this is precisely K.'s desire, too, albeit on his own terms, terms incompatible with castle-village culture.

K.'s Dream

Toward the end of *The Castle* and just after Frieda abandons him, K. finds himself in the room of Bürgel, a "connecting secretary" from the castle. This accidental encounter provides K. with his closest contact to castle officialdom in the novel. Bürgel, unlike other officials, is friendly to K., seducing him with promises of intervening positively in his case. But K. is too tired to engage with Bürgel. The weariness that has been with him for the entirety of his time in the village—exacerbated by days of interrupted sleep—overcomes him just as Bürgel seems to divulge to K. the hidden secret to achieving one's desires at the expense of the system. The secret is to approach a sympathetic castle official by night, when he is most vulnerable, and to extract the desired result—an extraction that the weak, vulnerable official cannot help but relinquish. The parallels between the hypothetical scenario outlined by Bürgel and the present circumstances K. finds himself in are obvious: Bürgel is offering himself to K. It is in this context that K. has the only dream in the novel:

> K. slept, but it wasn't really sleep, he was still hearing what Bürgel was saying, perhaps better than earlier when he was still awake but dead tired, one word after another accosted his ears, but that irritating awareness was gone, he felt free, it was no longer Bürgel who kept him, but he, K., who now and then groped about for Bürgel, he had not yet reached the depths of sleep, but he had dipped into it and now no one was going to steal this from him. And it seemed to him as though in this way he had achieved a great victory and a group of people was already there to celebrate it and he or even somebody else was raising a champagne glass in honor of the victory. And in order to let everyone know what it was all about, the battle and the victory were being repeated once again, or perhaps they weren't being repeated but were taking place for the first time and had been celebrated earlier and kept on being celebrated, because there was fortunately no doubt at all about the outcome. A secretary, naked, very much like the statue of a Greek god, was being hard pressed by K. in battle. That was quite comical, and in his sleep K. smiled gently at the way the secretary was being constantly startled out of his proud posture by K.'s advances and quickly had to use his raised arm and clenched fist to cover up his exposed parts, but he was not yet quick enough. The battle didn't last long, for step by step, and very big steps they were too, K. advanced. Was this even a battle? There was no real obstacle, only every so often a few squeaks from the secretary. This Greek god squeaked like a girl being tickled. And then finally he was gone; K. was alone in a large room; ready to fight, he turned around and looked for his opponent, but there wasn't anybody there anymore, the group of people

> had scattered as well, only the champagne glass lay broken on the ground, K. stamped on it. But the splinters hurt; with a start he woke up feeling sick, like a small child on being awakened; nevertheless, at the sight of Bürgel's bare chest a thought from the dream came to him: "There's your Greek god! So pull him out of the sack!" (Kafka 1998: 264–265)

The movement into the dreamscape represents the only moment in the novel when the setting moves beyond the territory of the castle-village complex, which up to this late point in the book has been a nearly totally "sealed up" world. K. escapes this world by slipping into a hypnagogic state—not entirely awake, not entirely asleep, but enveloped by the emerging dreamscape. The significance of this shift is reflected in the startling phrase: "but that irritating awareness was gone, he felt free…." This is a shocking revelation—the notion that a failure of awareness opens up a potential space for freedom. The winning of this freedom is, for the dreamer-K., a "great victory" and the subsequent dream translates this notion of victory into a narrative.

K.'s movement into the dreamscape results in the loss of "awareness." This awareness or consciousness is what defines his relationship to the specific setting and to others present, in this case Bürgel. The "awareness" is irritating to K., presumably because it acts to register these surroundings and relationships, and to define them always within the dominant understanding of the castle-village system. The loss of awareness opens up new configurations—and immediately the loss of consciousness produces a shift between K. and Bürgel: "…it was no longer Bürgel who kept him, but he, K., who now and then groped about for Bürgel…." It is not entirely clear what this means, except that K. has turned from a passive object to an active subject.

The startling result of this loss of awareness and, with it, the disintegration of the castle-village system, is that K. "felt free." This feeling of freedom precedes the narrative report of the dream, the formation of the dream-text. The feeling of freedom reflects the rupture in consciousness and the movement into the territory of the dreamscape. As "irritating" awareness fades and the dreamscape emerges, freedom presents itself. The central question, though, is what is meant by this freedom. How should it be understood in relation to the power structures of the castle-village system? On the one hand, it seems clear that the freedom is of a radical type—that it is not limited by any qualifying statements, not a "freedom from" anything or a "freedom to" do anything. It is a pure state of being free. This freedom results from the falling away of awareness or consciousness, implying that pure freedom emerges with a relinquishing, at least momentarily, of a situated understanding of selfhood. Since the castle-village power structure is built precisely on the ability of the system as a whole to locate and define each individual member in relation to all others, this relinquishing of position is tantamount to a radical rejection of the system's reality.[10] On the "waking" side of the hypnagogic line, Bürgel explains to K. a seemingly effective strategy to deal with the castle authorities, namely by exploiting his immediate situation with Bürgel himself. But this seeming grasp at power, that is, the advancement of K.'s interests, contrasts directly with the feeling of freedom in the dreamscape, revealing that there is no freedom possible from within the castle-village system; one must escape the system to discover freedom. The bitter irony here is that this feeling of freedom exists but for a single moment—it can be nothing other than fleeting, ephemeral, and partial. The dream-text itself writes the feeling of freedom back into the structure of power and upon waking K. carries none of its potential radicalism with him.

The freedom K. experiences is not, at first, related to a victory over the castle-village system. The link between the feeling of freedom and the notion of competition and domination only comes when the dream-K. starts to translate the primordial understanding of freedom in narrative terms. First, the freedom is equated with the state of sleep—again a state of total but temporally limited erasure of identity. The achievement of sleep, however, invites the notion of "victory"—and this notion leads to the idea of contestation. The achievement of sleep and thus of freedom, then, is reframed as an inversion of hierarchy. Instead of K. being oppressed by the castle officials and village society, he now oppresses or dominates the representative official and wins the support of the villagers. In the dream-text, the castle authority is symbolically naked and helpless—exposed and ashamed of itself. Dream-K. exploits this shame to push his advantage. However, the quest for domination proves futile. The end result is that the crowd vanishes. The idea that one can invert power relationships or wrestle power from the authorities proves barren. The initial feeling of freedom is not experienced again through victory. Dream-K.'s stamping of the champagne glass and his injuring himself mean the end of the party—and the angry recognition that his (apparent) victory over the castle authorities is meaningless. Freedom cannot be found there.

Despite the limited appearance of freedom in the dream in *The Castle*—occupying no more than a single sentence, perhaps extending into two, its political implications are significant. The freedom does not, in its spontaneous upwelling, depend on any hierarchical relationships. It imagines a state of being outside of power. Of course, it is impossible to exist entirely beyond hierarchies and outside of flows of power. *The Castle*, however, invites the reading of the possibility of experiencing this type of a-hierarchical zone as waking reality crumbles, the dreamscape emerges, and the dream-text has yet to displace the pre-narrative dreamscape. The depth of the dreamscape is a space beyond the reach of both the castle-village system and the opposing dominant system of the modern state that K. unwittingly embodies. K., in this moment, is stripped of his identity—that "irritating awareness"—and one can intuit that it is not only Bürgel who appears naked, but K., too, and that this nakedness is a stripping away of "dress" in the physical and non-physical sense. Bürgel's artificiality (he appears as an animated statue of a Greek god) reflects back on the dream-K.—for he, too, is not K. but an empty vessel, in which any and all possible identity formations could be poured. This artificiality is further emphasized by the performative nature of the dream scene. The action consists of repeated reenactment—implying that the actor playing the combatant K. is not the dream-K., but a stand-in for the dream-K., who watches the performance along with the crowd. When K. attempts to claim the mantle of victory, the spectators vanish, suggesting that they cannot recognize him or distinguish between the real dream-K. and the actor-K. in the dream performance.

If the two key ideas about dreams from Kafka's diaries discussed above are read into this moment of *The Castle*, the significance deepens. The first idea is that of radical displacement: "Again pulled through this terrible, long, narrow crack; it can only be forced through in a dream" (Kafka 1988: 390). In *The Castle*, the transition into the dreamscape means both the unmaking of the self, including the location of the self within the social system, and the emergence of a type of anarchic zone of freedom. Indeed, its "narrowness" in the novel is quite severe—the width of one sentence among thousands. In Kafka's "A Report to an Academy," the juxtaposition of freedom with social identity construction is made explicit. In the story, the narrator, an ape, describes the choice he makes to give up his ape-ness and to become human in order to find his "way out" of his cage—"I had to stop being an ape" (Kafka 1995: 253). The narrator elaborates:

> I fear that perhaps you do not quite understand what I mean by "way out." I use the expression in its fullest and most popular sense. I deliberately do not use the word "freedom." I do not mean the spacious feeling of freedom on all sides. As an ape, perhaps, I knew that, and I have met men who yearn for it. But for my part I desired such freedom neither then nor now. In passing: may I say that all too often men are betrayed by the word freedom. And as freedom is counted among the most sublime feelings, so the corresponding disillusionment can also be sublime....No, freedom is not what I wanted. Only a way out... (Kafka 1995: 253)

The ape's "report" describes his assimilation into the ways of human beings in order to live a life beyond the cage and in open society. The "way out" was to become human, to imitate human actions (like drinking schnapps) and human speech. It is speech, the saying of "Hallo," that allows the ape to "[break] into the human community" (Kafka 1995: 257). This "way out," of course, has come at considerable cost to the ape—freedom has been abandoned and a deep sense of self-alienation accompanies the ape's reaching the "cultural level of an average European" (Kafka 1995: 258).[11] If the "way out" was an abandonment of ape-ness in order to conform to the norms of human society, freedom, in the "Report," meant choosing for death. Even had the ape fought through the cage, he says, he would have to fight his way onto deck, only then to throw himself overboard into the deep sea to drown. Like the ape in "A Report to an Academy," K. faces the choice between the freedom of the dreamscape or the "way out" proposed by Bürgel—that is, how K. can work within the castle-village system. Unlike the ape, K. achieves neither. He cannot embrace the radicality of the opening toward freedom and fails to comprehend Bürgel's instructions about how to operate within the social system, in other words how to speak the language of the castle-village, the ape's "Hallo."

The second idea about the radicality of dreaming in the diaries concerns its power to write over, inscribe on, or deface the "stubborn material" of waking life—marking the body of the sleeper. In *The Castle*, this marking is enacted through the stabbing of the shards of broken glass, which serves to obliterate the dreamscape. The initial feeling of freedom, then, has evolved into a feeling of pain. This sensory evolution suggests that the feeling of freedom must be preserved through pain—a scratching of the stubborn substance without which the whole process would be swiftly forgotten in the unforgiving light of wakefulness.

While the dream-text can be woven into various interpretive schemata of *The Castle*, the moment of freedom in the transition from wakefulness to the dreamscape cannot be assimilated into the constructs of power that structure the novel. The freedom is not won through an assertion of power over the castle authorities, either by someone within the castle domain or by an intruder from beyond it. The freedom, thus, does not correspond to the kind of rights-based freedom of the modern state that both K. and Joseph K. in *The Trial* are attempting to assert. While an external assertion of force—for example of the bank world against the trial world—would reinstitute hierarchy and authority in the name of liberation, K.'s moment of freedom escapes this trap. Finally, K.'s freedom does not depend on a shifting of the social hierarchy in the village. In this sense, it is a type of freedom directly opposed to Brunswick's inversion of the master/apprentice relationship with Barnabas's father and the use of political strategies to win social power in the village. K.'s freedom, in fact, cannot be public—as the dream-text makes clear, the spectatorship of K.'s so-called victory serves to quash the moment of freedom and to cause the transition back into the world of wakefulness.

The value of K.'s moment of freedom in *The Castle* is enormous—made enormous by its very smallness in comparison to the novel's complex portrait of a system of power and authority in a state of clear decline, though so hermetic as to be (partly) unaware of the acuteness of the crisis. The scene between K. and Bürgel is fundamentally about the vulnerability of the castle authority—the limits of its power. Bürgel's advice is for

K. to seek the advancement of his interests by exploiting the system's vulnerability. While seemingly plausible, this working within the structures of power is an authoritarian answer. The alternative, which wells up in parallel to this authoritarian approach, emerging in the movement into the dreamscape, is the anarchic possibility of knowing one's freedom—not as a part of the system of power, not as a product of a certain identity construct (like that of land surveyor), not as an ally of a specific faction (that of Brunswick or the Barnabas family) but rather as a subject momentarily emancipated from all definitions, all notions of identity, all strategies of resistance or self-interest—all narratives of one's life. Only here in *The Castle*, in the depths of what seem like the most hopeless circumstances, does Kafka propose—as the dreamscape emerges—a type of radical freedom that could be characterized as anarchistic. I can only speculate that for Kafka the potential of the emerging dreamscape to rupture constructed reality and to refashion it through its intense power reminded him of the potential of the creative act of writing—the inscribing of a vision on the *stubborn material* of the page. K.'s freedom, seen in this light, is Frost's shattering ice, Eve's polyvalent desire, the serpent's chaos, Job's terror—it is the disordering force of chaos and unmaking that precedes—and is the very foundation for—any true creative act. These are acts of anarchy.

Conclusion

Recent studies of Kafka have attempted to locate him as an anarchist, radical, or subversive writer.[12] Michael Löwy reads *The Castle* through a late nineteenth-century, early twentieth-century anarchist lens, concluding that Kafka is "questioning…the despotic basis of all states, of the state in general (as anarchists do)…" (2004: 50). My discussion has called into question the appropriateness of equating the castle-village structure with the modern state, as Löwy does, and contests his assertion that "the castle maintains a seamless dominance over the village population and inspires fear and obedience" (2004: 52).[13] I have argued that the situation in the castle-village system is much more dynamic, fragile, unsettled, and contested than Löwy describes. Against the dominating bureaucratic system,

Löwy submits that Kafka proposes the individual in the "libertarian tradition" as the potential emancipatory agent. The individual best embodying this tradition, for him, is not K. but Amalia, who defies the authority of the castle when she refuses to submit to its demands for sexual exploitation and abuse (2004: 56–57). While I agree with Löwy that Amalia's act is heroic, it also seems like a kind of Bartleby-like refusal; it is powerful, disruptive, and yet doomed to failure. The libertarian individual can resist power, then, as K. and Joseph K. also do, but it cannot (re)imagine freedom.

More radical and politically anarchic than Amalia's forceful refusal is the type of freedom that emerges from K.'s movement into the dreamscape. This movement causes a rupture in K.'s understanding of himself. To dream, then, for Kafka, is to unmake the self, opening up the opportunity for self-(re)creation. This process of unmaking and refashioning reminds of the constructed nature of selfhood and identity and proposes the active creation of alternative constellations. Together with the momentary obliteration of the self, the movement into the dreamscape escapes the trap of hierarchical notions of freedom. Freedom in the dreamscape cannot be won at the expense of another—the constructions of hierarchies and hierarchical inversions are the product not of the movement into the dreamscape but of the reverse movement from the dreamscape into the narrative construct of the dream-text.

As such, it could be argued that this "freedom" and this "anarchy" are politically toothless and nothing but a literary flourish with no resonance in actual political struggle. In fact, Kafka's conception of dreaming contains the core of his most radical political expression as well as the foundation for anarchic thinking and action—the dissolution of self and other and a return to a state of "primordial chaos" as the beginning of the creative act of becoming free. I say this because the essential element of Kafka's notion of power is its hermetic quality, the illusion (or delusion) that power is total, ubiquitous, and unquestionable. Perhaps this is why Kafka chooses the name "Klamm" to represent the human form of the castle—taken either from the German *Klamm* (gorge or ravine) or (and seemingly more likely) from the Czech word *klam*, meaning deception, deceit, fallacy, sham, or illusion. Power might be *klam*, but it is so in a way that is total, unapproachable, incomprehensible, and irrefutable.

One cannot lessen the oppression of power by challenging this deception through counter-deception (like pretending to be a land surveyor)—the real challenge to *klam* is in escaping it, fleeing the deceptive totality of the system of power through the pinprick of the dream into the domain of freedom. Once experienced, this freedom makes the system of total power both explicable and (one would hope) unbearable.

Notes

1. Hannah Arendt makes this point already in 1944: "That *The Trial* implies a critique of the pre-war Austro-Hungarian bureaucratic regime, whose numerous and conflicting nationalities were dominated by a homogeneous hierarchy of officials, has been understood from the first appearance of the novel. Kafka, an employee of a workmen's insurance company and a loyal friend of many eastern European Jews for whom he had had to obtain permits to stay in the country, had a very intimate knowledge of the political conditions of his country. He knew that a man caught in the bureaucratic machinery is already condemned; and that no man can expect justice from judicial procedures where interpretation of the law is coupled with the administering of lawlessness, and where the chronic inaction of the interpreters is compensated by a bureaucratic machine whose senseless automatism has the privilege of ultimate decision" (Arendt 1994: 71). Brian Danoff argues that Arendt "found revealed in Kafka's fiction many of the crucial elements of totalitarianism that she wrote about in *Origins of Totalitarianism*" (2000: 211). On Kafka and bureaucracy, see: Clegg et al. (2016); Danoff (2000); Hodson et al. (2013); Löwy (2016); Stach (2005); Stach (2015); Warner (2007); and Wolf (2018).
2. Walter Benjamin, while seeing the realms of power in Kafka as representations of officialdom, bureaucracy, and the state, correctly describes the trial world when he claims, "Filth is the element of the officials" (1969: 114).
3. After the woman is summoned to the Examining Magistrate and submits to this demand, the novel states: "K. slowly walked after them [the woman and the student], he recognized that this was the first unequivocal defeat that he had received from these people. There was no reason, of course, for him to worry about that, he had received the defeat only

because he had insisted on giving battle. While he stayed quietly at home and went about his ordinary vocations he remained superior to all these people and could kick any of them out of his path. And he pictured to himself the highly comic situation which would arise if, for instance, this wretched student, this puffed-up whippersnapper, this bandy-legged beaver, had to kneel by Elsa's bed some day wringing his hands and begging for favors" (Kafka 1992: 59).

4. Josephus, in *The Jewish War*, captures the terror the *sicarii* spread in a Jerusalem under Roman rule: "When the countryside had been cleared of [bandit chief Eleazar's men], another type of bandit sprang up in Jerusalem, known as 'Sicarii.' These men commit numerous murders in broad daylight and in the middle of the City. Their favorite trick was to mingle with festival crowds, concealing under their garments small daggers with which they stabbed their opponents. When the victims fell, the assassins melted into the indignant crowd, and through their plausibility entirely defied detection. The first to have his throat cut by them was Jonathan the high priest, and after him many were murdered every day" (147). The *sicarii* were much more than "bandits"—they represented the most extreme wing of Jewish national resistance to Rome. They eventually occupied the fortress at Masada, the final redoubt of resistance to the Roman army's successful campaigns against the Jewish lands. Josephus writes of the final Roman siege of Masada, "The fortress was Masada, occupied by the Sicarii under the command of an influential man called Eleazar, a descendent of Judas who had persuaded many Jews…not to register when Quirinius was sent to Judea to take a census. At that time the Sicarii combined against those prepared to submit to Rome, and in every way treated them as enemies, looting their property, rounding up their cattle, and setting their dwellings on fire: they were no better than foreigners, they declared, throwing away in this cowardly fashion the freedom won by the Jews at such coast, and avowedly choosing slavery under the Romans" (1984: 393).
5. Though Mark Nanos argues against the authenticity of the claim of widespread use of the epithet "dogs" for gentiles in the ancient Near East, the link became strongly developed in its reversal—the later Christian designation of Jews as dogs (Nanos 2009).
6. Schwenger provides an interesting discussion of this diary entry in his chapter in *At the Borders of Sleep* on insomnia. For Schwenger, Kafka is referring to a hypnagogic state or even to a series of "waking dreams" that

one might read as hallucinations of sorts. Schwenger writes, "The dreams that haunt the insomniac Kafka, then, are the product not of sleep but of a psychological night…The insomniac becomes aware of an incessant inner turbulence that dreams tap into but can also surge forward without the intermediary stage of sleep" (2012: 62).

7. I agree with Ron Smetana's claim, "The Castle is not an independent entity. It is immanent as well as transcendent. Its existence and meaning lie with the villagers; there is no Castle other than the social realm." Power and authority, Smetana asserts, are not attributes of the Castle and/or its officials; power lies with the villagers: "Castle officials, in fact, have no greater influence over the social order than do other villagers…. authority is immanent in all village life, not just in official actions." Smetana concludes, "[K.'s] unique and unsatisfying status in the village comes from his refusal to act on the knowledge that society is immanent—that the peasantry is the Castle" (1991: 54–58).
8. Corbella is on target when he calls this relationship a "disturbance" in the system of power (2007: 75).
9. Reiner Stach, in the third volume of his biography of Kafka, nicely compares the village in *The Castle* to the real village of Spindelmühle, where Kafka began writing the novel. In contrast to the tourist town of Spindelmühle, Stach writes, "An outside world does not seem to exist for the villagers…" of the novel (2015: 433–434). He adds, and this will be important for my discussion below, "The world of The Castle is arcane and sealed up tight" (2015: 443).
10. This freedom that results in the movement into the dreamscape should be compared with the other moment of "freedom" in the novel. This comes after K. has attempted to waylay Klamm on his way out of the Gentlemen's Inn by hiding in the sleigh that is ready to take him to the castle. K.'s attempt prevents Klamm from leaving and eventually the coachman gives up waiting and parks the sleigh and the horses in the stable. When only K. remains in the courtyard, the narrator provides access to his reflections: "…it seemed to K. as if they had broken off all contact with him, but as if he were freer than ever and could wait as long as he wanted here in the place where he was generally not allowed, and as if he had fought for this freedom for himself in a manner nobody else could have done and as if nobody could touch him or drive him away, or even speak to him, yet—and this conviction was at least equally strong—as if there was nothing more senseless, nothing more desperate, than this

freedom this waiting, this invulnerability" (Kafka 1998: 106). While the freedom of moving into the dreamscape is a result of the move beyond or outside of the structures of authority, the freedom "won" by K. in the courtyard is a product of competition and confrontation, which results not in a kind of false or sham sense of freedom but in a purer, transcendent experience of being free.

11. At the end of the "Report," the ape describes the costs of his process of conformity: "Nearly every evening I give a performance, and I have a success that could hardly be increased. When I come home late at night from banquets, from scientific receptions, from social gatherings, there sits waiting for me a half-trained little chimpanzee and I take comfort from her as apes do. By day I cannot bear to see her; for she has the insane look of the bewildered half-broken animal in her eye; no one else sees it, but I do, and I cannot bear it. On the whole, at any rate, I have achieved what I set out to achieve. But do not tell me that it was not worth the trouble" (258–259).
12. Much of the debate about Kafka's politics concerns the extent to which he identified as an anarchist, took seriously the anarchist ideas he was exposed to, and participated in Prague's anarchist circles. The positions range from considering Kafka as a committed anarchist to seeing him as being only superficially involved. These debates do not play a significant role in my analysis of Kafka's politics of the dreamscape, as the radicalism I read there is not dependent on a systematic presentation of anarchist theory.
13. This type of analysis leads Löwy to see Kafka as a kind of prophet of totalitarianism. "The libertarian inspiration is inscribed into the heart of Kafka's novels. When he speaks to us of the *state*, it is in the form of 'administration' or 'justice' as an impersonal system of domination which crushes, suffocates, or kills individuals. This is an agonizing, opaque, and unintelligible world where unfreedom prevails. *The Trial* is often presented as a prophetic work. With his visionary imagination, the author had foreseen the justice of the totalitarian state and the Nazi or Stalinist show trials" (1997: 10).

References

Arendt, Hannah. *Essays in Understanding: 1930–1954*. Ed. Jerome Kohn. New York: Harcourt Brace, 1994.

Benjamin, Walter. *Illuminations*. Ed. Hannah Arendt. Trans. Harry Zohn. New York: Schocken, 1969.

Clegg, Stewart, et al. "Kafkaesque Power and Bureaucracy." *Journal of Political Power* 9.2 (2016): 157–181.

Corbella, Walter. "Panopticism and the Construction of Power in Franz Kafka's *The Castle*." *Papers on Language & Literature: A Quarterly Journal for Scholars and Critics of Language and Literature* 43.1 (2007): 68–88.

Cumberland, Ruth. "Inscribed Bodies: The Cruel Mirage of Imperialistic Idealism in Kafka's 'Penal Colony.'" *Papers on Language & Literature: A Quarterly Journal for Scholars and Critics of Language and Literature* 49.2 (2013) 203+.

Danoff, Brian. "Arendt, Kafka, and the Nature of Totalitarianism." *Perspectives on Political Science* 29.4 (2000): 211–218.

Hodson, Randy, et al. "Rules Don't Apply: Kafka's Insights on Bureaucracy." *Organization* 20.2 (2013): 256–278.

Kafka, Franz. *The Castle*. Trans. Mark Harman. New York: Schocken, 1998.

Kafka, Franz. *The Diaries*. Trans. Joseph Kresh and Martin Greenberg. New York: Schocken, 1988.

Kafka, Franz. *The Complete Stories*. Ed. Nahum Glatzer. New York: Schocken, 1995.

Kafka, Franz. *The Trial*. Trans. Willa Muir and Edwin Muir. New York: Schocken, 1992.

Kafka, Franz. *Letters to Milena*. Ed. Willy Haas. Trans. Tania Stern and James Stern. London: Vintage, 1999.

Josephus. *The Jewish War*. Eds. Betty Radice and E. Mary Smallwood. Trans. G.A. Williamson. New York: Penguin, 1984.

Löwy, Michael. *Franz Kafka: Subversive Dreamer*. Trans. Inez Hedges. Ann Arbor: U of Michigan P, 2016.

Löwy, Michael. "Kafka and Libertarian Socialism." *New Politics* 6.3 (1997): 120.

Löwy, Michael. "Paper Chains: Bureaucratic Despotism and Voluntary Servitude in Franz Kafka's *The Castle*." *Diogenes* 51.4 (2004): 49–58.

Nanos, Mark. "Paul's Reversal of Jews Calling Gentiles 'Dogs' (Philippians 3:2): 1600 Years of an Ideological Tale Wagging an Exegetical Dog?" *Biblical Interpretation* 17.4 (2009): 448–482.

Pan, David. "The Persistence of Patriarchy in Franz Kafka's 'Judgment.'" *Orbis Litterarum* 55 (2000): 135–160.

Schwenger, Peter. *At the Borders of Sleep: On Liminal Literature.* Minneapolis: U of Minnesota P, 2012.

Smetana, Ron. "The Peasantry and the Castle: Kafka's Social Psychology." *Twentieth Century Literature* 37.1 (1991): 54–58.

Sokol, Walter. "Perspectives and Truth in 'The Judgment.'" *The Problem of the Judgement: Eleven Approaches to Kafka's Story.* Ed. Ángel Flores. New York: Gordian, 1977. 193–237.

Stach, Reiner. *Kafka: The Decisive Years.* Trans. Shelley Frisch. Orlando: Harcourt, 2005.

Stach, Reiner. *Kafka: The Years of Insight.* Trans. Shelley Frisch. Princeton: Princeton UP, 2015.

Tulley, David. "'To Live Outside the Trial': Anarchist Implications in Foucauldian Readings of Franz Kafka's In the Penal Colony and The Trial." *Anarchist Studies* 26.2 (2018): 12–31.

Warner, Malcolm. "Kafka, Weber and Organization Theory." *Human Relations* 60.7 (2007): 1019–1038.

Wolf, Burkhardt. "Kafka in Habsburg." *Administory* 1.1 (2018): 193–221.

7

J. Allan Hobson's *Dreamstage* in Context

Introduction

In April 1977, the exhibition *Dreamstage: A Multi-Media Portrait of the Sleeping Brain* opened at Harvard's Carpenter Center. The exhibition was the brainchild of psychiatrist and neurophysiologist J. Allan Hobson, who, together with Robert McCarley, had been exploring the neurophysiology of the brain during sleep, attempting to describe the biochemical mechanisms behind the dreaming process. Two visual artists collaborated with Hobson on *Dreamstage*: the photographer Theodore J. Spagna Jr. and the media artist and composer Paul Earls. Central to the exhibition was a live sleeper, readings of whose heartbeat, brain waves, eye movements, and muscle tones were converted into visual laser displays and synthesized music (College Museum News 1977: 333). The exhibition, combining science and art, exhibition with performance, proved popular, drawing some 6000 visitors during its first few weeks and over 10,000 in total (Dolnick 1990). A few months later, in December 1977, Hobson and McCarley would publish their groundbreaking study of the dreaming brain in *The American Journal of Psychiatry*, "The Brain as a Dream State Generator: An Activation-Synthesis Hypothesis of the Dream

© The Author(s), under exclusive license to Springer Nature Switzerland AG 2021

S. Rogoff, *The Politics of the Dreamscape*,
https://doi.org/10.1007/978-3-030-74796-1_7

Process." One of the explicit aims of the article was to offer a "final" refutation of Freudian dream theory from the perspective of neuroscience. Its other, related aim was to locate dreaming firmly in the biochemical processes of the brain.

While the attempt to describe the dream state in neurophysiological terms is not inherently authoritarian or anarchic, the production history of *Dreamstage*, its aestheticization of scientific processes, and Hobson and McCarley's search for a specific "dream generator" overlap with a number of contexts and discourses that recruit sleep and dream science into their political logics. The first discursive context for the rise of dream (neuro) science is the movement in psychotropic pharmacology from the effects-oriented tranquilizer era to the cause-oriented Prozac era. Blockbuster psychiatric medicines, starting in the late 1980s with Prozac and continuing until the present (2020), were marketed as intervening in highly localized brain functions. The quest for the "depression-generator" mechanism in the brain, notably, runs parallel to that for the "dream-generator," the holy grail of Hobson and McCarley's work. Second, Hobson and McCarley's work on dreaming contributed to the anti-Freudian wave in psychiatry and psychology, culminating most famously in the important anti-Freudian revision to the *Diagnostic and Statistical Manual of Mental Disorders*, published as the *DSM-III* in 1980. In other words, dream science and its related neurobiology were part of the transformation of the definitions and borders of psychiatric and psychological practice. Third, Hobson and McCarley's thesis about dream generation fit the mold of technological or material determinism that permeated an increasingly technophile West. Dreaming, in this mode, became part of the utilitarian *work* of the brain, serving primarily to more efficiently fulfill *functions*, such as learning—the brain as bureaucratic machine. The combination of increased pharmacology of the brain and the idea that sleep was part of an individual's daily "work" further encouraged the intrusion of medicine into the domain of sleep through the development and marketing of sleeping pills—with the entire structure of sleep oriented around the hours of the capitalist workday. Dream science, especially in its public manifestation in *Dreamstage*, was an important testing ground for pharmaceutical advertisement and the visual language of science's commodification. Accordingly, this chapter first discusses Hobson and McCarley's work on dreaming in relation to these overlapping discursive contexts before shifting to an analysis of *Dreamstage*. The first section charts the parallels between the discourse on the science of dreaming and the parallel discourse surrounding the precision understanding, targeting, and commodification of neurobiological structures. The second section argues that a critical component of the rise of dream science was its push to overcome the Freudian legacy. This allowed dream science to define dreaming in purely materialist terms, as one discernible phase of the biological sleep cycle (REM sleep). The third section places dream science of the late 1970s and 1980s against the backdrop of discourses on technology and capitalism, focusing specifically on the relationship between sleep/dreaming and work.

The Science and Commodification of Sleep

The opening of Hobson's *Dreamstage* at Harvard's Carpenter Center in 1977 came at a pivotal moment in the treatment of sleep disorders (and mental disorders in general) between the euphoria of the early tranquilizer period and the rise in the mid-1980s of a new class of drugs based on the regulation of neurotransmitters like serotonin (Herzberg 2010; Lewis 2006; Tone 2008). Prozac, the most famous of the neurotransmitter drugs, hit the market in 1987, ushering in a sea change in the pharmaceutical industry as it related to psychotropic drugs and in the public's relation to brain science. By the late 1980s and early 1990s, the first sleeping pill to utilize the new paradigm, Ambien, became available. Use of pharmaceutical sleep aids grew steadily throughout the following decades to tens of millions of prescriptions per year. By 2014, an estimated five percent of women and around three percent of men in the United States used sleeping pills to combat sleep disturbance (Romm 2014).

In the late 1970s, the glow of prescription tranquilizers had faded, giving way to a period of panic about the side effects of tranquilizer use (Herzberg 2006). The primary target of critics of the use of tranquilizers was the drug Valium, a benzodiazepine sold by the pharmaceutical company Hoffman-La Roche. It was Hoffman-La Roche that provided twenty of the thirty thousand dollars necessary to launch *Dreamstage* at the Carpenter Center, thereby bringing Hobson's dream science together with the producer of the then dominant sleep-aids: Valium, of course, and the more specific Dalmane—another drug in the benzodiazepine family (Institute of Medicine Staff 1979: 48–52).

Hoffman-La Roche's first blockbuster benzodiazepine tranquilizer was not Valium but the chemically related Librium, which went on sale in 1960 and immediately became the top-selling medication for an array of perceived psychic ailments—most significantly "anxiety," the forerunner of "depression" (Tone 2008: 135). Since sleep disturbance was considered a key symptom of psychic trouble, Hoffman-La Roche made sure to advertise Librium's soothing nighttime effects. Designer Rolf Harder's "Escape to Reality" advertisement for Librium, for example, proclaimed that it was an effective treatment for alcoholism; its message read, in part: "In the treatment of acute episodes such as impending or active delirium tremens or hallucinosis, injectable Librium relieves tremor, fear, anxiety and restlessness and induces restful sleep" (Harder 2019).

The connection between tranquilizer use and improved sleep recurred in most Librium advertisements. In another ad, it is stated, "A college student with 'long-standing anxiety neuroses' showed an immediate improvement after he began taking 25 mg of Librium three times a day. His nightmares stopped, he became more affable and relaxed, and his grades improved" (Tone 2008: 134). Librium's advertising budget was immense for its day, reaching two million dollars in its first year on the market. By the mid-1960s, Librium was targeting the seemingly ubiquitous nervous disorder of anxiety—contributing to the creation and maintenance of this ubiquity. A 1964 advertisement for Librium positioned the drug as a palliative "for the Age of Anxiety," featuring a pair of anxious male eyes above scenes of everyday stress and allusions to Cold War fears (Tone 2008: 136).

A few years later, an infamous Librium ad, "College Girl," appeared in a medical journal directed at college physicians. Its appearance makes explicit what had been implicit in much of the Librium campaigning up this point: the gender targeting of the advertising and the link between tranquilizer use and the social, cultural, and political position of women in American society. In the ad, a young and seemingly distressed woman is carrying books. The headline beneath her says: "A Whole New World … of Anxiety." The text of the advertisement runs:

> Exposure to new friends and other influences may force her to reevaluate herself and her goals … Her newly stimulated intellectual curiosity may make her more sensitive to and apprehensive about unstable national and world conditions … Today's changing morality and the possible consequences of new freedoms may provoke acute feelings of insecurity. (Colen 1980)

In its first year in the market, Librium won twenty percent of the tranquilizer market, "with doctors writing more than 1.5 million new prescriptions for Librium each month" (Tone 2008: 137–138).

The gender, race, and class targeting of the tranquilizer market did not begin with Librium. It had its roots back in the context of the explosion of the first great postwar blockbuster tranquilizer drug, Miltown (Herzberg 2010: 54–56). Though advertising for Miltown and its successor drugs stressed its potential as a treatment for both men and women of the middle and upper classes, minor tranquilizers such as Librium and Valium were predominantly prescribed for women. By the 1970s, Valium had far outpaced all other tranquilizers in the market and had established a powerful consumer identity built around the alleviation of everyday stress, tension, and anxiety.

One of the key symptoms Valium targeted, according to its advertisements, was insomnia—the same claim that had been made for Miltown and Librium. "High prescription rates reflected medical responsiveness to women's expressions of distress but also a willingness among doctors, more than 90 percent of whom were male in 1970, to code nervousness, stress, and insomnia as distinctly 'female' problems" (Tone 2008: 96). Hoffman-La Roche capitalized on the soporific effects of drugs like Librium and Valium by launching another benzodiazepine, flurazepam, specifically as a sleeping pill under the name Dalmane. Dalmane dominated the sleeping pill market in the 1970s, all but eliminating competition from barbiturate drugs and other older modes of sleep drug therapy (Institute of Medicine Staff 1979: 48–52). As myriad advertisements from the 1970s and 1980s indicate, the prototypical insomnia patient was an "anxiety-ridden" white woman.

What is perhaps more interesting about the Dalmane campaign, however, is how "scientific" the marketing strategy is. References abound to the latest trends in sleep research, including the ability to measure brain waves during sleep to determine the episodic stages of sleep. The advertisements present visualizations of data to support claims about Dalmane's efficacy. Technology is emphasized in the form of the EEG and other apparatuses. In one advertisement, a sleep scientist appears in contour outlines above the scene (God-like) to oversee the sleep cycle of the woman patient. The intended message is quite clear—the regulation of sleep by Dalmane is a modern and scientifically sound practice ("Proved in the sleep laboratory…. Proved clinically…. Proved over time," the advertisement reads), rooted in the most advanced understanding of the brain and the brain's functioning during sleep.

Despite Hoffman-La Roche's attempt to create a sophisticated science-based marketing campaign around Dalmane, the underlying vagueness of the science supporting benzodiazepines combined with the multilayered movement that arose in the mid-1970s against tranquilizer use—focusing on Dalmane's "cousin" Valium—pushed pharmaceutical companies to exploit new neurological discoveries to develop an emerging class of drugs that focused on regulation of the release, reception, and reabsorption of neurotransmitters. The rhetoric of this move from the coarse-acting or rudimentary benzodiazepines to the more "targeted" neurotransmitter regulators emphasized scientific breakthrough, technological advancement, precision, and (perhaps the sum of these parts), the ability of doctor and patient to gain control over the patient's mental functioning.

The move from benzodiazepines to a new class of psychotropic drugs was accompanied by a transition from the vague term "anxiety" to the more clinical term "depression." Much of the nervousness or anxiety discourse was reframed in the rhetoric about depression, which came to be seen as the root cause of these other symptomatic problems. Among the symptoms of depression was insomnia (Bei et al. 2018; Buysse 2013; Staner 2010). In fact, the link between sleep disorder and depression had been established well before the emergence of drugs targeting the neurotransmitters, as can be seen by the Hamilton Rating Scale for Depression (HRSD), which was developed in the 1960s to quantify a patient's depression. Three of the HRSD's seventeen categories asked the subject about insomnia, thus establishing a strong link between the two categories (Hamilton 1960). The degree of specification became even more pronounced as the science of the brain developed throughout the 1970s and 1980s, providing neurophysiologists with a more detailed understanding of the functions of the brain on both micro and global levels. The understanding of depression, for example, moved from a quantitative psychological approach represented by the HRSD to a neurobiological analysis of localized brain function. In the case of depression, this meant primarily an identification of the root cause of depression in the brain's regulation of the neurotransmitter serotonin. In *Happy Pills in America*, David Herzberg gives a compelling account of the scientific optimism (or euphoria) surrounding neuroscience and related pharmacology that permeated the era of the development and eventual commercialization of the next "wonder drug," Prozac. This optimism did not stop at managing psychic illnesses or disorders; it boldly imagined what Dr. Peter Kramer called the "cosmetic" improvement of everything from sexual performance to memory to intelligence and creative achievement (2010: 171–173). Despite this optimism, the ability to convert deeper knowledge of the brain into effective pharmaceuticals remained elusive. The exceptions to this were drugs that relied on the manipulation of the neurotransmitter serotonin.

Prozac, the first "selective serotonin uptake inhibitor" went on sale in 1987 and quickly became the first blockbuster mood drug following the rise of the benzodiazepines and the subsequent (or even synchronous) panic over the ill-effects of Valium in the mid-late 1970s:

> What made Prozac so special was its supposed selectivity and relative lack of serious side effects, which allowed whole new populations of less seriously ill Americans to take it. Not surprisingly, numerous utilization studies revealed that these new populations of pill takers tended to be well-off, white, and female—those with the resources and habits that gave them ready access to prescription medicines, and also those culturally prepared

> to embrace as "sickness" the kinds of mental states now open to treatment with Prozac. (Herzberg 2010: 177)

The specificity of Prozac differentiated it from the earlier tranquilizer treatment of anxiety and depression. This, in turn, allowed the drug, as Herzberg demonstrates, to fit into a variety of shifting cultural discourses about mental illness, gender roles, class, and race. The commercial and cultural discourse around Prozac was less about managing anxiety or depression and more about overcoming both in order to seize personal opportunity (Herzberg 2010: 179–180). The transformation occurred during the day and night—one of the promises of Prozac being the regulation and the sleep-wake cycle and the mitigation of sleep disorders, including insomnia, without soporific effects on the pill's consumer (Herzberg 2010: 182). The confident claims about "restful nights," however dressed up in seemingly scientific garb, were nothing more than empty advertising—as studies reveal that SSRIs have unpredictable effects on a consumer's sleep with some experiencing better sleep and others seeing sleep actually worsen by the antidepressant treatment (Wichniak et al. 2017: 1). But the discursive assertion is what matters here: the science of neurotransmitter manipulation gives doctors and especially patients a sense of understanding about, and control over, the functioning of their brains.

The emphasis on the targeted and simplistic—and therefore less invasive—treatment method is famously on display in one of the first major television ad campaigns to promote the SSRI Zoloft. The advertisement came after the US FDA shifted its policy for consumer-targeted television ads, thereby spurring a massive increase in pharmaceutical advertisements (Donahue 2006: 683–689). The campaign stars a small, white "depressed" blob that, through its implied treatment by Zoloft, overcomes depression and finds happiness and the companionship of others—like butterflies, birds, and ladybugs. Sunshine and chirping replace storm clouds, rain, and thunder. An almost giddily positive reflection on the success of the campaign appeared in *The New York Times* in 2005:

> Zoloft's blob advertisements began running in May 2001. They are directed and illustrated by Pat Smith, an animator whose résumé includes directing

> the former MTV cartoon show "Daria." The popularity of the commercials can be measured not only in their longevity, but also in the volume of online commentary the blob has inspired. On one message board, participants discuss how sweet-looking the blob is and express a desire for a stuffed animal version.
>
> The commercials' appeal may lie in their simplicity: childlike animation and elementary-school explanations of mental illness. But the Zoloft campaign is much more sophisticated than its basic elements suggest. For the drug itself, the two commercials successfully communicate a complicated biochemical fact: that anxiety and depression can be treated with the same pill. (Arthur 2005)

The "biochemical fact" underlying the Zoloft television ad campaign is the regulation of serotonin. The advertisement "dramatizes" this regulation in a language, both textual and visual, that can be easily understood. The thrust of the advertisement's presentation of the regulation of the neurotransmitter serotonin is quite clear. Zoloft forms blockages at the border of the "nerve," increasing the level of serotonin present in the brain. The increase in serotonin makes consumers of the drug happier. The ad's slogan, "When you know more about what's wrong, you can help make it right," fits into the key discursive element of the Prozac era: the message that precise knowledge translates into consumer control. This idea of control or even self-sufficiency underlying (rather paradoxically) the decision to take Zoloft is emphasized at the start of the ad. A smoothing but confident male narrative voice asserts, "You know when you're not feeling like yourself." The narrative voice then presents the viewer with a number of potential symptoms. The implication is that these symptoms are somehow at odds with the true or deeper self: "You may feel sad and cry a lot"; "you lose interest in things you once loved"; "you may feel anxious and can't even sleep." This segment of the ad ends with, "You just know when you don't feel right" (Nudd 2016). The contrast between the seemingly simple science and the vagueness, subjectivity, and indeterminacy of the diagnostics produces an internal tension in the Zoloft advertisement, one that it attempts to overcome through its confidence, soothing tone, and the binary clarity of its visual strategy.

It is important that from Miltown to Prozac (and Zoloft)—so from the 1950s to today—the marketing of psychotropic medication for common "nervous disorders" has emphasized the benefit of balancing relief during the waking hours with more restful sleep. Sleep improvement, in this rhetorical zone, is vital for the success of any "nervous disorder" medication that targets a wide consumer base. The evolution of more targeted sleeping pills traces the path from the Valium era to the Prozac era quite closely. Benzodiazepines like Dalmane and Halcion were almost entirely pushed out of the pharmaceutical market by drugs that targeted neurotransmitters. The first of these drugs to hit the market, Ambien, became, like Prozac, both a mode of treatment and a consumer product with a distinct identity, fusing with discursive constructs about science, technology, and the user's socioeconomic status. While the marketing strategy for Prozac was to establish the regulation of serotonin levels as the key to understanding and treating depression, that for Ambien focused on a lesser-known neurotransmitter, GABA: gamma-aminobutyric acid (Parker 2013: 50). Like Prozac, Ambien discourages GABA from being received by receptor neurons and thus promotes an increase in the presence of the neurotransmitter, which works to slow the brain, encouraging its transition from a state of being awake to a state of being asleep. The keys to the success of Ambien, like that of Prozac, were the purported lack of negative side effects (in contrast to the benzodiazepines) and the drug's simplicity, targeting precisely one chemical in the brain instead of the coarser "global" approach of the earlier treatments.

Ambien's "works like a dream" commercial (2000) captures the key points of this post-Prozac discursive structure, albeit without illustrating the specific science of GABA "balance" in the brain, since GABA does not have the "brand-power" and marketing appeal of serotonin. Still, the ad places Ambien firmly in the era of sleep science. The commercial opens with a confident and smoothing female voice telling the viewer, over a dynamic soundtrack, "There is a rhythm to life. We sleep at night and wake in the morning." The voice goes on to claim, "It's the sleep cycle that helps keep us in a healthy balance" (Works like a Dream 2019). After a brief introduction to the idea of insomnia and sleep disturbance, the commercial presents the viewer with an array of visual images that indicate the vibrancy of the moment of waking up refreshed. These images include a nest of birds chirping, the slow-motion unfurling of a purple morning glory, and a litter of five puppies scampering away from a shared bed. These "nature" images precede the scene of a man waking up well rested and, having regained the "natural balance" between waking and sleeping, being ready to embrace the day.

Dreaming becomes part of the economy of the sleeping pill market, according to the marketing schemes. Ambien's slogan "works like a dream" communicates both that Ambien works really well and that it works to enable access to the oneiric state. This idea of sleeping pills as gateways not only to sleep proper, but to dreaming, is made explicit in a 2005 television commercial for Rozerem, a drug targeting the transmission and reception of melatonin. In this "dream-like" scenario, the protagonist of the commercial, a middle-aged white male suffering from insomnia, encounters Abraham Lincoln and a talking beaver in his kitchen—along with a figure in an old-fashioned diving suit preparing something at the counter in the background. The thrust of the ad is that the figures from the man's dream life miss him and want him back. This obvious point is underscored with the text "your dreams miss you," which appears about two-thirds of the way through the minute-long spot. A male narrative voice then explains to the viewer, "If you can't sleep, you can't dream," implying that Rozerem will help its consumer overcome insomnia and re-discover a more active dream life (Nudd 2016).

Since the 1950s and the discovery of REM, sleep science and dream science have been closely joined. By the time Hobson began his quest for the dream-generator mechanism in the brain in the late 1960s, much was already known about the physiology of sleep. The key discovery of modern sleep science was that the state known cumulatively as "sleep" was in fact a conglomeration of diverse sub-states with the core difference appearing between non-REM or "deep sleep" (also called "slow wave sleep") and REM or Rapid-Eye Movement sleep (Rock 2004: 7–8).

The discovery of the phasic nature of sleep presented two key initial questions for sleep research. First, what accounted, neurologically speaking, for the shift from one state to another? Second, was dreaming sleep, or "D sleep," as Hobson terms it, related to one or more particular phase(s) in the sleep cycle—and if so, how? It was this second question that Hobson and McCarley confronted in their 1977 article, "The Brain as a Dream Generator." The central thrust of this article is that the event of the dream is "determined and shaped" by "physiological processes"; it is not the product of specific and traceable psychological dynamics. Dream impulses, claim Hobson and McCarley, are activated as the brain undergoes its transition into the physiological state of dreaming sleep. These impulses are then organized as a "dream" by a process of "synthesis" of the information provided by the brain stem to the forebrain. Thus, Hobson and McCarley name their theory the "activation-synthesis hypothesis." The article summarizes the main contours of the idea:

> The most important tenet of the activation-synthesis hypothesis is that during dreaming the activated brain generates its own information by a pontine brain stem neuronal mechanism… We hypothesize that this internally generated sensorimotor information, which is partially random and partially specific, is then compared with stored sensorimotor data in the synthesis of dream content. (Hobson and McCarley 1977: 1336)

The triggering mechanism for the process of brain state change between non-dreaming and dreaming sleep, as between non-REM and REM sleep, was neurochemical, in this case the strengthening presence of the neurotransmitter acetylcholine. Though preliminary, Hobson and McCarley claim that cholinergic agents (those stimulating acetylcholine) or agents that inhibit the reception and absorption of acetylcholine can artificially generate and otherwise influence the length and intensity of D-sleep. They write: "In summary, these results support the hypothesis that the pontine brain stem is the generator zone for the D sleep state. The trigger mechanism for the whole system, including the eye movement generator, may be cholinoceptive and the executive zones are probably in the reticular formation" (1977: 1339). They continue:

> …the activation-synthesis hypothesis of dreaming can be stated as follows: during D sleep, a cholinergic mechanism in the reticular formation of the pontine brain stem is periodically activated. The consequences of this activation are as follows:

1. The forebrain is tonically activated, probably via the midbrain reticular formation that is also responsible for its activation during waking. Thus the forebrain is made ready to process information.
2. The spinal reflexes are tonically inhibited, possibly via the bulbar reticular formation and the LC; thus motor outflow is blocked despite high levels of activity in the brain, including the motor cortex.
3. The oculomotor and vestibular systems are phasically activated by the pontine reticular formation so as to produce eye movements. This circuitry, in its entirety, is an internal information source or generator that provides the forebrain with spatially specific but temporally disorganized information about eye velocity, relative position, and direction of movement. Information may similarly be derived from the brain stem generators of patterned motor activity.
4. At the same time that internal information feedback is being generated by the activation of various motor systems, exteroceptive input to sensory systems is phasically blocked. They may intensify the relative impact of the endogenous inputs to the brain, accounting for the intensity of dream imagery and preventing sleep disruption by the externally generated excitation. (1977: 1340)

With these hypotheses, Hobson and McCarley propose that the process of dream activation, duration, and intensity can be understood physiologically—and that such an understanding opens up these processes to manipulation and control. The idea of biological control over sleep and dream inducement and duration overlaps with the general scientific thrust in the late 1970s and 1980s to assert a scientific control over the micro-processes of the brain. Writing ten years after the publication of the 1977 article, Hobson makes a specific connection between dreaming and mental illness:

> If even the minute imbalance of chemicals in a minute region of the brain can influence the whole system and change its state, our conceptual model is important in understanding not only normal conditions (such as REM sleep and dreaming) but abnormal ones (such as mental illness). (Hobson 1988: 202)

Hobson and McCarley's work is part of the neuroscientific drive to define the precise functioning of the human brain in terms of the relationship between local function, information transmission, and general brain "states." According to Hobson and McCarley, dreaming could be physically defined. It was no longer merely a set of images or emotional attributes—dreaming was a brain state with a certain triggering mechanism, a periodicity, and an underlying neurochemical foundation that could be manipulated or even controlled by external chemical assertions. This discourse of precise understanding of brain chemistry and neuron relationships, coupled with the idea that control could be achieved through chemical inputs, contributed to the shift from popular conceptions of the brain as a largely inscrutable entity to the notion of the brain as a relatively open target for pharmacological enhancement. The "dark continent" of the brain suddenly appeared mapped. Views on sleep and dreaming, likewise, were subsumed into this increasingly scientific/technological and pharmacological discourse.

Dream Science, Freud, and Power

Hobson and McCarley begin their pioneering 1977 essay "The Brain as a Dream State Generator" with a claim that they are engaged in nothing less than leading a paradigm shift in how people think about dreams. "Since the turn of the century," they claim at the article's opening, "dream theory has been dominated by the psychoanalytic hypothesis that dreaming is a reactive process designed to protect consciousness and sleep from the disruptive effect of unconscious wishes that are released in sleep" (1977: 1335). This rhetorical move allows Hobson and McCarley to construct the terms of the paradigm shift. Dreams are no longer primarily a psychological phenomenon. They are first and foremost a neurobiological phenomenon—and if they have psychological importance, it is only accidental and either minimal or quite transparent, lacking the complex dream-censor and difference between manifest and latent content of the Freudian system. After their presentation of the activation-synthesis model of dream generation and formation, Hobson and McCarley turn to its implications for psychology, explicitly contrasting their paradigm with psychoanalytic theory. They identify four major implications. First, dreams are not generated for psychological reasons but as a product of physiological phenomena, casting doubt on the primary importance of the psychological significance of dreaming. Dreaming has a "preprogrammed, neurally determined genesis." In other words, wishes, urges, or impulses do not generate dreams, neurons do. They add, "In fact, the neural mechanisms involved can now be precisely specified" (1977: 1346). Second, the specific dream imagery is stimulated by the neurobiological processes of the pontine brain stem and not by the "cognitive areas of the cerebrum," meaning that unlike what is claimed by Freud and psychoanalysis, "the dream process is thus seen as having…little or no primary ideational, volitional, or emotional content" (1977: 1347). While there might be content that is grafted onto the dream imagery in later stages, the dream content does not indicate psychological conflict between impulse and censor but is "genotypically determined"—dream imagery is biologically hardwired, occurring automatically. Third, the relationship between the dream- and image-producing brainstem and the more "advanced" forebrain is one of raw production and synthesis. The forebrain takes what the brain stem offers and weaves the dream together, synthesizing the impulses the best way it can, based on what it receives and what it knows. This role of synthesis contrasts directly with the idea of "censorship" in Freudian theory. A dream's strangeness, then, has no inherent psychological meaning; it is the result of a forebrain trying desperately to organize a flood of random, meaningless impulses. Finally, fourth, while Freud posits that the forgetting of dreams is a mode of repression, Hobson and McCarley demonstrate that this forgetting is a result of natural neurochemical processes: "dream amnesia can now be modeled in a testable way as the result of a different balance between cholinergic and aminergic neuronal activity and the resulting effects on second messengers and macromolecules" (1977: 1347). In sum, according to the activation-synthesis paradigm dreams are not provoked by impulses or wishes; dream imagery has no symbolic meaning; dream content is not censored—there is only manifest content—but rather an attempt to synthesize non-ideational stimuli from the brainstem; and dreams fade upon waking because of a shift in the brain's state and not because of psychological repression.

For Hobson, the 1977 article with McCarley and the launching of *Dreamstage* at the Carpenter Center mark the beginning of the composition of a more detailed historical and popular scientific presentation of the activation-synthesis theory of dreaming. An important stage of this process was the publication of Hobson's book *The Dreaming Brain: How the Brain Creates Both the Sense and the Nonsense of Dreams* (1988). The book places Hobson in the middle of two related movements in psychiatry: first, the attempt to locate psychiatry on a more rigorously "scientific" and "empirical" foundation; second, the campaign to rewrite the history of psychiatry in order to present psychoanalysis as an aberrant and unfortunate "interlude" between an initial wave of scientific psychiatry in the nineteenth century and a "New Psychiatry" emerging in the 1970s and 1980s with roots in the first postwar decades. In this sense, the "Acknowledgments" section of the book is telling, as it places Hobson both at the center and at the intersection of these two movements:

> Critical feedback and support for my thinking about the book's subject grew out of two related groups. On the inside was the New Psychiatry Seminar, a quasi-revolutionary band of young psychiatric malcontents who creatively complained to and quarreled with me from 1983 to 1986 in the New Psychiatry Seminar. Willard Quine wryly dubbed us "Freudians Anonymous." Ned Hallowell, John Ratey, and David Mann were the ringleaders of this band. On the outside was the still evolving discussion among a group of critics that includes Charles Brenner, Frank Sulloway, Adolf Grunbaum, Paul Roazen, and Frederick Crews. (Hobson 1988: xvi)

This is a noteworthy cast, to be sure, announcing to the reader that the book is a product of discussion among the most vociferous anti-Freudian thinkers of the 1980s (Grünbaum, Crews) and a collaboration with the leaders in New Psychiatry movement, which sought to uproot any and all Freudian influence from psychiatric discourse and to rebuild psychiatry on a purely neurobiological foundation with a diagnostic practice based on seemingly more empirical and demonstrable criteria. Most interesting among this acknowledged group are Hallowell and Ratey, who popularized attention-deficit hyperactivity disorder (ADHD) in the book *Driven to Distraction: Recognizing and Coping with Attention Deficit Disorder from Childhood Through Adulthood* (1994), which advocates for professional psychiatric diagnoses of the "disorder" and drug treatment to manage its neurologically based symptoms (1995). ADHD, like depression and dreaming, was claimed to be about neurons, not neurosis.

Hobson's dream science, then, should be situated in the overlapping contexts of the emergence of a "New Psychiatry" based on "empirical" diagnostics and neurological information, the increasing specialization of neuroscience and its related pharmacology, and the rise of a generation of critiques of Freud and his psychoanalytic system. In this light, it is not surprising that Hobson shared discursive strategies with the most influential piece of the "New Psychiatry" movement, the *DSM-III*. The *DSM-III* represents a major revision to the categorization and diagnostic analysis of mental illnesses. The central thrust of the shift from the *DSM-II* to the *DSM-III* was to eliminate traces of the psychoanalytic tradition and to ground psychiatric diagnosis on what the authors of the revision claim was empirical, scientific evidence that could be verified through clinical testing. The framework of the approach to the *DSM-III*, according to the analysis of Bradley Lewis, matches the framework of Hobson's dream theories in several significant ways. Lewis defines *DSM-III*'s medical or "disease model" thusly:

> Though the DSM-III developers claim to use a neutral rhetorical frame, when we connect their work with the models-of-madness literature, we see that they actually use a very rigid "disease model" (also called the "medical model"). The central tenets of the disease model include the following:
>
> - Mental pathology is accompanied by physical pathology
> - Mental illness can be classified as distinct disorders that have characteristic common features
> - Mental illness is biologically disadvantageous and handicapping
> - The causes of mental pathology are explicable in terms of physical illness
>
> The disease model in psychiatry forces psychiatric observation and research to emphasize signs, symptoms, formal mental-status exams, lab tests, differential diagnosis, pathophysiology, etiology, medical treatments, and prognosis. The larger rhetorical frame for the disease model is based on natural science frames of objectivity, precision, and reliability. (2006: 107)

For Lewis, the *DSM-III*'s rhetoric of "objectivity, precision, and reliability" leads to a number of problematic outcomes. He writes:

> The rhetorical frame of the disease model tends to
>
> - naturalize and reify "mental illness";
> - feed into the medicalization of deviance;
> - feed into psychiatry as an agent of normalization, state control, and multicultural oppression;
> - feed into the pharmaceutical industry boondoggle; and
> - rest on a natural-science model approach to humans that excludes other approaches and excludes multiple approaches. (2006: 109)

DSM-III was produced by a closed circle of psychiatrists all dedicated to the same professional direction—a return to the roots of biological, empirical/scientific psychiatry and a rejection of psychoanalysis and psychodynamic models. The *DSM-III* team was almost exclusively male, white, and academic, and their categorizations reflected these social and cultural positions. Beyond the individuals involved, the *DSM-III* set out to eliminate any conflicting or alternative approach to dealing with mental, psychological, or behavioral issues. The explicit target, of course, was Freudian analysis—but other perspectives that diverged from the official *DSM-III* line were also excluded. Furthermore, the *DSM-III* justified and strengthened the transformation of traits into symptoms, and symptoms into diseases, thereby providing physicians with the tools to understand patients (Lewis 2006: 112–113). This "understanding" furnished psychiatrists with the means by which to intervene in the patient's case, most often pharmacologically. The combination of the perceived systematization of diagnostics in the *DSM-III* and the rise of "precision-based" psychotropic drugs like Prozac, based on the latest "targeted" neuroscience, formed a potent node of social and professional authority, one that would dominate the cultural sphere of psychiatry and psychology for the following two decades (at least) before it began to unravel. *DSM-III*, New Psychiatry, and the emergence of "targeted" neuroscience converged to create by the 1990s the dominant and dominating figure of contemporary medicine, society, and culture—the drug-prescribing psychiatrist, a marginal figure in the 1970s. It would take the professional annihilation of the Freudian establishment to secure its power, and a central pillar of Freudian power was its hold on the interpretation of dreams.

Hobson's dream model is framed by the discursive regimes outlined above: the rhetoric of precision and targeting that fueled the pharmaceutical industry, the biological determinism that underpinned the New Psychiatry, and the exclusivity that discourages or banishes modes of conceptualization other than empirically based "objective" science. Hobson deploys these discursive strategies in his battle with the shadow of Freud. In the opening of *The Dreaming Brain*, he writes, "A new way of viewing dreams, as transparent, their significance available to the dreamer unaided by prophet or psychoanalyst, derives from the objective studies of modern sleep science and neurobiology" (1988: 3). This "objective" approach, Hobson claims, goes beyond dreaming. Since dreams exhibit common features with "mental illnesses," knowledge of one area leads to enlightenment in the other:

> Dreaming could thus be a mental product of the same *kind* of physiological process that is deranged in mental illness. This conclusion gives the scientific study of the dream process implications beyond the realm of dreaming itself: since all of the major signs of mental illness can be imitated by normal minds in the normal state of dreaming. The study of dreams is the study of a model of mental illness. (Hobson 1988: 9)

The conflation of dreams with mental illness pathologizes the dream. As part of this drive to see dreaming as only a physical brain state, dreaming itself is redefined as part of the sleep cycle (REM sleep). It is no longer a "third" state between waking and sleep. Toward the end of Hobson's *The Dreaming Brain*, the "dream" has merged, blended, or become coterminous with REM sleep. Hobson writes:

> The emerging functional picture is of a tidelike shift of chemical predominance within our brains as we sleep. Underlying—and explaining—the change from our waking orientation (toward external information and externally directed action) to our REM-sleep orientation (toward internally generated information and suppressed action) is a major shift in the metabolic orientation. Waking is concerned with information acquisition,

> catabolic energy expenditure, and action upon the world; REM sleep is concerned with information shuffling, anabolic energy conservation, and suspended animation. Sleep may thus serve development and maintenance of the nervous system, perhaps with reorganization of the nervous system's own information. It appears that our brains and our minds are in a tidal ebb and flow: from concern with the outside world to concern with the internal events that are brain activity itself. (Hobson 1988: 194)

Hobson's conflation of dreaming with REM sleep pushes in the direction of the full biologization and materialization of dreaming. This definition of dreaming shifts a discussion of a dream's meaning to a dream's function, in this case "the development and maintenance of the nervous system."

Hobson's notion of dreaming as having a material function was pushed by contemporaries in varying directions, some very much beyond the scope of Hobson's own conclusions. For Francis Crick and Graeme Mitchison, dreams function to purge unneeded or useless information created by neural connections during the day in order to avoid "overloading" the brain. Dreams, in other words, promote *forgetting* in order to maintain the system. Crick and Mitchison see dreaming as a functioning of brain circuitry—and as more or less coterminous with REM sleep (1983, 1995). Contrary to this, other dream researchers advocate theories that dreams promote memory by re-inscribing memory impulses into the neural circuitry by a process of rehearsal. It is interesting that both the "overload" thesis and the "rehearsal" thesis connect the analysis of REM sleep and dreaming to the rising discourse about the functioning of computer systems. The brain, thus, is not only materially understood—but increasingly understood as the body's computer. Dream analysis in the brain-as-computer model was popularized by Christopher Evans in his book *Landscapes of the Night* (1983).

The renewed movement to banish the legacy of Freudian psychoanalysis from psychiatry in the mid-late 1970s and continuing into the 1980s necessitates a reckoning with Freudian dream analysis and a replacement of dream interpretation with the new paradigm of dream understanding that stems from the previous decades of sleep science research. Dreams, once seen as a set of internally generated images or sequences during sleep, are transformed into a set of external, material properties—observable and measurable. This diagnostic definition fits the mold of the rising New Psychiatry movement, which considers mental states and mental disorders as based on material, biological brain conditions. The conflation of dreaming with REM sleep solidifies dreaming's brain-based condition, thus putting pressure on (as I discuss below) the very conception of a dreamscape. Finally, the understanding of dreaming as a physical state connects the discourse on dreaming with discourses about analogous systems like computers, advancing the notion of dreaming as "functional," as a "tool" of a system's maintenance. The new paradigm for understanding dreaming thus becomes an expression at the nexus of science, technology, and capitalism.

Dreams, Technology, and Capitalism

In *24/7*, Jonathan Crary describes contemporary life's intolerance of sleep as a mode of being that resists the two central organizing activities of capitalist existence: work and consumption. Sleep, Crary says, is unproductive—one cannot simultaneously sleep and work. In addition, sleep disrupts an individual's process of consumption of material, services, and information—thus providing one of the only zones of non-acquisitive activity left in society. He contrasts sleep with its opposite, sleeplessness: "Sleeplessness is the state in which producing, consuming, and discarding occur without pause…" (2013: 17). Modernity's campaign against sleep, Crary argues, has been successful, reducing the average North American's sleep time from ten hours per night around 1900 to a mere six and a half hours in the twenty-first century. Not satisfied with this reduction, the military-industrial-technological complex (including the pharmaceutical industry) has its sights set on the complete eradication of the need for sleep, which would also eliminate dreaming.

Though sleep has not yet been replaced through technological means, it has been despoiled, according to Crary, by means of technology and pharmacology, both related to the broader culture of nonstop capitalism. Technology becomes the conduit for the continuous flow of goods, services, and information. The inability to disconnect from one's apparatus, to unplug from the flow of online activity, stretches the parameters of the workday into all of waking time. Even if a subject is not "working" while engaging in online activity, this subject is adding to the flow of work in some form, whether by consuming or simply by providing data for the generation of other business. A recent (though probably already outdated!) study indicates that the need to stay connected even during the traditional sleep period (the night) motivates around fifty percent of people under the age of thirty-five to check their phone at least once per night (White 2016). These intrusions into the nocturnal period are paired with people's growing desire to be looking into their screens before sleep and directly upon waking. More and more, in other words, sleep is becoming a period between check-ins with the screen-world, an interval that is increasingly intolerable to the technology-using subject. According to PEW, twenty-five percent of people in the United States are "almost constantly" online, with the percentage rising to nearly forty percent for those under the age of forty (Perrin and Jiang 2019). Such "encroachments" into sleep, for Crary, create the conditions for a contemporary type of insomnia, which necessitate a market response: "All of the encroachments on [sleep] create the insomniac conditions in which sleep must be bought (even if one is paying for a chemically modified state only approximating actual sleep)" (2013: 18). Crary presents a definition of contemporary sleep in the following way: "…sleep is now an experience cut loose from notions of necessity or nature. Instead, like so much else, it is conceptualized as a variable but managed function that can only be defined instrumentally and physiologically" (2013: 13). From the instrumental perspective, sleep is connected to productivity or a subject's ability to wake up and continue working.

The connection between sleep and work is a fundamental pillar of the medicalization of sleep. A 2009 television advertisement for the sleeping pill AmbienCR, for example, opens with a restless, insomniac woman unable to sleep (AmbienCR 2009). The scene then cuts to her at work the next day in her office cubicle looking bedraggled as she is unable to focus on her deskwork and instead gazes up at a hallucination of a rooster that crows from the top of her partition. After taking AmbienCR, the formerly incapacitated woman enters her office looking confident and ready for the workday. The confident woman is able to engage productively (talking on the phone) while her colleague in the adjacent cubicle is now plagued by the insomnia-rooster. This emphasizes the ubiquity of the problem—work is under direct threat from sleeplessness.

The storyboard of this AmbienCR commercial makes a direct connection between a restful night's sleep and a productive day of work—sleep, the commercial contends, is valuable because it facilitates work. In the Rozerem commercial discussed above, the sleepless man complains, "I just have all this stress at work," which by implication is preventing him from sleeping. Abe Lincoln reassures the man, "It happens to a lot of people," and the talking beaver adds, "… more than half of adults report experiencing some kind of insomnia at least a few nights a week" (Nudd 2016). The logic of the commercial is that work stress leads to insomnia, which can be overcome through medication—in this case Rozerem—allowing access back into one's dreamlife, and, presumably, a more productive workday. The harnessing of sleep in support of work (white-collar work) has its roots in the benzodiazepine movement, is central to the marketing of Prozac and other SSRI anti-depressants and other behavioral psychotropic medications, and is the dominant lens through which post-benzodiazepine sleeping pills are presented to the public.

The case of the advertising campaign for the drug Lunesta opens up another level of sleep's relationship to capitalism—in this case equating a good night's sleep and its dreamlike quality to the fantasy of white, upper-middle-class suburbia (Lunesta 2011). The television commercial follows the florescent green Lunesta Luna moth as it checks in throughout one night on three female sleepers. The commercial opens with the moth hovering above a woman at time intervals from 11:30 pm to 4 am, showing her blissfully asleep. The green moth then visits other sleepers and landscapes, gathering a set of images that contextualize the sleeping woman encountered at the beginning of the commercial. Three visual themes present themselves: the purity and beauty of nature, the wholesomeness of suburban life, and the security of the physical structure of the family house. The first theme, that of natural purity, reflects a merging of a kind of dreamscape (albeit a corporate construction of one) with upper-middle-class aspirations of living in a world free of pollution, trash, and mess—an untouched world with ample space and nonthreatening nature. The images of the town where the sleeper seems to live are likewise idyllic—the nighttime is peaceful, silent, and safe. The natural world as pure, beautiful, untouched, and nonthreatening, and the space of the town as quiet, peaceful, and (as symbolized by the church) wholesome frame the depiction of the private sphere of the single-family house as a zone of total safety. The commercial suggests that the bliss of the woman upon waking has less to do with the influence of the Lunesta than with her existence in a white, upper-middle-class fantasy world cleansed of anything that might violate this corporatized ideal—and that using Lunesta will provide access to this type of life.

Notably, in the realm of advertising, sleeping pill sleep is portrayed as empty, dreamless sleep. In some sense, this is accurate, as one of the recognized effects of sleeping pills is that they inhibit memory upon waking, thus erasing traces both of nighttime disturbances and of dreams. As Ian Parker writes in "The Big Sleep":

> …insomnia is a condition not just of losing sleep but of being disturbed by sleeplessness. Indeed, most people with prescriptions for insomnia never visit a sleep lab, trusting their own assessment of a sleep deficit. This emphasis on the subjective also makes the amnesiac effect of sleep drugs oddly advantageous to those who manufacture them: the drugs inhibit people from creating memories of waking during the night. (2013: 50)

While sleep, as Crary argues, exists in some tension to the world of non-stop capitalism, it might be more accurate to say that it has been adapted to the modern capitalist mode of work and consumption, and defined by a combination of scientific discourses and corporate representations. Dreaming, now one stage in the sleep cycle, is primarily thought about in terms of its biochemical properties, function, and utility—or it is erased entirely as an uncontrollable element with a potential for "disturbance." The *Dreamstage* exhibition, to which I will move now, was a key moment when the scientific discourses on neurobiology became public and aestheticized in ways that foregrounded the next phase of corporate, capitalistic pharmacology.

Dreamstage

The *Dreamstage* exhibition that took place at Harvard's Carpenter Center for the Arts was divided into two main parts—a "dark space" that featured a live sleeper and multimedia displays along with a "light space" for visual arts and scientific materials. In the dark space, readings from the sleeper were translated into laser displays and soundscapes. Blue laser traces represented rapid eye movement. EEG readings were translated into red, green, and multicolored beams. Muscle tone and heartbeat were registered in golden light. In addition to this laser-light show, the readings of the live sleeper were fed into a synthesizer and converted into soundscapes. The live sleeper remained visible through one-way glass. In addition to the laser displays and soundscapes, the dark space showed slide projections of a cat's brainstem tissue as well as stopgap photographs of sleepers taken at regular intervals throughout a single night. In the light space, *Dreamstage* turned into a more conventional science exhibition, documenting the rise of modern sleep science and the neurophysiology of the sleeping brain. The overarching thrust of *Dreamstage* was captured in the exhibition's press release, "Graphic material will illustrate aesthetically remarkable aspects of brain science; drawings and paintings will represent the scientist as artist; the beauty of the brain's form and function will be emphasized in other graphic media" (Dreamstage Exhibit Archive (n.d.)).

In the exhibition catalog, Hobson writes, "Dream theory has changed very little since Freud's time, whereas the state of neurophysiology has markedly matured, making it quite feasible to study the dream process at the level of the neuron" (Hobson et al., 1977). "The level of the neuron" refers to the examination of the physical attributes of the brain during sleeping and dreaming, which can then be read against the dream plot—not in order to "interpret" dreams but to explain the physical mechanisms underlying them. The move from interpretation to explanation relies on a set of strategies—both rhetorical and aesthetic—that together support a broader scientific-technological paradigm for understanding phenomena. *Dreamstage*'s scientific-technological discourse around sleep and dreaming mirrors the related discourses around the growing precision of psychopharmacology, the understanding of brain function, and the relationship between sleep and capitalist formations of work and consumption discussed previously in this chapter.

On the rhetorical level, *Dreamstage* presents a narrative of scientific progress that moves from the mysticism and dream analysis of the ancient world through Freud to the step-by-step scientific discovery of the basic building blocks of the physical properties of sleep and dreaming. The story *Dreamstage* tells is driven by a combination of intrepid (and objective) research scientists and an increase in technological sophistication. Scientific understanding and technological development, in other words, go hand and hand, with the former often predicated on the latter. *Dreamstage* begins this story by introducing the invention of methods to record brain wave activity (EEG) and the related discovery of sleep stages, including REM and non-REM sleep. *Dreamstage* describes the first recording of electrical waves in the brain as a moment of scientific clarity, banishing superstitious and outmoded beliefs:

> The discovery that electrical activity of the brain could be recorded in the form of brain waves (EEGs) by placing electrodes on the scalp was made in 1929 by Hans Berger…Berger's discovery voided, once and for all, the Aristotelian hypothesis that the mind was situated in the heart and clearly demonstrated that the physiology of consciousness was regulated by the brain. (Hobson et al., 1977)

EEG measurement was the technological basis for the distinction between REM and non-REM sleep. The *Dreamstage* catalog captures this moment:

> … the discovery of REM sleep and its association with dreaming did not take place until 1953. Two investigations, Aserinsky and Kleitman…happened to notice the sleep of their subjects was characterized by rapid eye movements and EEG activation, in the absence of external stimulation. Soon after, they established that this internally-induced brain arousal (REM) was the physical substrate of dream consciousness. (Hobson et al., 1977)

Like the banishment of "outmoded" and scientifically laughable conceptions of the heart as the center of consciousness, the discovery of the "physical substrate of dream consciousness" moves the discourse on dreaming from one of interpretation and mystery (or mysticism) to one of analysis and objective understanding—like Freud, utilizing the language of scientific objectivity and paradigm shift. As an observable phenomenon, then, dreaming could be fully explicated as a set of physical properties within a broader system of sleep, which could likewise be fully described as a physiological process:

> The discovery of the cyclic alternation of REM and NREM sleep was laden with scientific portent: first, it meant that sleep was highly differentiated, not as a single state or even a succession of states, but rather as a continuously changing process, an oscillation between extremes with peaks in REM and troughs in Stage IV; second, it implied that sleep was controlled by a brain oscillator, a biologic cock with a period of 90 minutes; third, it implied that sleep serves a continuously shifting set of functions instead of just one, that of rest. (Hobson et al., 1977)

The narrative here flows like a detective story—one discovery opens up new pathways for the scientist to pursue. In this case, the discovery that sleep was comprised of a set of states that cycled at fairly regular intervals through the night implied the existence of a certain neurochemical mechanism at work. To understand dreaming, therefore, one needed a sophisticated and precise understanding of the localized functions of the brain. The *Dreamstage* catalog presents this understanding in a pithy, unambiguous form—the confident and "factual" language of the scientist. The increasingly specific analysis of the brain and its localized function pushes toward Hobson's key conclusion, the discovery of the dream-generation mechanism. Hobson cannot claim certainty about this conclusion, but in the context of the progressive story of the triumph of neurophysiology, it is compelling:

> The electrical activity of giant pontine cells, as measured by the frequency of action potentials, is lowest during waking and highest during dreaming sleep. Exactly the opposite occurs in the nearby locus coeruleus, or LC,

> cells. In other words, the increase in the rate of giant cell activity at the onset of dreaming sleep is mirrored by a *decrease* in the activity of LC neurons, suggesting that the two cell groups are reciprocally mediated. It is thought that LC neurons probably inhibit giant cells, and that dreaming sleep begins when the inhibition is withdrawn and the excitability of the giant cells is allowed to increase. Giant cell excitation, probably mediated by acetylcholine, in turn may ultimately result in a restoration of the LC inhibition, which would bring the dreaming sleep episode to an end. (Hobson et al., 1977, italics in text)

The technological-scientific narrative of progress has set the key terms for the neurological understanding of dreaming. Dreaming no longer stands alone as a state; it appears in combination with sleep as "dreaming sleep." As such, dreaming is subsumed into the sleep cycle, understood as an automatic biological process that follows the circadian rhythms of the twenty-four-hour cycle. The mechanistic view of dreaming extends to its initiation and its conclusion, Hobson's on-off switch located in seemingly precise terms in the interface between the "giant cells" and the neurons of the locus coeruleus.

Hobson's dream takes place in the brain—and there is no longer a dreamscape but only the territory of biological materiality. While an anarchistic dreamscape is one that defies mapping, the new territory of the dream, the brain, can be mapped with increasing precision. The more the dream comes to belong to the territory of the brain, the more open it is to manipulation and control by the scientist. A key example of the implications of this shift in the territory of the dream can be seen toward the end of *Dreamstage*'s catalog:

> A specific example may help to clarify this concept: suppose you are dreaming and in your dream you see the back of a man who is standing at an intersection. Suddenly, the man turns to the left and runs across the street. The explanation for this event in the dream would be that REM-generating pontine cells activated nearby eye movement neurons, specifically those that move the eyes to the left. The cerebral cortex registered this activity and attempted to make sense out of it in light of what previously occurred in the dream. The logical solution, based on the speed and direction of the

> eye movements, was to move the man to the left and rapidly across the street. (Hobson et al., 1977)

This example of the tracing of movement and direction fits with Hobson's mapping of the brain. The dreamscape has transformed into a reflection or secondary generation of the territory of the brain, an illusion or delusion, opening the way to the establishment of the analogous relationship between dreaming and psychosis as both projections of physiological brain states. "Through the use of the dream we will show that the normal brain is functionally capable of generating many of the signs of psychiatric illness" (Dreamstage Exhibit Archive (n.d.)).

In its "light space" displays, *Dreamstage* presents a linear narrative of technology and scientific discovery. At the same time, in both the light space and the dark space the visualizations of the brain in the form of the laser displays, rendering of neurons and neural networks, projections of feline brain tissue, projections of "abstract landscapes" taken from photomicrographs of neurons, and so forth take on an aesthetic function as well as a rhetorical one (Dreamstage Exhibit Archive (n.d.)). On the aesthetic level, the exhibit aims to present the brain as an object of beauty and exceptional complexity, a view of the brain far removed from its typical depiction as a lump of rather unpleasant looking gray matter. As for the mechanisms of dreaming, which, according to the constructed narrative, one can only properly understand by moving to hyper-specific analysis of localized brain function, the exhibition presents the beauty of the brain as existing on the cellular level.

The "light space" exhibit, in keeping with its presentation of a short history of neuroscience, begins with early neuroscientific pioneers of the late nineteenth and early twentieth centuries. Images from Cajal and Facundo Valverde introduce the viewer to the concept of the neuron, or brain cell, and the community or environment of neural relationships. In the exhibition catalog, Cajal's drawings are paired with a representation of a human brain, producing the visual effect of combining the micro and the macro, the aesthetic and the objectively scientific gaze (Cajal's and Valverde's drawings operating, I think, on both levels; this was recognized by Hobson in his proposal for the exhibition: "The rendering of structural features of the brain, especially in the drawings of anatomists, is often nothing short of artistic…" (Dreamstage Exhibit Archive (n.d.)). Such a pairing of images of micro-level brain cells and a macro or global depiction of the brain establishes a key rhetorical position: the brain, far from consisting of undifferentiated "gray" matter, is complex and beautiful. Hobson stresses this depiction in his project proposal, writing in a way that reveals his attempt at rhetorical positioning:

> The humanistic orientation of the exhibit will counter trends…to view man as a machine and to view his behavior as subject exclusively to external control. We will stress the beauty, the order, and the creative capacity of the human brain; in doing so, we hope also to communicate a view of the scientist as humanist—man trying to understand himself. (Dreamstage Exhibit Archive (n.d.))

On the other hand, the brain—beautiful, creative, imaginative—is also *representable* and therefore in some way "simple." Simplicity was one of the key concepts that characterized the linkages between neuroscience, pharmaceutical advertisements, and psychiatric definitions. "The activation-synthesis model can account for dream nonsense and for dream meaning in terms of an extremely simple and economical set of principles," Hobson writes, "without recourse either to the collective unconscious or to a dynamically repressed unconscious in accounting for either the occurrence of dreams or for their unique properties" (Hobson 1988: 15). Hobson clearly wants to position the "simplicity" of his science against the "complexity" of Freudian theory. Part of what made Freudian dream theory "complex"—and this was exaggerated in subsequent psychoanalysis—was that dreams contained no "nonsense," every aspect of the dream-text was seen as containing layers of latent content.

The notion of a combined micro and global understanding of the brain was critical both for the mapping of what became the physical dream space, which depended on an understanding of specific neuron activity and how this activity was situated in the brain, and for the seeming achievement of mastery over brain function by dream scientists. The ability to represent the brain becomes tantamount to grasping it, to being able to manipulate it, to intervene in it. A significant moment in this story of increased scientific control over the brain came with the publication in 1968 of Alvin Berman's atlas of a cat's brainstem, *The Brain Stem of the Cat: A Cytoarchitectonic Atlas with Stereotaxic Coordinates.* Hobson utilizes images from the atlas for *Dreamstage*.

The mapping and aestheticization of the cat's brain point to a concealed layer of violence not only in the *Dreamstage* exhibit but also in the history of the study of the anatomy of the brain. Throughout the *Dreamstage* exhibition, the cat is situated in relationship to the human being. In the exhibition proposal, Hobson writes, "The use of animal models for neurobiology has implied validity through side-by-side demonstration of the sleep cycle in man and his pets" (Dreamstage Exhibit Archive (n.d.)). The work of Theodore Spagna Jr., who used time-elapse photography to capture a subject's full night of sleep next to his cat, creates precisely the homology between human and animal that Hobson calls for in the exhibition proposal (Figs. 7.1 and 7.2).

Figures 7.1 and 7.2 present, compositionally, themes of the relationship between science, technology, and the human (and animal) body. First, technology allows the artist to capture a series of identically framed photographs over the course of a single night. This capacity is predicated on an innovative use of technology, in this case the "intervalometer-controlled camera" (Hobson et al., 1977). The looming image of the device (in the catalog it appears as an overlaying onionskin) adds a dramatic effect to the image—symbolic of the outsized importance of technology in the analysis of sleep. The camera is also symbolic on other levels: it captures sleep science's project of monitoring subjects during sleep, a process pioneered by Aserinsky and Kleitman in their Chicago sleep laboratory in 1953; and it represents the scientist-artist as an agent of surveillance, with the human reduced to a subject to be studied and, by extension, controlled. In the photographs, the cat appears at first to be something of a prop, but as the exhibit continues, it becomes the homologous human and, thus, the medium through which the scientist can "penetrate" the human brain. Spagna senses this in the exhibition proposal when he writes, "…the sleeping humans appear to serve as zeitgebers for their pet dogs or cats," implying that the human and pets sleep cycles seem to have merged (Dreamstage Exhibit Archive (n.d.)).

The foundational step in establishing the homology of cat and human is the direct brain comparison—cats have human-like brains. Figure 7.3

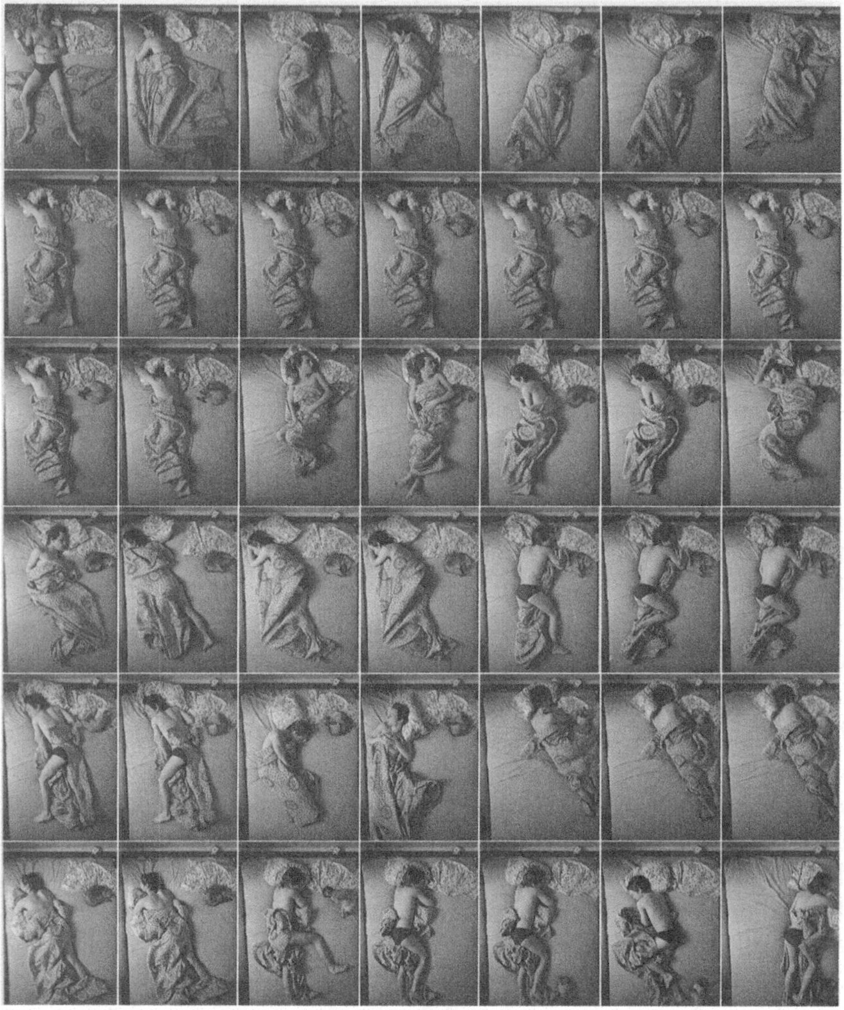

Fig. 7.1 Theodore Spagna Jr., Time-Elapse Photography of Sleeping Man with Cat. Dreamstage Catalog (Hobson et al., 1977)

depicts an onionskin with similar brain diagrams and labels overlaid on the sleeping human and cat.

The imagery is backed up by text in the catalog, "…the similarity in cat and human brain electrical activity tend to make the cat an ideal

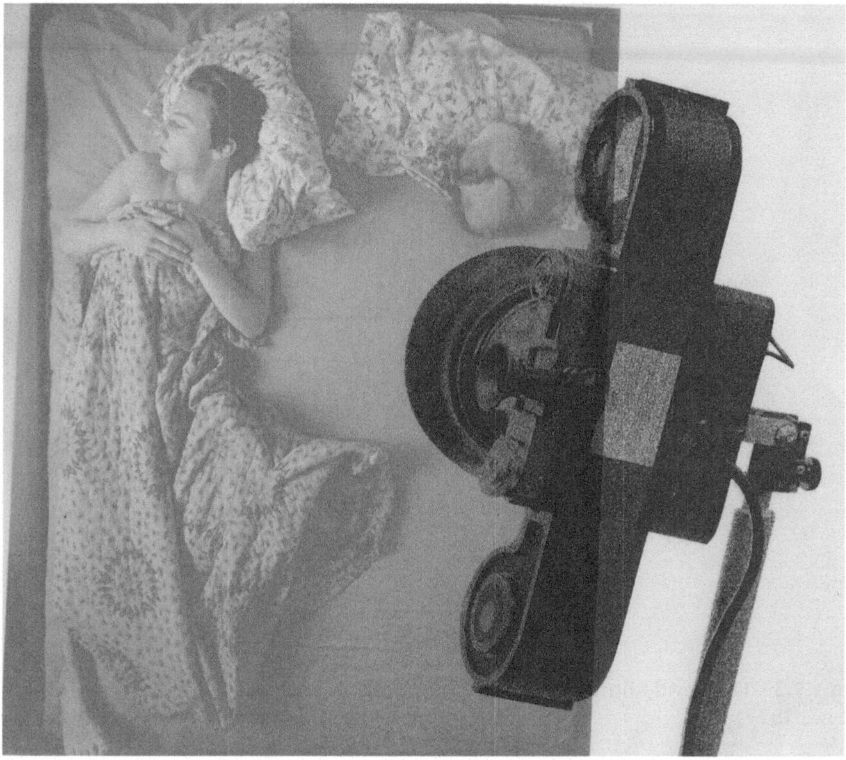

Fig. 7.2 Theodore Spagna Jr., Sleeping Man with Cat, Onionskin Overlay with Camera. Dreamstage Catalog (Hobson et al., 1977)

animal model for studying sleep and dream phenomena" (Hobson et al., 1977). It is noteworthy that the cat is not simply an "animal" but an "animal model." In fact, the "animal model" provides the basis for nearly all of the subsequent conclusions about brain function featured in *Dreamstage* and in Hobson and McCarley's theories in general. These conclusions rest on the physical manipulation of the cat's brain through techniques like measuring EEG activity in the sleeping cat's brainstem through the insertion into its brain of microelectrodes; scarring or "lesioning" the cat's brain in order to isolate certain interactions and functions; and performing lobotomies on cats (decerebration) to isolate brain regions from one another. From this viewpoint, then, Berman's *Atlas* of

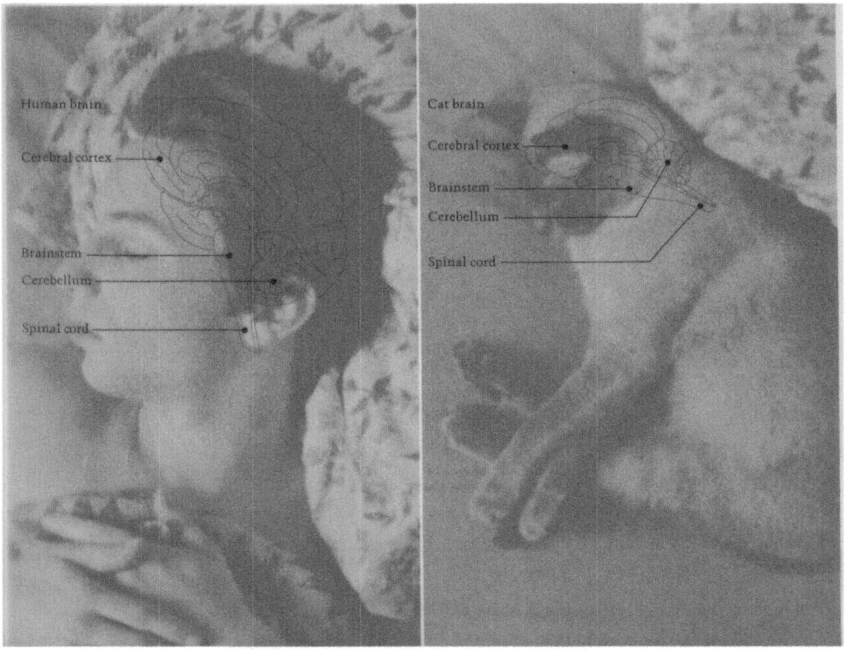

Fig. 7.3 Cat and human brain compared. Dreamstage Catalog (Hobson et al., 1977)

the cat's brainstem is more than a simple mapping—it is a strategic charting of terrain in the service of violent conquest.

Though the cat becomes the "animal model" and subject for nearly all of the significant brain experimentation in the realm of sleep and dreaming, it vanishes when the scientific gaze zooms in, allowing the viewer to cross back over the species-border to the human. If the cat's brain has become (at least in part) an aesthetic entity through the photography and multimedia exhibitions, the processes revealed through its violent manipulation turn into something like animations or cartoons with the animal feature (and certainly the violence) nowhere to be seen. The link between the visual language of Dreamstage's presentation of neural transmission and that of the Zoloft advertisement discussed in a previous section of this chapter cannot be missed. The commercially powerful Zoloft image is but the close cousin of this easily digestible expression of the neuro-transmission process in *Dreamstage* (Fig. 7.4).

The core or central attraction of the *Dreamstage* exhibition was the "performance" of a live sleeper, whose brain and body measurements were expressed in colored projections and as a soundscape. At the heart of the exhibition's concept, then, was a sleight-of-hand—the sleeper appeared to the exhibitgoer as the human subject upon observation of which the scientists had made their leaps of knowledge into sleep and dreaming. In fact, beyond the measurement of electrical activity in the brain (and quite imprecisely in terms of localization of activity), the vast majority of scientific experiments and discoveries had been not with the human subject but with the "animal model"—the cat. *The New York Times*, for example, covered the *Dreamstage* exhibition through the lens of the MIT student, Ben, hired to sleep in the exhibition environment. The article leads with a quote from Ben's journal in which he describes the feeling of trying to fall asleep in front of the thousand people who came to the exhibit on opening night. Later on, the article describes the sleep-performance:

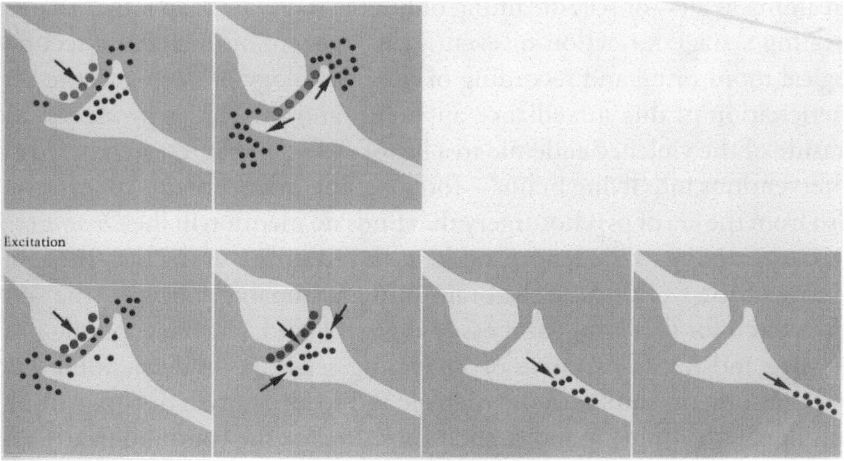

Fig. 7.4 Diagram of neuron transmission. Dreamstage Catalog (Hobson et al., 1977)

> While Ben sleeps—nude but covered with a silver lame spread—behind one-way glass in full view of visitors to Harvard's Carpenter Center for the Visual Arts in Cambridge, a dozen electrodes monitor his heart, muscle tone, eye movement and brain waves. The impulses are converted by a laser and a polyphonic synthesizer into light and music—squiggly, dancing lines of colored light projected on the exhibit's walls, and haunting, electronic music, hinting of some future world. (Winfrey 1977)

"Hinting of some future world"—this is the lingering promise of the seeming revolution in the understanding of sleep and dreaming. The "future world," despite the positive presentation of the *New York Times*, points past aesthetics to a world of monitoring/surveillance, manipulation, and control. Such imperious impulses are made manifest in a piece from *The New York Times* magazine in July 1977. When the discussion in the piece turns to nightmares and other stubbornly bothersome dreams, the article asserts a solution in the prevailing spirit of the times, and in line with the scientific discourse of the *Dreamstage* exhibition. "To help people beset with unproductive and unpleasant dreams, several researchers are developing methods for controlling dreams" (Cherry 1977: 34).

Dreamstage can be seen as presenting a techno-capitalist conception of dreaming. It could be argued that the exhibition does not, in fact, present dreaming at all—or sees dreaming only as a "stage" of sleep rather than as creating a stage for action or event. This conception includes a technological monitoring and recording of the physiology of sleep and the aestheticization of this surveillance apparatus and the data it produces; the erasure of the violence endemic to a history of scientific research based on interventions into living brains—foremost the "model brains" of cats, but also from the era of psychosurgery that finds no mention in the *Dreamstage* literature or any of the reports on it; a simplification of the massive complexity of the workings of the brain into consumable concepts (the "on/off" switch for dreaming) and easily digestible didactic imagery; the progressive and linear narrative of increasing scientific understanding and the banishment, similar to the rhetoric in Freud, of myth or superstition; and finally the implicit and explicit promises for the commodification of scientific knowledge in the notion of sleep and dream control, primarily targeted at removing the interference in the form of tiredness, moodiness, and so on with the capitalistic demands of work.

Conclusion

Dream science has threatened to erase the dreamscape and to put in its place a fully mapped neurophysiological territory of dreaming. This territory is defined geographically in terms of localized brain function, temporally in terms of circadian rhythms, socially or even "legally" in terms of the interaction of neurons through the substance of neurotransmitters, politically in terms of the hierarchies of brain function (the brain stem dominating the cerebral cortex), and economically in terms both of seeing dreaming as a maintenance mechanism and as part of the process of general state of productivity.

This creation of the new territory of dreaming, defined in scientific-technological-capitalist terms, did not begin or end with Hobson and McCarley's work in the 1970s or with the *Dreamstage* exhibition at Harvard's Carpenter Center in 1977. Nonetheless, *Dreamstage* was a key public event in a process of molding ideas about sleep and dreaming to the culture of postwar capitalism. The creation of the neurophysiological territory of sleep and dreaming helped foster and sustain the commodification of sleep (and by extension dreaming)—and of neural processes in general. This terrain helped launch "wonder drugs" like Valium and facilitated the transition from "primitive" psychotropic drugs—like the benzodiazepines—to the "sophisticated" drugs like Prozac, Zoloft, and so on. The same foundation for anti-depressants like Prozac propelled a wave of sleep-aids like Ambien and Lunesta, which grew into multi-billion-dollar drug empires. By the first decade of this century, this neurobiological territory was dominated by multinational drug-makers, who spent hundreds of millions of dollars blanketing the media with television (and then online) advertisements—advertisements that utilized the language and visual strategies of the cartographers of the brain. The discovery and "mining" of neurotransmitters like serotonin could be equated with the general capitalist impulse of massive natural resource exploitation in the name of profit and power.

Does this mean that in the era of dream science, the anarchic potential of the dreamscape has disappeared? Perhaps not. Dream science has shown a dreaming brain that makes a qualitative shift in state between waking and the various phases of sleep, supporting the notion that the dreamscape is, in fact, a discrete place or space, one just as "real" as the perception of waking life. Such state-changes put pressure on notions of rigid identity; subjects, judging from brain states, are always in flux, always adjusting to impute, to context, to stimuli. In addition, while the interface between science and the public tends to be through simplified notions of the brain function and claims to knowledge that are partial or hypothetical, more specific disciplinary work reveals a brain that is unimaginably complex, containing a system of connections and information exchange that is barely understood, perhaps barely understandable. This woven maze of connections challenges notions of the hierarchy of brain function and forms a biological model for democratic, anti-hierarchical thinking. In other words, it is not necessarily the dream science itself that is authoritarian; it is the instrumentalization of dream science through the discursive logic of advanced/digital consumer capitalism that lends the neurobiological dreaming sleep its authoritarian character.

References

"AmbienCR Rooster Commercial". *YouTube*, uploaded by SanofiAventisPharma, 26 October 2009. https://www.youtube.com/watch?v=NG1hdWb8yBM.

Arthur, Kate. "Little Blob, Don't Be Sad (or Anxious or Phobic)." *The New York Times*. 2 January 2005. Web. Accessed 10 July 2018.

Bei, B., et al. "Treating Insomnia in Depression: Insomnia Related Factors Predict Long-Term Depression Trajectories." *Journal of Consulting and Clinical Psychology* 86.3 (2018): 282–293.

Buysse, Daniel J. "Insomnia." *JAMA* 309.7 (2013): 706–716.

Cherry, Lawrence. "A New Vision of Dreams." *The New York Times*. 3 July 1977, 11–13, 34.

Colen, B.D. "Valium Ads—Sales Pitch or Product Information." *The Washington Post*. 20 January 1980. Web. Accessed 17 July 2018.

"College Museum News". *Art Journal* 36.4 (1977): 332–343.

Crary, Jonathan. *24/7*. Los Angeles: Verso, 2013.

Crick, Francis, and Graeme Mitchison. "The Function of Dream Sleep." *Nature* 304.5922 (1983): 111–114.

Crick, Francis, and Graeme Mitchison. "REM Sleep and Neural Nets." *Behavioural Brain Research* 69.1–2 (1995): 147–155.

Dolnick, Edward. "What Dreams are (Really) Made of: the Psychiatrist and Neuroscientist Allan Hobson Suggests Replacing the Traditional Freudian View." *Atlantic* (July 1990): 41+.

Donahue, Julie. "A History of Drug Advertising: The Evolving Role of Consumers and Consumer Protection." *The Milbank Quarterly* 84.4 (2006): 659–699.

Dreamstage Exhibit Archive. (n.d.). Cambridge: Harvard University Archive. CCVA accession 19724, box 5.

Evans, Christopher R., and Peter Evans. *Landscapes of the Night: How and Why We Dream*. New York: Viking Press, 1983.

Hallowell, Edward M., and John J. Ratey. *Driven to Distraction: Recognizing and Coping with Attention Deficit Disorder from Childhood through Adulthood.* New York: Simon & Schuster, 1995.

Hamilton, Max. "A Rating Scale for Depression." *Journal of Neurology, Neurosurgery, and Psychiatry* 23 (1960): 56–62.

Harder, Rolf. *Escape to Reality*. Museum of Modern Art. Accessed 11 March 2019. https://www.moma.org/collection/works/109233?artist_id=32655&locale=en&page=1&sov_referrer=artist.

Herzberg, David L. *Happy Pills in America: From Miltown to Prozac*. Baltimore: Johns Hopkins UP, 2010.

Herzberg, David L. "'The Pill You Love Can Turn on You': Feminism, Tranquilizers, and the Valium Panic of the 1970s." *American Quarterly* 58.1 (2006): 79–103.

Hobson, J. A. *The Dreaming Brain: How the Brain Creates both the Sense and the Nonsense of Dreams*. New York: Basic Books, 1988.

Hobson, J. A., and R. W. McCarley. "The Brain as a Dream State Generator: An Activation-Synthesis Hypothesis of the Dream Process." *American Journal of Psychiatry* 134.12 (1977): 1335–1348.

Hobson, J. A., Theodore Spagna and Paul Earls, *Dreamstage: An Experimental Portrait of the Sleeping Brain*. Exhibition Catalog. Harvard University: Carpenter Center, 1977.

Institute of Medicine Staff, National Academy of Sciences (U.S.), and Institute of Medicine (U.S.). Division of Mental Health and Behavioral Medicine. *Sleeping Pills, Insomnia, and Medical Practice: Report of a Study* vol. 79-004. Washington: National Academy of Sciences, 1979.

Lewis, Bradley. *Moving Beyond Prozac, DSM, and the New Psychiatry: The Birth of Postpsychiatry*. Ann Arbor: U of Michigan P, 2006.

"Lunesta". *YouTube*, uploaded by Steven Crutchfield, 17 August 2011. https://www.youtube.com/watch?v=kWdt7yn2BoU

Nudd, Tim. "6 Pharma Ads from the Past 15 Years That Were Just What the Doctor Ordered." *Adweek*. 27 March 2016. https://www.adweek.com/brand-marketing/pharma-feel-good-ads-170424/.

Parker, Ian. "The Big Sleep." *The New Yorker*. 9 December 2013, 50–63.

Perrin, Andrew, and Jingjing Jiang. "Almost a Quarter of U.S. Adults Say They are 'Almost Constantly' Online." Pew Research Center. 14 March 2018. Accessed 11 May 2019. https://www.pewresearch.org/fact-tank/2018/03/14/about-a-quarter-of-americans-report-going-online-almost-constantly/.

Rock, Andrea. *The Mind at Night: The New Science of How and Why We Dream*. New York: Basic Books, 2004.

Romm, Cari. "Americans are Getting Worse at Taking Sleeping Pills." *The Atlantic*. 14 August 2014. https://www.theatlantic.com/health/archive/2014/08/americans-are-getting-worse-at-taking-sleeping-pills/375935/.

Staner, Luc. "Comorbidity of Insomnia and Depression." *Sleep Medicine Reviews* 14.1 (2010): 35–46.

Tone, Andrea. *The Age of Anxiety: A History of America's Turbulent Affair with Tranquilizers*. New York: Basic Books. 2008.

White, Martha. "Here's Why You Can't Stop Hitting the Snooze Button." *Time Magazine*. 29 September 2016. http://time.com/money/4509796/smartphone-addiction-disturbs-sleep/.

Wichniak, Adam, et al. "Effects of Antidepressants on Sleep." *Current Psychiatry Reports* 19.9 (2017): 1–7.

Winfrey, Carey. "A Real Dream Job: Starring in 'Show' While Fast Asleep.' *The New York Times*. 16 May 1977, 31, 49.

"Works Like a Dream". *YouTube*. 11 March 2019. https://www.youtube.com/watch?v=uL4RD7tWWf0.

8

Conclusion

It might seem peculiar that something as ephemeral and "unreal" as the dreamscape would play such an important role in the history of the narrative construction of authority from the ancient world until today. Yet, as I have shown in the previous chapters, dreams structure the book of Genesis and many other ancient Mesopotamian and Near Eastern texts, like the Legend of Sargon and the Gudea Cylinders. Dreams also play a central role in *The Epic of Gilgamesh*. Ancient texts from other parts of the world add to the overall picture of the centrality of dreams to narrative construction. Canonical texts of Buddhism and Taoism contain key dream scenes, like Queen Maya's "White Elephant Dream" and Chuang Tzu's "Butterfly Dream," which I discuss in the introduction. Dreaming continues to occupy a central place in modern times, with dreams often coming at key points of narrative transition. I have demonstrated how concepts of dreaming function politically in a range of literary texts, from William Blake's *Job* and Robert Frost's "After Apple-Picking" to works by Franz Kafka, Philip Roth, and Jean Rhys, as well as in psychological or neurobiological accounts by Sigmund Freud, Carl Jung, and J. Allan Hobson.

© The Author(s), under exclusive license to Springer Nature Switzerland AG 2021

S. Rogoff, *The Politics of the Dreamscape*,
https://doi.org/10.1007/978-3-030-74796-1_8

The history of dreaming and dream analysis, of course, goes far beyond the material covered in this book. My goal has not been to provide a chronological or encyclopedic account of dream interpretation but to propose a structure for situating the dreamscape politically, particularly in relation to persistent attempts to assert interpretative and narrative control over it. Answering the theoretical or speculative question of what the politics of the dreamscape are or could be requires a conceptual framework. The one I have developed here is partly based on what I call an origin myth of the dreamscape. In this origin myth, the dreamscape emerges as a negative to the order and hierarchy of creation—as an anarchistic space placed, in the Judeo-Christian tradition, in juxtaposition to the territories of power that come to govern the postlapsarian world after the "fall" of Adam and Eve and their expulsion from Eden. As such, it puts pressure on structures of power, operating as a disordering or disintegrating force. I have referred to this force metaphorically as a "serpent"—the representative of the pre-creation "deep," a zone beyond control, hierarchy, and delineated structures of power. The dreamscape, in this conceptualization, is the serpent in the garden of order and power, a force always present to unmake, to disorganize or disintegrate, pointing away from hierarchy, individuation, and organization to a realm of harmony and unity, Chuang Tzu's *hundun*. This makes the dreamscape's power an anarchic one in the sense of a rupture or disruption that calls into question or undermines or shatters the building blocks of authoritarian power. Thus, the anarchism of the dreamscape is mainly conceived of as a mode of critique that challenges notions of fixed identity, the naturalness of hierarchy and inequality, and the strictures of narrative logic that support coercive power.

The dreamscape's anarchic power, in its very mysteriousness and ephemerality, invites authoritarian incursions or conquests. These incursions aim to harness the force of chaos in the dreamscape and to transform the primal dreamscape into an authoritarian political territory. This transformation is achieved through the representation and interpretation of dreams—from Joseph to Freud, from Sargon to Neil Klugman in Philip Roth's *Goodbye, Columbus*. The vast majority of representations of the dreamscape—or what I call dream-texts—attempt to weave the dreamscape into an authoritarian logic. This is especially strong in the neurobiological dream discourse, which attempts to conflate the dreamscape with physical properties of a specific sleep state in the brain, thereby denying the dreamscape its spatial dimensions. A countercurrent, which I have traced in texts by Jean Rhys and Franz Kafka, has sought to tap into the dreamscape's anarchic power, however partially. I have structured my readings of these anarchistic texts by aligning them with concepts that stress: (1) the disintegration of narrative coherence or structure; (2) the fluidity of subjectivity as opposed to rigid identities; (3) the inherent equality and connection of subjects in the dreamscape. While the current hyper-capitalist society attempts to exploit subjectivity as a basis for consumerism and as a distraction from growing inequalities and the deepening of authoritarian power, the anarchism of the dreamscape, as envisioned in these countercurrent texts, shows how ruptures in the daily flow of life can open up spaces for critique and repositioning—modes of escape from, and resistance to, the type of 24/7 consumer capitalist culture described by Jonathan Crary.

Beyond escaping or resisting the 24/7 assault of hyper-consumerism that currently plagues the world and its ecological health, it is imperative that a politics be developed or *imagined* that challenges the central pillars of authoritarianism. These include the tolerance for (and celebration of) hierarchical structures throughout society—foremost in social institutions (especially the workplace); notions of fixed or rigid identity derived from categorizations based on nationality, religion, race, gender, and so on (categories that are deeply interwoven with the structures of hierarchy); the fixed or "natural" view of the "real" with corresponding attempts to delegitimize alternative concepts as "fantasies," "delusions," or "fictions"; and narrative logics that underlie notions of fixed identity and hierarchy, contributing to the apparent naturalness of categories and the "reality" of the "real." The anarchic politics of the dreamscape seeks to break these pillars and to open up spaces subjective becoming, transformation, disintegration, and positive chaos—the conditions of freedom.

As I have demonstrated throughout this book, tensions between the dreamscape and its corresponding dream-text create fertile ground for analyzing the discursive practices and narrative structures of power. This is especially true at periods in the history of dream interpretation during which new modes of understanding attempt to push out and replace others. At these points, representations and interpretations of dreams seek to challenge and replace older modes—and thus cut in both radical and authoritarian directions. This is the case with most of the biblical dream interpretation, which seeks to undermine competing polytheistic practices while cementing the special relationship between the Hebrew's God and the "chosen" people as well as the authority and legitimacy of the patriarchs, priests, and kings. This is also the case with Freud and the psychoanalytic movement, which sought to overcome a diverse range of dream theories in order to locate the dream at the center of the individual's psychological drama, as Freud understood it. Psychoanalytic innovators like Jung and Lacan venture to reimagine the dream in relation to their structural challenges to the Freudian system. J. Allan Hobson explicitly works to dismantle this psychoanalytic system in order to assert the neurobiological foundation of dreaming. In these cases—biblical dreaming, psychoanalysis, and the neurobiology of dreaming—discussions of dreaming are interwoven with concurrent discourses related to power and authority. This book has asserted that these dynamics of power are central to the understanding of the cultural position of dreaming.

If, as this book reveals, innovations in thinking about dreaming are bound to discourses of power, then it is also the case, as I hope to have demonstrated, that certain representations of dreaming work to challenge authoritarian and hierarchical tendencies by attempting to capture the anarchistic attribute of the dreamscape. While these texts are politically powerful or radical, they are so only partially, often giving way to discursive structures of authoritarian power in one way or another, like Frost's "After Apple-Picking," which cannot fully commit to the reality of the dreamscape and instead grounds the dream-text in a context of the social and discursive structures of hierarchical waking life. In rare cases, like with Rhys and Kafka, the creator of a dream-text channels the chaotic, disintegrative energy of the dreamscape to rupture the discursive constructs and narrative strategies of waking life, the "reality" of which the dreamscape is fundamentally challenging.

Index[1]

[1] Note: Page numbers followed by 'n' refer to notes.

© The Author(s), under exclusive license to Springer Nature Switzerland AG 2021

S. Rogoff, *The Politics of the Dreamscape*,
https://doi.org/10.1007/978-3-030-74796-1

The manufacturer's authorised representative in the EU is Springer Nature Customer Service Centre GmbH, Europaplatz 3, 69115 Heidelberg, Germany. If you have any concerns regarding our products, please contact ProductSafety@springernature.com

Printed and bound by CPI Group (UK) Ltd, Croydon, CR0 4YY
30/09/2026
02225701-0008